Above, early C-124 concept drawing that was meant to illustrate the load carrying ability of the proposed C-124. The C-124s were illustrated with the bug-eyed cockpit enclosure, similar to that used on the C-74 aircraft. (Douglas via Earl Berlin)

SETTING THE STAGE

It's only been in the last thirty years that the United States Air Force has been able to efficiently airlift personnel and equipment to the site of a major military crisis or national disaster throughout the world. The Lockheed C-5 "Galaxy" was and remains the vehicle that made this possible. The newer C-17 enhances this ability to a remarkable degree, and will do so all the more as greater

numbers of the new airplane enter operational service.

Powered by huge fuel efficient turbofan engines, the C-5 hauls previously unheard of tons of cargo at jet speeds to hot spots around the world. Though it has a range measured in thousands of miles, its ability to refuel in mid-air allows it to be almost anywhere in the world in little more than a day.

During World War Two the desire for longer range and larger payloads resulted in the development of larger airframes and more powerful reciprocating engines. These were the years of the C-46, C-47 and C-54; they represented what were, for their time, the epitome of passenger and cargo aircraft. Though the C-46 led a some-

what checkered life in military and civilian service, the C-47 and C-54 came to be much loved and highly respected. Even today, the C-47 and its DC-3 commercial counterpart are recognized as classic examples of rugged, reliable and stylish cargo / passenger aircraft.

The answer to the need for larger and faster commercial and military airlifters was provided by the "big three" American aircraft manufacturers. Lockheed produced its elegant Constellation series, initially for the Army Air Corps and later for the world's airlines and several of the world's military arms. Douglas produced its DC-6 and DC-7 commercial airliners and the military DC-6 equivalent, the C-118, as well as the completely military C-74 and C-124 cargo

planes. Not to be left out, Boeing produced the military C/KC-97 transports and its civil equivalent, the Model 377 Strato-cruiser. Not mass-produced but representative of futuristic thinking of the times was Convair's massive six-engined XC-99, only one example of which was built.

In the commercial world, the Constellation, DC-7 and Stratocruiser represented the zenith of piston engined airliners. Yet, advanced as they were, they reigned for a relatively short period. Around the corner lay a revolutionary powerplant; one that would make all previous engines obsolete practically overnight.

Though jet engines had been in service with air forces around the world for several years, long before they were applied to commercial aircraft, they were nonetheless a novelty to the traveling public. Beginning in the early 1950's, commercial jet transportation came to be recognized as the only way to travel. But the early years of jet transportation brought tragic failures along with the huge successes. The DeHavilland Comet was born out of a wonderful dream turned into a tragedy as the beautiful plane's designers discovered that building jet airliners was far more demanding than building piston engined machines. Jet aviation proved to be a whole new world. Out of DeHavilland's initial trials came that company's later success and the subsequent success of American aerospace giants Boeing, Lockheed and Douglas.

Boeing answered the call for commercial jets with what was initially known as the Model 367-80. Flown in prototype form under this designation, the airplane was later called the Model 707 and, like its Douglas DC-8 competitor, represented American aviation technology at its best.

Top to bottom: Chinese AF Curtiss C-46; VX-6 Douglas C-47/R4D; MARS-37 Douglas C-54/R5D; VR-54 Douglas C-118B; Lockheed C-121C; Lockheed R60 Constitution. (Ginter collection)

The early 707s and DC-8s were powered by turbojet engines and, though reliable, left a lot to be desired in many areas. They were noisy and generated long trailing clouds of smoke that lingered in the skies long after the airplane was out of sight. While the public liked riding these airplanes, it wasn't nearly as fond of listening to them. The airlines, too, weren't altogether happy with the new jets. Sure, they were cheaper to operate than their piston engined predecessors, but they needed still more power and greater efficiency. And the noise just had to go!

The answer came in the form of a dramatically altered jet engine: the turbofan. Quieter, more powerful and significantly more economical, these new engines were greeted most enthusiastically by the public and the airlines. Early airliners that could be modified with the new engines were. American Airlines took the bold step of having all of its early 707s and later 720s reengined and enjoyed the fuel savings for years afterwards. New airliner designs took full advantage of the new engine.

The military, observing the airlines' success, wasn't overlooking the advantages of jet transportation. In the United States, early military jet transports were derivatives of then current jet airliners. The C/KC-135 (Boeing Model 717) family was derived from the Model 367-80, the first of what came to be known as the 707 family. Early versions of the C-135 were powered by J-57 turbojet engines. As the commercial 707s and 720s went to turbofan engines, so did the C-135s. As far as the Air Force was concerned, the C-135s were able and efficient airlifters. But it would be years before a true purpose-built jet cargo plane would be built for the Air Force and it would come, not from Boeing or Douglas, but from Lock-

Top to bottom: Boeing C-97G Stratofreighter; Douglas C-133A Cargomaster III; Boeing C-135A Stratolifter; Lockheed C-141B Starlifter; Lockheed C-5A Galaxy. (Ginter Collection)

heed. It would be called the C-141 Starlifter.

As commercial and military jet transports became accepted as the preferred means to travel and move cargo, the need arose for still larger and more fuel efficient airlifters. The U.S. Air Force was the first to speak up. Lockheed and Boeing responded with proposals and both were strong contenders for a production contract. Both spent large sums of money during the design and development stage. Watching from the sidelines, the airlines recognized the potential of such mammoth aircraft and dreamed of possible commercial versions. Boeing and Lockheed weren't blind to the commercial applications and the possibilities that lay just around the corner. Boeing ultimately developed its 747, which shows no

sign of ending production in the 21st century. Lockheed added to their sucess of the C-141 by producing the C-5.

PLACING THE C-124

The C-124 could be considered a sub-step in the passenger/cargo aircraft evolution. It was a product of lessons learned when a larger airframe and very large engines were brought together in the form of the C-74 Globemaster, itself the next step up from the C-46, C-47 and C-54 era of military transports. The irony of the C-124 is that it improved on the C-74 "step" and survived to serve into the period or "step" represented by the C-5 "Galaxy". It wasn't just the weight the C-124 could carry that extended its service life. It was the <u>volume</u> it could handle. No other airplane could

Above, beautiful bug-eyed C-74, 42-65410, close-up and personal. Maximum capacity was 125 passengers or 72,000 lbs. of cargo. (Douglas)

carry the outsize cargo into less-than-well-prepared landing strips like the C-124 could. Even the C-5 proved unable to go where the C-124 could. So the C-124 continued to serve and might have served past the mid 1970s had not wing fatigue problems forced retirement of the fleet.

EVOLUTION

The C-124 evolved from an earlier Douglas design, the C-74 Globemaster. No, the C-124 wasn't called the Globemaster. Officially, it

4

was the Globemaster II. But the name had no more appeal to the drivers and fixers than "Thunderbolt II" had to A-10 operators and maintainers. The C-124 came to be called "Old Shaky" or just plain "Shaky" and, as time passed, the name was more often than not uttered with a kind of reverence.

To fully appreciate Shaky's contribution to military airlift, it's necessary to examine the advance represented by the C-74. Remember, the C-74 represented a major evolutionary step in airlift development.

The C-74 evolved from needs identified by strategists and aircraft manufacturers in the tense days immediately following Japan's surprise attack on Pearl Harbor. The C-47 and DC-4 (which would serve the Army Air Corps as the C-54) were in production and proving to be strong and dependable airplanes. But they weren't going to be big enough or long-legged enough to get supplies and personnel where they were most needed, in large enough quantities in the shortest possible time. The C-46 would soon come on the scene and make an important contribution to the war effort but it was in the same league as the C-47 and C-54.

Engineers at Douglas Aircraft Company saw what was needed and immediately began work on an airplane that would be anything but fancy but would be highly functional. The plane was designed to accommodate the Army's large trucks, tanks and other mechanized equipment. It was also designed to be relatively easy to mass produce and, once in service, maintain in the field.

The airplane was originally, in 1942, designated Model 415. Army Air Corps engineers looked at the initial design, suggested weight be reduced and the modified design became the Model 415A. Power was provided by Wright R-3350 engines, genuine heavyweights in their time.

Douglas received a letter of intent in March 1942. The Model 415A became the C-74 and the contract

Above, C-74 42-65402 was the first Globemaster built. (via Craig Kaston)

that followed, in June, specified the construction of 50 C-74s at a total cost of over $50,000,000. Also included in the contract was one non-flyable static test airframe. A total of 14 C-74s were actually built, their serial numbers ranging from 42-65402 to 42-65415.

A very large airplane, for its time, the C-74 was nonetheless built entirely state-of-the-art. New features had to be designed, built and proven in time to be incorporated in the final design or were left out. So urgent was the supposed need for these airplanes that the designers weren't given the benefit of building and testing a prototype or service test models. The C-74s were expected to be a production standard right off the drawing board.

As it turned out, the R-3350 engines specified in the initial contract weren't installed. A delay in the arrival of the powerplants, combined with the discovery that the engine wouldn't provide the rate of climb required for safe operation during over-the-weather flight at high altitude, led to a March 1943 decision to adopt the newer R-4360 Wasp Major engine. The R-4360 would go down in aviation history as a huge, powerful and generally reliable engine but would also be recognized as one that wouldn't tolerate being kicked around.

The new engine's arrival was also delayed. Meanwhile, because the R-4360 was heavier and increased the airplane's overall weight, the gross weight of the C-74 was raised to

145,000 lbs.

The ever-changing war situation affected the production of goods back home. Combat aircraft, naturally, had the highest priority and nothing was allowed to detract from their production. Such was the case when the Army directed that a large number of C-74 program personnel be transferred to the Douglas Long Beach A-26 attack plane tooling project. The C-74 went on a very low priority, but work didn't stop altogether. The first major jig was completed in August 1944 and the first C-74 rolled out of the factory at Long Beach in 1945.

The C-74 was, for a brief period, the world's largest airplane. With a 124 foot length and possessing a wing span of 173 feet, the airplane grossed out at 145,000 lbs. and carried more than 11,000 gallons of fuel in six wing tanks. The 6,800 cubic foot cabin could accommodate 125 passengers or numerous outsize cargo items. Cabin length was 75 feet. The R-4360-27 engines featured full-feathering Curtis Electric reversible propellers. This reversing feature allowed the airplane to back up under its own power, a novelty at the time.

The fuselage was of circular cross-section and could have been adapted to pressurization. However, during the C-74's entire service life, it remained an unpressurized aircraft. And, when the airplanes transferred into the private sector, they were used

Above and below, left and right hand views of the first C-74 42-65402 shows its large size and striking form. Once remade into a C-124, the C-74's graceful lines disappeared. (Douglas)

for cargo carrying where pressurization wasn't required.

A novel and quite noticeable feature was the two canopies for the pilot and co-pilot. Often referred to as "bug eyes," they were intended to give these crew members a 360 degree field of vision much like that enjoyed by fighter pilots. As it turned out, the crews didn't like the arrangement, claiming it restricted communications between them. The twin canopies were later replaced by a more conventional cockpit covering.

The first C-74 made its maiden flight on September 5, 1945. The flight test program went relatively smoothly, the only accident taking place on August 5, 1946; the airplane was destroyed but no injuries or deaths were recorded. The accident was caused by out-of-control elevator oscillations which, in turn, caused a violent "porpoise" that over-stressed the wings and caused both to shear off at the same time. Douglas found a cure, fixed the problem and the tiny fleet of C-74s kept flying.

After the accident, there were a total of 12 C-74s available for service. The second C-74 had crashed and the fourth was diverted for static test duties. The last C-74 was delivered in 1947 and, as with most aircraft being produced during the war, what further orders there might have been were canceled as the nation eagerly looked forward to peace-filled years.

Initially, the C-74 was cleared for carrying cargo only. Until the airplane

was thoroughly tested, passengers couldn't be carried "legally." Problems were identified and handled during the first four months of C-74 operations. The new R-4360 engines were "bugged", but even harder to handle were problems with cargo handling at the receiving terminals the planes flew into. Ground personnel just weren't prepared for the kinds of loads the C-74 could carry and valuable time was lost unloading and loading the airplanes.

In March 1947, a C-74 was flown to Pope Field (now Pope Air Force Base) for evaluation by Troop Carrier Command. After a thorough inspection and evaluation, in the air and on the ground, the board concluded that the airplane was sound but not suitable for operations with paratroops. With this evaluation concluded, the plane was flown to Randolph Field, Texas, where Air Evacuation personnel inspected it and were favorably impressed. There, it was determined that loading and unloading patients would not present undue problems, especially if the built-in elevator was employed.

As mentioned earlier, the R-4360-27 engines gave flight crews and maintenance personnel problems and, in the fall of 1947, a modification program was begun that reengined all the C-74s with R-4360-49 engines.

In June 1948, the Russians closed all land routes into divided allied sectors of West Berlin. The Berlin Airlift, that massive operation that supplied an entire city with all of its essential needs, was launched. The C-47s and C-54s that took part in the operation are well remembered, but the single C-74 was not. Though the plane did a fine job, it had to be withdrawn from the operation because it couldn't fit well into the traffic flow, and was more airplane than the runways were stressed to handle. Furthermore, the Russians protested that its built-in elevator allowed the airplane to function as a bomber.

Though withdrawn from the airlift operation in September, the C-74

nonetheless continued to support it by hauling C-54 engines and other parts needed to keep the participating cargo planes in the air. C-74 flight operations during the Berlin Airlift demonstrated the need for an airplane that could carry more in the way of bulky items. The C-74 easily handled the load but volume limitations caused it to be full before it had reached its weight limit. Douglas answered the Air Force requirement with a design based on the C-74: the C-124 Globemaster II.

1949 was a year of record-setting for the C-74. In May, a C-74 carried 75 passengers across the Atlantic, to England; the largest passenger load ever carried by an airplane across that ocean. In November, 103 passengers were carried to England on a 24 hour flight that originated at Brookley AFB and terminated at Marham, England.

From 1953 on the utilization of the C-74 steadily declined until when in 1955 maintenance and parts prob-

Above, C-74 42-65408 in MATS markings in 1949. Note the "bug-eyed" canopies have been replaced. Below, C-74 42-65409 with its outsized cargo door open during 1952. (USAF)

lems brought about a reduction of the C-74 fleet utilization rate to two hours a day. During the last six months of the fleet's service life, the planes were grounded twice for faulty fuel and flight control system components. On November 1, 1955, the C-74s were placed in flyable storage at Brookley AFB and in the first quarter of 1956, the C-74s were flown to Davis-Monthan AFB for storage.

That the C-74's mission capability declined in its later years is a reflection on planning and the supply system; not on the airplane itself. The C-74, properly maintained and flown, was a capable and reliable airplane and its contribution to the art of military airlift was significant beyond what its last years of service seemed to indicate.

At left, the first YC-124 was basically a refuselaged C-74. It is seen here on a foggy morning in September 1949 with its new clam-shell doors open. Below left, after fuselage of C-74/YC-124 42-65406 with C-74 42-5414 in the background and the X-3 in the foreground. (Douglas via Harry Gann)

over to the Air Force for regular airlift work.

Later, the airplane was equipped with R-4360-35A engines, each having a 3,800 horsepower rating, and redesignated YC-124C. Like the C-74 before it, this airplane had four bladed propellers. Photos of the airplane, as it appeared at the Air Force Museum, show that these were fitted with square-tipped blades. The C-124s that followed had three bladed propellers, initially having rounded tips and, on later models, the square tipped configuration.

The service testing of the C-124A was conducted by the 1258th ATS. Later, as the 3rd ATS, this unit tested the C-124C, as indicated in a photograph showing a C-124C in service with the squadron. Exactly how long the 1703rd ATG continued testing the C-124 isn't clear but that the process

EVOLUTION—THE C-124

As mentioned earlier, the C-124 evolved from the C-74. It retained the wing, tail surfaces and engines of the C-74, though the tail surfaces were slightly modified. The landing gear was also slightly modified and the built-in elevator, a novelty on the C-74, was retained. The engines were R-4360-49s.

The first C-124, designated YC-124 Globemaster II, was built by converting the fifth C-74, serial number 42-65406, at the Douglas Long Beach plant. The airplane made its maiden flight in the new configuration on 27 November 1949. Testing of the airplane was conducted over the following four years. With water ballast tanks installed, the airplane's stability and control characteristics were checked. By July 1954, the test equipment had been removed, the airplane refurbished and it was turned

Below, the first YC-124, 42-65406, prepares for its first flight on 27 November 1949. (Douglas via S. Nicolaou)

Above, the first flight of the YC-124 occurred on 27 November 1949. (Douglas via S. Nicolaou) Below, prototype 42-65406 on a early test flight over Los Angeles. The C-124 had an upper passenger deck, thus the two rows of windows. (Douglas via Berlin)

Above, YC-124 demonstrates load carrying capacity at the Douglas plant. (Douglas via Earl Berlin) Below, early C-124A lands at Muroc AFB after a test flight. (Douglas via Earl Berlin)

was a thorough one is indicated by the fact the Globemaster IIs were flying with the unit until at least 1956.

Accelerated Service Testing

While the 1703rd ATG conducted service tests of the C-124 on established MATS routes, other testing took place at specialized centers within the Continental United States.

These tests evaluated the airplane in terms of stability and control, maintenance requirements, reliability and a host of other important considerations.

The C-124A's Accelerated Service Tests were conducted at Wright-Patterson AFB from May 4, 1950 to May 23, 1951. C-124A, serial number 49-232, was used for the tests and a total of 457 flying hours were accumulated before the airplane crashed and burned, bringing this particular test program to a close. By the end of the program, 180 unsatisfactory reports had been written, though none were serious enough to ground the airplane.

As stated in the final report WCT-2350 and dated 7 December 1951, the purpose of the tests was as follows:

(1) Accumulate sufficient maintenance and flight experience to determine the reliability of the C-124A aircraft.

(2) Evaluate the aircraft from the maintenance standpoint, with particular emphasis on the amount of maintenance necessary and adequacy of prescribed procedures for maintenance and servicing.

(3) Discover and recommend corrective action on material failures.

(4) Obtain information on supply requirements.

At least eight different types of missions were flown during the course of the program. As will be seen in the following table, the number of missions required to complete a given phase of the service testing varied with the complexity of the specified task. Likewise, the number of flying hours required to complete a test series depended on the number of missions required and how long each mission had to be.

TABLE ONE   MISSION SUMMARY

Type Mission	# Of Flights	Hours
Transition and checkout	12	30
Cargo and cross country	54	280
Radio evaluation	10	14
Service ceiling flights	2	10
2 and 3 engine flights	2	10
Maximum range	1	24
Special test	14	49
Total	99	347

MISSION DESCRIPTIONS

Cargo and Cross Country Missions: These consisted of flights with high priority cargo transported to various points throughout the zone of interior. Various helicopters, an F-86 Sabre jet fighter, jet engines, bombs, guided missiles, etc. were carried. Whenever possible, special tests were conducted in conjunction with the cargo missions.

Radio Evaluation: Radio and electronic equipment check missions were flown to locate and correct operational discrepancies.

Special Test Missions: These were flown to obtain vibration data on engine driven generators and equipment in the lower cargo compartment, conduct spark plug tests, carburetor fuel flow checks, automatic power control unit checks, autopilot tests, simulated inflight refueling, and evaluation of pilot's revised flight instrument panel.

Maximum Range: A 24-hour flight was made to spot check some of the cruise data provided in the pilot's operating instructions.

Approximate Service Ceiling: Flights were flown to check the service ceiling of the aircraft. Approximately 26,850 feet was the maximum pressure altitude reached, using a take-off gross weight of

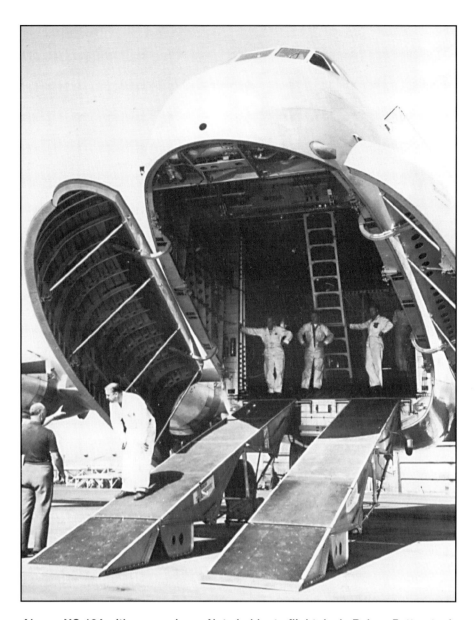

Above, YC-124 with ramps down. Note ladder to flight deck. Below, Patton tank is unloaded from a C-124A. (Douglas via S. Nicolaou)

Purpose: Present the results of performance and stability tests of the C-124A airplane, USAF No. 49-234. Flight tests of the aircraft were requested to obtain the data necessary to demonstrate and confirm performance guarantees, stability and maneuverability, operational utility, and to provide the contractor with sufficient data for compilation of the Pilot's Handbook Charts and Summaries.

The test program was conducted from 28 Septebmer to 14 November 1950 at the contractor's plant, Douglas Aircraft Comapny, Incorporated, Long Beach, California, and from 15 to 19 November 1950 at Edwards AFB, California. The program consisted of 45 flights totaling 152 hours and 10 minutes. A basic radius mission and a ferry flight on 11 March 1951, combined to bring the total flight time required to 163 hours and 5 minutes.

Performance tests were conducted at various weights, ranging from the maximum overload condition of 210,000 pounds to a light gross weight of 130,000 pounds. Stability and control tests were flown at both the forward CG limit of 18% mean aerodynamic chord and the aft limit of 34% mean aerodynamic chord. In-flight load changes were accomplished by an eight-tank water ballast system capable of holding approximately 4600 gallons of water.

The results of the Phase IV tests failed to confirm the guaranteed performance of the aircraft at a gross weight of 175,000 pounds for the following items:

High Speed
Four-engine rate of climb at sea level
Three-engine rate of climb at sea level
Three-engine service ceiling
Range at 10,000 feet
(66,600 pounds of fuel)

135,265 lbs., normal rated power with the oil coolers full open and engine cowl flaps set at 8 degrees.

Power Settings: A power setting of 60 inches of mercury at 2700 RPM with and without water injection was used for most take-offs. A power setting of 50 inches of mercury and 2250 RPM was used for all climbs, and the cruise power setting covered the range of settings given in the T.O. [technical order] 01-40NUA-1.

Gross Weight: The take-off gross weight varied from 142,000 to 175,000 pounds, with a center of gravity range from 24% to 30% mean aerodynamic chord, landing gear down

Author's Note: The simulated inflight refueling mentioned under Special Test Missions was done to evaluate the C-124 as a possible inflight refueling tanker, not as a receiver. As will be seen later, Douglas proposed a turbo-prop version of the C-124 for pure cargo carrying missions and developed an inflight refueling tanker variant of that airplane. Though the cargo carrier flew in a single prototype form, the tanker version never

went beyond the design proposal stage.

Also, power settings are measured in inches of mercury; which is, in turn, the scale by which engine manifold pressure is measured.

As mentioned in the beginning of the report, the test aircraft crashed and burned, bringing the program to a close. Cause of the crash was not stated in the report.

Conclusions: The performance and stability data presented in this report are representative of the C-124 A aircraft and are adequate to provide the information necessary for the handbook of Flight Operation Instructions.

Phase II and IV Flight Tests

The following information relative to these tests comes from the Memorandum Report, Serial Number MCRFT-2337, dated 20 April 1951. Though the actual report is quite lengthy, the data provided here gives the reader a basic idea of what is sought and found during tests such as these. What follows is taken directly from the report:

Above left, the 13th production C-124A 49-242 shortly after delivery. (via S. Nicolaou) At left, unmarked C-124A 50-107 taxis into Oakland with its nose loading doors open. (L. Smalley via William Swisher)

A comparison of the guaranteed performance and test results is presented in the following table:

DS-1129A Guarantee Phase IV Results
High speed with normal rated power
258 kts versus 251 kts
Four-engine rate of climb at sea level
800 fpm versus 730 fpm
Three-engine rate of climb at sea level
400 fpm versus 280 fpm
4-engine service ceiling/normal rated power
22,050 ft versus 22,050 ft
3-engine service ceiling/normal rated power
13,900 ft versus 12,100 ft
Range (NM) at 10,000 ft with 66,600 lbs of fuel
5,240 nm versus 4,910 nm
Average speed (knots)
177 kts versus 183 kts
Radius of action, 10,000 ft at 99% max range/speed
740 nm versus 740 nm
Average speed - cruise out (knots)
184 kts versus 197 kts
Maximum cargo (lbs)
47,961 lbs versus 48,050 lbs
Take-off distance over 50-ft obstacle at S/L and 208°
flap 5,209 ft varsus 5,050 ft
Landing distance over 50-ft obstacle at S/L,160,000
lbs., 40° flaps 3,340 ft versus 3,335 ft

Recommendations:

1. A study be made to determine:

    a. means of providing adequate stall warning with wing flaps down.

    b. means of providing adequate aileron trim for asymetric conditions

2. The use of the automatic power control unit be discontinued on this type of aircraft.

3. The effectiveness of the oil cooler be investigated to obtain better cooling during climb.

4. The throttle action be improved to provide a more proportional control of engine power over the entire movement of the throttle.

5. The brake system be improved to provide the pilot with adequate "feel".

6. Sufficient cold air ventilation be provided for the flight deck.

7. The pilot's and co-pilot's oxygen regulator be relocated for greater accessibility.

8. E-1 or B-1 attitude gyros be substituted for those now in use.

9. The C-5 directional gyros be replaced by C-1 gyros.

10. The emergency brake be relocated to allow operation by the pilot's right hand.

11. The emergency exit from the flight deck be modified to utilize the escape chute as provid-

ed for the test airplane.

12. The effectiveness of the windshield wipers be improved to accomplish their designed purpose.

Testing of the C-124, as can be seen, was a somewhat drawn out process but was nonetheless thorough. But there was still more to be learned and those lessons would come from the men in the field who would use the airplane day in and day out. These lessons would reveal the true nature of the plane; its versatility, ruggedness and ability to carry the most unusual cargoes to even more unusual places.

Above, mass parachute drop from C-124A Globemasters was observed by a C-119. (Douglas via Harry Gann) Below, paratroopers hook up for the jump. (Douglas via Harry Gann)

SERVICE WITH THE ACTIVE DUTY AIR FORCE

Old Shaky served for many long and honorable years. She served with but one air force, that of the United States. Naturally, she served with the Military Air Transport Service (MATS), which later became the Military Airlift Command (MAC). Many readers will, perhaps, remember that she served

The C-124 showed off its load carrying ability during the Korean war. Below, F-84s overfly C-124 in Japan on 10-17-52. (via Nicolaou)

MILITARY AIR TRANSPORT SERVICE/MILITARY AIRLIFT COMMAND

with the Tactical Air Command (TAC). But how many know that she served with Curtis Lemay's Strategic Air Command (SAC) and with the Air Materiel (AMC) and Air Force Logistics Command (AFLC)? How many remember what units she served with PACAF? Remembered or not, she served proudly with all of these commands and performed duties that, if appearances were any indicator, she didn't look like she could undertake.

As might be guessed, the Military Air Transport Service (later Military Airlift Command) was the largest user of the mighty Globemaster II. For this reason, I've chosen to address these commands first and not to address each as a separate operating agency. MAC continued the MATS mission,

essentially being the product of a name change only. Naturally, the change in command name carried over to the affected units, causing them to receive new numerical designations along with their new titles. For example, the 1607th Air Transport Wing (MATS) became the 436th Military Airlift Wing (MAC).

Because this section is a historical look at the MATS/MAC units, the units are discussed first as they were designated and controlled by MATS and then as they were designated and controlled by MAC, where applicable. This should help the reader better grasp the historical flow of events.

C-124s In The MATS Inventory (1951 - 63)

51	52	53	54	55	56	57	58	59	60	61	62	63
10	30	57	119	170	172	168	324	310	311	299	312	377

1501st ATW/60th MAW

The history of the 1501 ATW, with respect to C-124 operations, begins with the unit's redesignation as an Air Transport Wing, on 1 July 1955; having been an Air Transport Group (ATG) prior to that date. Unit historical records weren't too clear as to when the C-124 was first taken into the unit's inventory, though other historical references indicate the C-124 went into service at Travis AFB (1501 ATW's home base) in 1955. At that time, five squadrons were assigned to the wing: 28th ATS (Hill AFB), 55th ATS, 75th ATS, 84th ATS and 85th ATS. Two other squadrons, the 56th ATS and 77th ATS were deactivated, presumably in June 1955.

The historical records don't reflect much about the activities and accomplishments from 1955 through 1959. However, a wealth of information is available about unit activities from 1960 onward.

From 14 to 28 March, 1960, the unit was involved in the joint Air Force-Army operation BIG SLAM / PUERTO PINE. The mission was divided into three phases:

(1) **preplanning,**
(2) **execution and**
(3) **recovery.**

MATS OPLAN 102A-60, "BIG SLAM" was conducted as a test of the Strategic Transport Forces' ability to attain war time utilization rates safely and efficiently. The motive behind this test was the fact that MATS aircraft were flying an average of five hours per day. In a war time situation, the number of hours each airplane would fly daily would rise in proportion to the increased number of taskings. MATS' concern was whether the aircraft could be flown safely under the additional load. As a result of the exercise, MATS learned that its units could, indeed, meet additional taskings safely.

Like all MATS units, the 1501 ATW performed its share of humanitarian missions; one of the most unique being MOD 714-61, which took place between 13 and 18 August 1961. Two C-124s and their crews flew to Andrews AFB, Maryland, and picked up thirty tons of insecticide and flew on to Cairo, Egypt. The insecticide was destined for the United Arab Republic for use against an insect invasion.

Another particularly interesting mission was SWIFT STRIKE, conducted between 15 and 23 August, 1961. Four C-124s and eight crews supported the deployment and subsequent redeployment of Strategic Army Corps forces from Fort Campbell, Kentucky, to several staging areas. In addition to the aircrews, 36 maintenance technicians and air freight specialists took part in the exercise. 565 flying hours were accumulated during the exercise, the largest peacetime maneuver, up to that date, since 1941.

By 1962, the 1501 ATW was operating three different airlifters: the C-124, C-133 and C-135. The 28th, 75th and 85th ATSs flew C-124s, while the 84th ATS flew C-133s and the 44th ATS flew C-135s. The 55th ATS had apparently been deactivated. A new squadron, the 86th ATS [flying C-130s], would join the wing in June 1963.

1962 was a year of numerous exercises involving all of the wing's

aircraft. Those involving the C-124 included:

Long Thrust V Southern Cross (1 - 15 October)
Swift Strike II (10 August - 30 September)
Three Pairs (20 September - 10 October)
Guam Disaster (12 - 16 November)
Cuban Crisis (October - November)
1963 was yet another year of exercises and special missions. These included:
Sergeant Missile Deployment (First Quarter)
Joint Airborne Operation (23 and 24 March)
Long Thrust VI and VII (January - March)
Joint Airborne Operation (May)
Coulee Crest (April - May)*

In addition to utilizing C-124s from Travis AFB, additional Globemaster IIs from the 28th ATS were employed. It's interesting to note that this was the first time the computer

Above, 85th ATS C-124A 51-133, unloading in Japan in 1953. The forward fuselage markings were yellow highlighted in dark blue. Pacific Division was white on a dark blue stripe bordered by yellow. Rear fuselage markings were red, (Harry Sievers via Jack Friell & Nick Williams)

Below, 85th ATS C-124A 50-116, at Travis AFB on 15 May 1954. The yellow and blue nose markings were removed and painted over with U,S. AIR FORCE. (Lional Paul collection via Nick Williams) Bottom, 85th ATS C-124A 51-131, taxis in 1955. (L. Smalley via William Swisher)

Above, C-124A 50-0093, at Oakland on 26 September 1954. Tail was red. (Smalley via Swisher)

flight planning system was tested. Cross-checked throughout the exercise, the system was found to be extremely accurate.

Tidal Wave (May - June 1963)

1963 also brought the utilization of a new drop zone, at Beale AFB, California, for use in tactical qualification of wing aircrews. Of special significance was the training conducted with the 101st Airborne Division at Campbell AAF, Kentucky. September

saw the use of 12 C-124s for these operations, alongside four C-130s. Eight more C-124s were employed for this work in October and 16 were utilized in November. Training operations were curtailed in December because of the holiday season, 12 C-124s being utilized.

The following operation recaps give a good idea of the number of hours flown in direct support of major exercises during the last half of calendar year 1963. Note the number of hours flown by both C-124 squadrons from July through October. Note also the dramatic drop in the number of hours flown by the C-124s and the dramatic increase in hours flown by the C-135s and C-130s during the month of November. Interestingly, the

C-124s were the only aircraft involved in support of major exercises during December, though the number of hours flown was relatively small.

Swift Strike III
(21 July - 4 September 1963)

C-124s flew 792 hours during this exercise, compared to 151.5 hours flown by C-135s and 87.5 hours flown by wing C-133s.

Big Lift
(19 - 26 October/10 - 25 November 1963)

Again, the C-124s carried the bulk of the load; 41 C-124s being employed compared to 20 C-130s, 14 C-133s and 20 C-135s.

FY 1964 (October 1963 to September 1964) was a less than spectacular period for wing C-124s. While the rest of the wing performed well, the C-124s suffered a decrease in reliability rate, with an overall 68% recorded for the year and a documented reliability rate below the 70% standard for eight of the twelve

Below, aerial MATS family portrait (C-97, C-124, C-121) off the coast of Hawaii in 1956. (SDAM)

Above, 1502 ATW C-124A 51-5187 at Oakland on 11 March 1956. The upper fuselage has been painted white with a black cheat line. (Smalley via Swisher). Below, 1501 ATW C-124A 50-118 taxing at Oakland on 21 April 1956. (Smalley via Swisher) Bottom, 1501 ATW C-124A 50-1255 at Oakland on 1 July 1956. Note upper engine nacelle is painted black. (Smalley via Swisher)

Above, C-124C overflies San Francisco bay in route to Travis AFB, California. (via S. Nicolaou)

months of the FY. A low of 45% was recorded for January and a high of 81% was recorded for July. The C-124 FY 64 special mission tasking was only 64% of the FY 63 tasking.

Below, two C-124s on the flight line at Hickam AFB, Hawaii, in the late 1950s. C-97s, C-118s and C-121s can be seen in the background. (USAF via Nick Williams)

Overall C-124 reliability rate for FY 63 was 73%. As will be noted in the chart below, the C-124 flew the second highest number of special assignment airlift missions for the wing between January and June 1964, the C-133 flying the majority of the missions.

FY 1964

	C-124	C-130	C-133	C-135
Jan	20	23	64	12
Feb	49	27	55	8
Mar	29	26	76	29
Apr	30	1	83	12
May	32	2	71	13
Jun	39	12	46	25
Total	199	91	395	99

Between January and June 1964, the wing participated in the following major exercises:

Polar Siege (15 January - 20 February)

Quick Release

(24 January - 28 February)

Delaware (2 - 28 April)

Long Thrust XI (April, canceled)

Desert Strike (20 April - 15 June)*

Northwind (6 - 14 June)

Indian River [Phase I] (10 - 28 June)

Indian River [Phase II] (22 - 24 July)

It's interesting to note the C-124 carried the load during the deployment phases of this exercise. The C-133s carried the next highest portion of the load for the wing during the exercise. See the chart below.

Deployment Flying Time (Hours)

	Prime	Support	Total
C-124	1030.1	297.5	1327.6
C-133	680.9	127.9	808.8

Redeployment Flying Time (Hours)

	Prime	Support	Total
C-124	1933.0	401.0	2334.0
C-133	544.0	165.0	709.0

"Goldfire I" was the main exercise the wing was involved in during the last quarter of 1964. In addition, during December, the 28 ATS was given control of aircrew tactical training at Hill AFB, unit aircraft being utilized to provide training to student flight engi-

neers. Pilots received training as a by-product of the flight engineer training. Tactical operations moved to Marine Corps Air Station Yuma, Arizona, and the unit flew 1,000+ training hours during the month.

Again called upon to perform in the humanitarian role, wing C-124s were used to provide aid to the disaster stricken northeastern United States during the Christmas season. Floods ravaged the area and the C-124s hauled aviation fuel in support of the Army and Marine helicopters flying rescue missions in the region.

During the first quarter of 1965, the C-135B aircraft, assigned to the 44th ATS, were phased out in favor of the C-141. Proven reliable during their years of service with the wing, they were nonetheless unable to handle the heavy airlift mission as well as the newer Lockheed Starlifter.

The first quarter also saw the C-124s carrying the load as a result of the phase-out of the C-135Bs and the grounding of the C-133s. By the second half of the year, the C-133s were flying again.

Above, 28th ATS C-124C 52-0999 was stationed at Hill AFB, Utah, and was assigned to the 1501 ATW. (via Nick Williams)

Between July and September, 1965, the 75th ATS phased out the C-124s assigned to that squadron and began preparation for C-141 operations. Nonetheless, the C-124s of the remaining squadrons flew 87 special assignment missions, amounting to more than 50% of the wing's quarterly tasking for this kind of mission.

The figures below reflect what portion of the wing's airlift tasking was being handled by the C-124 during the last half of 1965. Note that as the C-141s came on line, the tasking load on the C-124s decreased. It's interesting to note too, that the figures below are supposed to represent hours flown, according to the official historical record they were taken from. I'm inclined to believe these fig-

Below, 28th ATS C-124C 52-0944 was assigned to Hill AFB, Utah. (via Nick Williams)

ures may, in fact, represent missions flown. The reader will note the small figures in each column and understand why this conclusion was drawn.

1965

	C-124	C-130	C-133	C-141
Jul	44	13	10	6
Aug	32	23	13	1
Sep	23	12	5	4
Oct	23	9	6	10
Nov	30	11	13	12
Dec	23	14	20	15

During the second quarter of the year, practically the entire MATS C-124 fleet was grounded as a result of a fatal accident on the East Coast. The subsequent accident investigation revealed serious cracks in the C-124 wing spar structure. Severe restrictions were placed on C-124 flight operations, tactical operations being eliminated during this period. By the end of June, 40 C-124s were grounded for wing spar cracks and another 160 aircraft were yet to be

Above, C-124C 52-1031 in flight over Northern California. Note the American flag has been added to the rudder. (Douglas via Earl Berlin) Below, C-124C 52-1035 from 1501 ATW over Northern California. Note black wing-walk lines and upper-rear engine nacelles. (Air Force via Williams)

inspected. The C-124s continued to be used in support of the building crisis in Viet Nam, despite the flight restrictions.

The chart below reflects, in flying hours, how well the C-124 continued to meet its taskings during the first half of 1965. Note that during the second quarter of the year, the C-124s carried the load. Note also the February through April time frame where the C-133s are shown flying no sorties. It was during this period that they were grounded. The reduced number of C-135 hours reflects the operational draw down of these aircraft.

1965

	C-124	C-130	C-133	C-135	C-141
Jan	229	186	442	228	0
Feb	1090	147	99	0	0
Mar	1682	354	0	335	0
Apr	2203	752	0	464	0
May	2697	757	61	58	8
Jun	2526	522	319	38	0

Steve Brown was an R-4360 engine mechanic with the 1501st Maintenance Group (MG). His first assignment was to the flightline where ....

"I enlisted in the USAF in late May 1957. I spent 4 wks at Lackland, and then Aircraft Reciprocating Engine School at Sheppard AFB, Wichita Falls, TX. Jets would have been my first choice by far, either airframe or engines. Anyway our instructors told us the Recip School was a lot harder because the engines were more complex. At Sheppard we worked on R-1820's (B-17 leftovers) a little on R-3350s (B-29 leftovers) and did run up R-2000 (C-54) engines in some test cells. Of my engine class we split about 50/50 to Travis and Dover, Del. My first active duty work was in the 1501 Flightline Maintenance Squadron doing Postflight inspections on C-97A and C-97C Boeing Stratocruiser / Stratofreighters. We looked for loose connections, leaks, and fixed the minor maintenance squaks on the R-4360-65 engines.

Travis was a big operation. The 1501 Maint Group was composed of the 1501 Flightline Maintenance Squadron, 1501 Periodic Maintenance Squadron and 1501 Field Maintenance Squadron. FLMS did Post Flight and Pre-Flight & Turn Arounds, PMS did the hourly inspections in their "docks" (early wooden creatures), soon replaced with better facilities. I think the hourly interval was 300 hr inspections. Planes were in the hangar about 3 days and FMS had all the specialty shops. I got transferred to FMS after about 9 months to 1 year. My first reaction on going to FMS was a little cool because I liked where I was. That soon changed as I made friends and a bunch of the guys had all been through Sheppard at about the same time.

FMS had at least six shops: Instruments, Propellers, Fabrication, Aero Shop (flight controls), hydraulic shop and engine shop. The engine work was done in a big building, P-16. There were three engines in P-16 in the "EBU" Engine Build-up, R-4360-20WA for C-124As, R-4360-63A for C-124C's, and R-4360-65 for C-97A and C-97C. EBU was one shop and about 2/3 civilian, engine change was another section. About 1959 there was some reorganization. An Engine Conditioning Section was established. Engine conditioning's goal was to increase the TBO [Time Between Overhaul] of the engines. Vibration analysis equipment was used. A vibration pickup was fastened to each cylinder and a harness connected the whole thing to an oscilloscope box. Engines were started and run up to about cruise power briefly to get patterns and see if any abnormal patterns showed up. As I recall, some of the cowling and baffling was removed. Engines tended to heat up so you had to move right along, but not a big problem. The patterns of valve opening and closing, spark plug firing, could be observed and problem cylinders or magnetos out of time could be retimed. We had cylinder change crews also. An engine change could be done in 6 - 8 hours, cylinders varied depending on location, top side and front row were easiest, a rear bottom ... location was difficult. 60 weight oil was black and made it hard to see everything and lighting wasn't always the best. Some special tools were required.

I made earlier reference to the EBU. The overhauled engines in the Blue or OD [olive drab] cans needed a lot of work before allowing an engine change. All our powerplants were put into a "QEC" Quick Engine Change configuration. The engine mount system was bolted to the raw engine, then to a mobile engine stand. This went through several work stations in a production line arrangement. Things that had to be added - carburetor, oil coolers, turbosupercharger (R-4360-65 only), cowl flaps, exhaust system, fuel air manifolds, generator or alternators, fuel flow meter, some instrumentation. It was about a 4 - 5 day process with 1 - 3 workers. Then these were brought out to the "Test Beds". I worked here for my final assignment. The QEC was transferred from the Engine Stand to the Test Bed via a forklift with a boom and cables. This was often done in Engine Change on the Flight Line

Above, C-124A from the 1501 ATW at Travis AFB in 1958. (Steve Brown via Earl Berlin) Below, engine test stands at Travis AFB. C-97 unit is followed by a C-124 unit. (Steve Brown via Berlin)

60TH MILITARY AIRLIFT WING

Maintenance Area. In the hangars, we had a overhead crane. The QEC's weight was about 6,000 lbs. Once we had the QEC mounted on the Test Bed, throttle, fuel, oil, instrument connections were made and propeller installed. This was about 1 hour job. A brief run to 800 - 1000 rpm was made. This on half set of spark plugs to blow out the pickling fluids in the cylinders. Yeah, it was a little messy and Test Bed got quite a few washings. With the rest of the plugs installed, the rest of the bafles and the complete cowling, we were ready to see if the engine would deliver its advertised power. Power was measured in T.O.P., Torque Oil Pressure at takeoff rpm and 60" manifold pressure max. Temperature was a factor, of course. Travis was 58' above sea level. Hot dry summer, cool, and sometimes very wet winters. I can't remember for sure where the engines were overhauled, but I am pretty sure it was SAAMA [San Antonio Air Material Area], Kelly AFB—maybe a few from SMAMA McClellan AFB. Some were also overhauled at civilian plants. One was Aerodex in Miami, Fl. Engines passed 98% of time. A marginal engine was done early in the morning before it got too hot (OAT) [Outside Air Temperature]. In 1960 most of the engines I saw had been thru overhaul 6, 7, 8, 9 times as evidenced by the stamping on the nose case by the Depot. All the P&W Eagles (brass) had been removed. I got one from a buddy in EBU."

On January 1, 1966, Military Air Transport Service became Military Airlift Command. What had been the 1501st ATW became the 60th MAW, the Air Transport Squadrons becoming Military Airlift Squadrons. The numerical designations for the Airlift Squadrons didn't change, the 85th ATS becoming the 85th MAS.

The wing continued to operate two C-124 squadrons, one at Travis AFB and one at Hill AFB, Utah. The C-133s of the 84th MAS were fully operational after a grounding period in 1965. Conversion of the 75th ATS (subsequently the 75th MAS) to C-141s was complete.

During the first half of 1967, the wing prepared for and executed the termination of C-124 operations. Both flying squadrons and the associated maintenance squadron (60th Organizational Maintenance Squadron [OMS]) were deactivated. With the termination of C-124 operations, the wing was left with four flying squadrons, three operating the C-141 and one flying the C-133.

Though the C-133 continued in service with the 60th MAW, it would some time later fall victim to wing spar cracks that couldn't be economically repaired. The airplane would be permanently grounded, while the C-124 continued to serve elsewhere. Additionally, the C-133 never served with the Air National Guard or the Air Force Reserve. The C-124 served admirably with both of these organizations, finally being retired in 1974 when wing spar cracks brought its service to this country to an untimely end.

1502nd ATW/61st MAW

The history of the 1502nd ATW/61st MAW is filled with triumph, tinged at times with tragedy. No military organization is ever perfect, no matter how much its leaders and personnel strive to reach that elusive goal. Nonetheless, this wing came as close to perfection as a military airlift unit is apt to get. The mind boggling number of safely flown flying hours, most flown in day-to-day airlift operations, is a solid testimonial to the superiority of this unit's leaders, the effectiveness of its training programs and trainers (human and mechanical) and the dedication and motivation of its personnel in all career fields. As will be seen, this unit didn't just accumulate thousands of safe flying hours. It accumulated hundreds of thousands of safe flying hours, and that this was done while flying an airplane as mechanically demanding as the C-124 is an achievement of the highest proportions.

Effective July 1, 1955, the 1500th Air Transport Group (ATG) became the 1502nd ATG per Military Air Transport Service General Order Number 105, dated 14 June 1955. The unit, at this time, had three Air Transport Squadrons (ATSs): the 47th, flying C-97 aircraft; the 48th, flying 12 C-124A aircraft; and the 50th, flying 16 C-124A aircraft. Maintenance was provided by the 1502nd Maintenance Group and its associated squadrons.

Some time before 1958, the 47th ATS was either disbanded or transferred to another group or wing. This left the 1502nd with two C-124 squadrons, their composition not changing. By June 1960, the 48th transitioned from C-124As to C-118 "Liftmasters". Remarkably, the 48th accumulated some 130,000 accident-free flying hours before the last Globemaster II was phased out.

Above, 1502nd ATW, 50th ATS C-124C 51-0119 at Tachikawa AFB on 17 May 1958. (via Craig Kaston)

The beginning of 1960 saw the two C-124 equipped squadrons participating in Operation Big Slam, a mobility exercise that saw the units airlift 1,364 troops and 401 tons of cargo and equipment belonging to the 25th Infantry Division between Hickam AFB and General Lyman J. Field, Hawaii. As mentioned above, by mid-year, the 50th ATS was flying all of the wing's C-124 airlift missions, utilizing 16 C-124A aircraft. While the role of the C-118 within the wing was significant, time would prove that the C-124s would play the most significant role in meeting the wing's mission taskings and, in time, the wing would again be completely C-124 equipped.

Operation "Blue Straw", flown in support of Joint Task Force 8, was supported by both 1502nd airlift squadrons. Various islands in the Pacific were to be working locations for units involved in the Pacific nuclear testing program. Some of these island landing strips were in relatively poor condition and were considered less than safe to use, conditions being measured against normal MATS operating criteria. The priority of the missions, however, dictated that missions be flown to all the islands involved. The 1502nd by this time had become the prime mover of personnel and equipment associated with the Task Force mission.

The early phase of the operation was largely exploratory and the number of missions involved was relatively small. Once definite locations were identified, movement of personnel and equipment increased in steady

increments. At the peak of the movement process, 12 - 13 aircraft were flying daily to Christmas Island and 4 - 5 aircraft were flying daily to Johnston Island. Both islands were identified as the center of delivery operations during this period.

The construction phase of the operation saw the wing fly 599 of the 890 total airlift missions flown in support of JTF-8. With the completion of this phase, a resupply phase was initiated and this required far fewer support missions, the number flow monthly dropping by as much as 60 percent.

By the end of June 1962, the wing had flown 1,073 missions in support of JTF-8. Of these, 795 missions were flown by C-124 aircraft moving more than 3,500 passengers and nearly 10,000 tons of cargo. As thought was given to the end of the program, and discussions of how personnel and equipment would be returned to their home stations, plans were made to move the majority by land and sea means.

Personnel and aircraft of the 50th ATS were involved in 528 missions airlifting more than 11,000 soldiers and better than 5,500 tons of equipment between the islands of Oahu and Hawaii, in support of the 25th Infantry Division. 515 of the missions departed on time, resulting in a 97.5

At left, 60th MAW, 28th ATS C-124C leaves Hickam AFB, Hawaii. MATS has been replaced with MAC on the tail stripe. (Nick Williams via Berlin)

Above, 50th ATS C-124C 51-0102 in overall natural metal during Operation Long Sabre II. (Air Force via Nick Williams)

percent reliability rate. The missions were flown over a five month period, from January to May 1962. A better idea of the effectiveness of the airlift effort during this period can be gained by examining the chart below.

#Missions	#Delays	Reliability	#Passengers	Tons
16 - 19 Jan				
90	3	96.7%	1,166	595.3
6 - 9 Feb				
90	1	98.9%	2,294	1,141.7
1 - 4 Mar				
90	3	96.7%	2,250	1,130.5
25 - 28 Mar				
88	1	98.9%	2,098	1,107.9
17 - 20 Apr				
90	3	96.7%	2,194	1,095.8
14 - 17 May				
80	2	97.5%	1,063	475.2
Total				
528	13	97.5%	11,065	5,546.4

The 1502nd ATW participated in the first ever Military Air Transport Service worldwide paradrop competition which was held at Scott AFB from 16 to 22 April 1962. Two aircrews and a ten man ground crew beat six other MATS crews in the competition that tested the effectiveness of unit training programs and C-124 crew proficiency in aerial delivery procedures. The two-day competition involved day and night parachute drops.

Beginning in July 1962, JTF-8 support requirements to Christmas Island decreased dramatically. On the other hand, support of operations to Johnston Island increased substantially. The wing flew a total of 422 missions in support of JTF-8 during the last half of 1962. Of these, 266 were flown by wing C-124s. Wing C-118s focused their efforts on moving passengers and small amounts of cargo while the C-124s moved far greater proportions of cargo but smaller numbers of passengers.

Cuban Missile Crisis

The wing was called upon to support U.S. operations in response to the Cuban Missile Crisis in October 1962. Peak operational readiness rate for wing C-124s during this period was 96 percent; for C-118s it was 95 percent.

During the crisis, 28 percent of the wing's personnel were deployed. Wing personnel augmented personnel from the 1501st ATW at George AFB, California, and manned control teams at two Florida bases.

Lava Ridge

From January to April, 1963, the wing participated in joint Army-Air Force airborne training exercises between Hickam and General Lyman Field, Hilo, Hawaii. The exercise, conducted in five phases, was known as Lava Ridge. Exercise dates were:

January 7 - 10; 28 - 31
February 18 - 21
March 11 - 14
April 1 - 4

During the first phase of the operation, 46 missions were flown with an overall reliability rate of 84.8 percent. The second phase saw the reliability rate rise to 98 percent and the third phase saw the reliability rate climb to 100 percent. The third phase was flown by 28 C-118s and 76 C-124s. Reliability rate for the fourth phase of the exercise, involving 110 missions, was 98.2 percent. The fifth phase of the exercise was completed with a 96.3 percent reliability rate. Overall reliability rate for the exercises was 97.2 percent for 532 departures.

C-118s were recorded as 100 percent reliable during the entire exercise. C-124s were 96.5 percent reliable over the same period. C-124 reliability at Hickam was 93.5 percent while that recorded at Hilo was 99.5 percent.

Exercise High Top — 1964

During the latter part of 1963, the Department of Defense directed a massive airlift of personnel and equipment from the 25th Infantry Division between Hickam AFB, Oahu and Hilo, Hawaii. Very similar to the previous Hilo and Lava Ridge exercises, this exercise involved the airlift of 12,800 troops and 5,200 tons of cargo. The 1501st and 1502nd ATWs participated, the 1502nd ATW providing the majority of the airlift and functioning as the controlling agency. The exercise was conducted between January and May 1964 and was broken down into five deployment phases and five redeployment phases. Each phase was expected to last approximately two days.

In March 1964, orders were published by Headquarters, Pacific Air Forces, directing the 6th Troop Carrier Squadron, Heavy, to move from Tachikawa Air Base, Japan, to Hickam AFB, Hawaii. The requested move was to be completed as soon as practical after June 1, 1964. With 16 C-124s assigned, the unit came be a welcome addition to the 1502nd ATW.

Operation Long Sabre

This operation was divided into three phases, conducted from September through December 1964. The 1502nd's part of the exercise involved moving the 1st, 2nd and 3rd Brigade Task Forces of the 25th Infantry Division between Hickam AFB and General Lyman Field, Hilo, Hawaii. All three of the wing's squadrons were involved in the airlift operation.

For the C-124 crews, the exercise involved a significant amount of formation flying. The Globemaster IIs were flown in three and six aircraft formations, flying in designated air corridors, and the goal was to simulate a paradrop over Molokai Island on each mission.

Execution of the exercise was governed by MATS OPORD 30-64, prepared by the 1502nd ATW. Plans called for the airlift of approximately 10,300 troops and 4,680 tons of equipment. To accomplish this, 680 missions involving some 1,190 flying hours were expected to be flown. Each deployment was expected to airlift approximately 1,800 troops and 780 tons of equipment. An Airlift Control Force was established at Hilo and at Hickam for the exercise.

Long Sabre I involved the deployment and redeployment of the 1st Infantry Brigade Task Force. Advance party personnel were airlifted on September 13, departing from Hickam AFB.

The actual deployment phase began on September 14. It continued on the 15th, 17th and 18th. Two C-118s and six C-124s were committed to each day's support of the exercise, with one C-118 and two C-124s acting as backup machines. 1,280 passengers and 838.6 tons of cargo were airlifted during this phase. Airlift reliability at Hilo was 100 percent and at Hickam was 98.2 percent. Total mission reliability was recorded as 98.2 percent for this phase.

Long Sabre II involved the deployment and redeployment of the

2nd Infantry Brigade Task Force. Again, an advance part was prepositioned before the main airlift began. Daily aircraft commitment was two C-118s and nine C-124s. Again, reliability was very high, that at Hilo recorded as 100 percent and at Hickam as 93 percent, with an overall average of 97 percent.

Long Sabre III also involved the deployment and redeployment of the 3rd Infantry Brigade Task Force. Advance party prepositioning followed the previous practices and again two C-118s and nine C-124s were committed daily. Reliability rates for the deployment phase recorded at Hilo and Hickam were the same: 96.5 percent for a 96.5 percent overall average.

For the redeployment phase of Long Sabre III, two C-118s and eight C-124s were committed daily. During this phase, aircraft and personnel from the 1501st ATW and 62nd Troop Carrier Wing (TCW) were involved, flying a total of 25 redeployment missions. Three C-124s and five crews were provided by the 1501st ATW while two C-124s and four crews were provided by the 62nd TCW.

Reliability statistics for the redeployment phase of Long Sabre III were as impressive as they were for the first two phases. Hickam recorded a 96.7 percent reliability while Hilo recorded a 97.9 percent figure. Overall reliability was 97.9 percent.

Overall, the 1502nd's performance during Long Sabre was out-

Above, 1502 ATW C-124C 51-0142 with tail stand fitted to the tail skid and the elevator belly doors open aft of the wing. (via Nick Williams)

standing. Of the 698 missions flown, 680 departed on time. This allowed the recording of a 97.4 percent reliability rate for the overall exercise. Just under 7,900 troops and 5,300 tons of cargo were airlifted.

500,000 Accident-Free Hours Flown

In July, 1964, the wing recorded an accomplishment that went down as a first in aviation history. On 23 July, the wing commemorated the event. The accomplishment: the accumulation of 500,000 accident-free flying hours. Flying day and night for over eight years, carrying passengers and cargo all over the world, the wing built up the best safety record in aviation history.

The wing was justly proud of this achievement, for it represented military professionalism at its best. To achieve this kind of statistic required the best in leadership, training, dedication, motivation and pride. This achievement was no accident and a lot of hard work and determination were expended to achieve it.

600,000 Accident-Free Hours Flown

In September 1965, the wing bettered its previous flying safety record

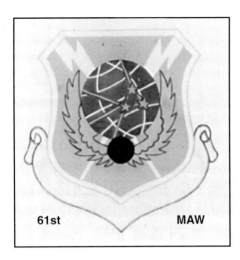

61st   MAW

61st MILITARY AIRLIFT SUPPORT WING

by reaching the 600,000 accident-free flying hours mark. General Howell M. Estes, Jr., MATS Commander, said in his congratulatory remarks:

"The completion of 500,000 hours of accident-free flying by the 1502d Air Transport Wing was greeted by the aviation world as a phenomenal feat, unparalleled in flying history. Now you have added another 100,000 hours to that remarkable record.

This is added proof that the many complex and individual elements of your mission have been welded into a smooth, effective whole by superior management techniques. With this operational harmony there is no practical limit to the goals you can achieve in the future.

I congratulate you and each member of your command for the obvious pride in individual excellence which made this record possible. I have every confidence that you will continue to achieve even greater results in the demanding years ahead. Well done."

The wing continued to perform in an outstanding manner and when, in January 1966, the wing came under the control of the Military Airlift Command and gained a new numerical designation, it didn't merely start over. As the 61st Military Airlift Wing, it continued the proud traditions established by the 1502nd ATW.

The wing proved its ability during a "No-Notice" Operational Readiness Inspection (ORI) in late August 1966. The exercise lasted four days and involved flying 27 missions. In addition to exercise missions, the wing flew regularly scheduled missions and averaged an overall 96.3 percent maintenance reliability rate.

By 1967, the wing had three squadrons, two at Hickam (6th and 50th) and one at Tachikawa, Japan (22nd). Total aircraft possessed was

48, 32 located at Hickam and the remainder at Tachikawa. Operational readiness was well above the standard. The chart below shows the monthly readiness, in percent, for the first six months of 1967. Note that the two squadrons at Hickam didn't perform quite as well as the single squadron in Japan, but the difference was just under 10 percent.

C-124s At Hickam

Jan	Feb	Mar	Apr	May	Jun	Avg
Operational Ready (Percent)						
84	81	79	78	78	79	79.8

C-124s At Tachikawa

Jan	Feb	Mar	Apr	May	Jun	Avg
Operational Ready (Percent)						
89	88	89	90	93	83	89.3

The wing accumulated 33,371 accident-free flying hours during the

Below, 61st MAW C-124C 51-7276 lifts off from Hickam AFB, Hawaii. 61 MAW was painted on each nose gear door on the white stylized FB-111 silhoutte. (Nick Williams 1968-69)

Above, 61st MAW C-124C 51-7282 thunders across the runway at Hickam on 31 January 1968. (Nick Williams)
Below, lightly loaded C-124C 51-7276 leaving Hickam in 1968. (Nick Williams)

first half of 1967. This brought the grand total of accident free flying hours to 723,444 since 1956. Also during this period, the wing received its third Outstanding Unit Award, the period covered being July 1964 to June 1966. The award was given in recognition of the wing's successful gearing up to meet the ever increasing airlift demands brought about by the Vietnam conflict. The citation read:

"The 61st Military Airlift Wing, Military Airlift Command, distinguished itself by exceptionally meritorious service from 1 July 1964 to 30 June 1966. During this period, the performance of the personnel of the 61st Military Airlift Wing made significant contributions to the furtherance of United States national policy and objectives worldwide, with particular emphasis on support of military objectives in Southeast Asia. In doing so, the Wing wrote new chapters of meritorious service constituting achievement of truly international significance, including both trans-Pacific airlift operations to meet general theater logistics requirements and direct specific support of organizations facing hostile action by unfriendly forces in Southeast Asia. While doing so, the Wing flew 161,513 accident-free flying hours to reach the unparalleled cumulative total of 656,032 hours without accident. The outstanding initiative,

resourcefulness, and professionalism displayed by the members of the 61st Military Airlift Wing reflect credit upon themselves and the United States Air Force."

In the midst of this superb flying, the wing was recognized for reaching the 700,000 accident-free flying hours mark. On February 23rd, a 6th MAS crew landed at Wake Island, having surpassed the significant milestone. Looking back, the achievement was recognized for what it represented in terms of individual flying squadron accomplishments. The 6th and 22nd had flown for four years, accident-free. The 50th had accumulated ten years of accident-free flying, total flying hours numbering 300,000.

About this achievement, Major General Joseph A. Cunningham remarked, "This record can only reflect on the commanders, aircrews, supervisors and support people. It proves the Air Force philosophy, 'accidents are not inevitable—they are avoidable.'"

Moon Dust Exercise:

The Hawaiian islands had been the site of numerous airlift exercises, involving the 1502nd ATW, over the years, and these had come to be known as the "Hilo Airlift" because they involved movements between Hickam AFB and Hilo, Hawaii. These exercises continued in Fiscal Year

1967, though they were now called "Moon Dust".

"Moon Dust" was supported entirely by C-124s and crews from the 61st MAW. Aircraft flew at a constant interval on a round-the-clock basis. "Moon Dust I, II and IV" were ultimately canceled. But "Moon Dust III, V, VI and VII" were completed, "Moon Dust III" commencing on 3 October 1966. "Moon Dust" exercises V, VI and VII took place during the first half of 1967.

The flight time to Hilo was approximately one and a half hours. C-124s arriving at Hilo, without cargo but filled with troops, would leave their engines running as the troops deplaned. Sometimes, this troop offload took only eight minutes and the C-124s were able to immediately depart for Hickam afterward. Remarkably, the 61st Wing maintained a 100 percent reliability rate during the "Moon Dust" exercises.

The unit received its fifth Outstanding Unit Award during 1968, being recognized for airlifting more than 900,000 tons of cargo, processing more than 6 million passenger movements, giving medical care to 88,665 wounded and sick patients airlifted from Vietnam and other Pacific locations and supporting more than 124,000 aircraft departures throughout the many areas of respon-

Below, 61st MAW C-124C 51-5205 being loaded at Hickham AFB in 1969. Note red prop warning line on inboard engine cowling. (Nick Williams)

sibility it maintained in the Pacific region. In addition, the wing flew 60,950 accident-free hours during the reporting period (1 July 1967 through 30 June 1968).

Leprechaun Laughter

This exercise, like the previous "Moon Dust" exercise, was similar to the former "Hilo Airlift" exercises and was conducted as shown below.

Exercise Actual Operating Dates
Leprechaun Laughter I (Deployment)
25 August and 28 - 30 August 67
Leprechaun Laughter I (Redeployment)
02 October and 07-09 October 67
Leprechaun Laughter II (Deployment)
02 October and 07-09 October 67
Leprechaun Laughter II (Redeployment)
27 - 29 October 67
Leprechaun Laughter IV (Deployment)
08 April and 15 - 17 April 67
Leprechaun Laughter IV (Redeployment)
19 - 22 May 67

In the midst of the demands of the Vietnam Conflict, the wing continued to maintain its excellent flying record. It was indeed notable that the wing passed the 800,000 accident-free flying hour mark while returning from Vietnam. What made the achievement truly noteworthy was the fact the giant C-124s were flying into and out of some of the smallest airfields found in Southeast Asia.

Safety Awards For 1968

Because the wing flew its own missions and provided enroute support for all MAC aircraft flying throughout the Pacific areas, its responsibilities were quite large when compared with those of other MAC wings. The wing had been maintaining these responsibilities for some years and this made its flying safety record all the more remarkable. To do its job, the wing had 41 subordinate units in 26 locations all over the Pacific. Some were in Hawaii, others in Vietnam, still others were in New Zealand and Australia. Altogether, the wing picked up 12 safety awards for 1968.

1969: Achievement and Termination

During the first six months of 1969, the wing flew 18,755 hours; 14,403 hours being flown by the Hickam based C-124s and 4,352 hours being flown by the Tachikawa based aircraft. The second half of the year saw the wing fly 10,450 hours. The wing also flew more actual hours during the second half of the year than were programmed. The monthly breakdown, shown below, reflects the accomplishment.

Jul	Aug	Sep	Oct	Nov	Dec
% of Programmed Flying Schedule					
102	103	99	101	106	-

The 22nd Military Airlift Squadron, one of two still assigned to the 61st Military Airlift Wing by 1969, was deactivated on 8 June. The final mission was flown on April 2, some two months before. The unit had flown 120,000 accident-free hours over a period of just under seven years. 15,000 of those were flown under hazardous conditions within the combat zone. With the deactivation of the squadron, a brilliant 27 year history, 20 years of which were recorded in Japan, came to a close. The 22nd MAS ended its operations recognized as the most decorated airlift squadron in the Military Airlift Command. It's interesting to note that the squadron didn't slow down its flying operations in anticipation of its deactivation. It kept right on doing its job, right on up to the final moment when the powers-that-be yelled "STOP!"

Following not far behind the 22nd MAS, deactivation-wise, was the 50th MAS, the last operational flying squadron in the 61st MAW. Formally

Below, 61st MAW C-124C 51-5202 landing at Hickam AFB in 1969. Note landing flap position. (Nick Williams)

Above, 1502rd ATW 22 TCS C-124A 51-0178 with red nose and tail stripe and wing-tip heaters. (via Nick Williams)

deactivated on December 22, 1969, the unit closed out the wing's flying operations with a total of 838,670 accident-free hours, the record dating back to June 1956. The 50th MAS had accumulated a total of 376,345 accident-free flying hours. While some of the accident-free hours had been logged by C-118s and C-97s, the majority were logged by the giant Globemaster IIs.

The 50th MAS, as the last flying squadron in the 61st MAW, was among the last three C-124

Below, 1503rd ATW C-124A 51-0126 at Osan AB, Korea in April 1959. The upper cabin area was painted white with a black cheat line. (Norm Taylor collection via Earl Berlin)

squadrons in the active duty Air Force. The other two squadrons were at McChord AFB, Washington, and Kelly AFB, Texas.

The 50th had come to the 1502nd ATW as a C-124 outfit, having converted to the giant cargo plane while assigned to the 1500th Air Transport Group. The conversion took place in 1955. In 1958, the squadron joined the 1502nd ATW and when, in 1966, the 1502nd became the 61st MAW (under MAC), the 50th ATS became the 50th MAS. It served the 61st MAW with honor from then on.

With the deactivation of the 50th MAS, C-124 operations within the 61st MAW came to a halt. The unit history, from which this information was taken, does not reflect known plans, at that time, to begin airlift operations with a newer type of aircraft.

1503rd ATW/65th MAG

The 1503rd Air Transport Wing

operated in the Pacific region, the unit being based in Japan. Unit historical records pick up operations being conducted in 1956 and reflect the unit's involvement in accelerated testing of the C-124A.

The purpose of the accelerated testing was to establish whether aircraft utilization could be doubled without adversely affecting safety of flight and mission accomplishment. To test the idea, the amount of cargo that would normally be airlifted in one month was to be airlifted in ten days. The conclusion drawn, at the end of the test, was that such operations could be safely conducted. On the other hand, the test was viewed as not totally realistic, with respect to simulating a war-time scenario. This conclusion was drawn based on the fact that the units involved were given advance notice and were able to gather necessary augmentees and additional equipment to make the test a success. There was speculation that, in a war-time situation, such a flying schedule would be more difficult to maintain as fewer augmentees would be available and the doubled airlift tasking would begin on short notice.

1959 was the year of Operation Handclasp V, a joint US-Australian airpower display conducted to demonstrate the spirit of cooperation between the two countries through a mutual aerial display of military might. The exercise was held in conjunction with Australia's commemoration of the Battle of the Coral Sea and ANZAC day. ANZAC day originated during World War I but honors Australian and New Zealand war dead of both World Wars, according to the 1959 report. The commemoration may well honor war dead of the Korean and Vietnam conflicts today. It is similar to Memorial Day, celebrated in the U.S.

The exercise, conducted from April 25 through May 7, saw C-124s from the 6th and 22nd Troop Carrier Squadrons deliver 72,000 pounds of communications equipment to various sites in Australia, to be set up prior to the arrival of RF-101s, RB-

66s, KB-50s and C-130s which were used for aerial demonstrations, flybys and static displays throughout the operation. These activities took place in Brisbane, Sydney, Richmond, Amberly, East Sale and Melbourne.

1960 historical records for the wing reflect two C-124 squadrons (6th and 22nd) and one Navy squadron (Detachment Alpha, VR-7) assigned to the wing. The Navy unit was under the operational control of the 315th Air Division but under administrative control of VR-7 at Moffett Field, California. As noted in the records, the 1503rd's C-124s were the only such aircraft assigned to the Far East at this time. It's primary commitment was to carry passengers and cargo between Japan, South Korea and Iwo Jima. Approximately 45 percent of the wing's mission came under the "special" classification and these were controlled by the 315th Air Division. Not surprisingly, the wing maintained a mobility commitment and was prepared to support emergency (natural disasters, etc.) and wartime commitments as necessary.

In early October 1961, the wing dispatched six C-124s from Yokota AB, Japan to Cambodia. The airplanes were carrying heavy cranes and tractors to help with flood relief operations. The tractors and cranes were delivered completely intact so that they could be put to work immediately upon arrival. Each airplane five in all, the sixth being a backup carried an average of 46,000 pounds of equipment.

The historical records of 1962 reflect one operation that, though small in concept, was significant in that it demonstrated the kind of quality airmanship the men of the 1503rd were capable of. A group of military personnel were snow-bound at Cheju-do Island, South Korea, and needed to be supplied with food and mail. A C-124 dropped a total of 7,000 pounds of goods from an altitude of 1,500 feet. The drops were so well performed that the gentle landings allowed eggs to arrive unbroken.

Southeast Asia Treaty Organization (SEATO) Exercise Dhanarajata/Tidal Wave was con-

ducted during late May and the first half of June 1963. The exercise involved aircraft and personnel from all over MATS and was the largest the wing had ever been involved in. Flights of 4,000 miles in length, through precise corridors, in formation at times, were recorded and believed to be the longest ever in MATS for aerial deliveries. Nine C-124s and two backups were used during the initial phase and ten C-124s were used during what was called the retrograde phase.

The wing historical records record routine operations, mostly, up to the first part of 1964, when its support of Operation Wingover is mentioned. Wing C-124s supported the participation of F-105 Thunderchief aircraft in New Zealand Air Force Day ceremonies held at Ohakea, New Zealand. The celebration, held on 22 February, required support missions that lasted until the first week in

---

Below, MAC C-124C 52-1024 unloading cargo in 1966. (USAF)

Above, 1607th ATW C-124C 52-0992 with red tail and wing markings. Upper fuselage was white with a dark blue cheat line. (via Williams)

March. A total of fourteen C-124 missions were flown to New Guinea, Australia, and New Zealand in support of the celebration.

In March, the wing participated in Exercise Silver Leaf, a two-phased operation that tested the wing's ability to fly corridor and formation missions, dropping joint personnel on an established schedule. Wing performance was excellent as seventeen of the eighteen C-124s blocked out of the chocks ahead of schedule. Included in the first phase of the exercise was a 24-plane formation paradrop at Yontan Drop Zone, Okinawa. This marked a first for the Military Air Transport Service as it represented the largest number of aircraft to participate in a single paradrop mission. The second phase of the exercise was to have included a 25-plane mission to Yontan, but inclement weather caused this phase to be canceled after the first fourteen airplanes had been launched.

At the beginning of 1964, the wing had 33 C-124s assigned, all distributed between the 6th and 22nd Troop Carrier Squadrons. This was an increase of 7 C-124s over what the wing had in its inventory at the beginning of 1963. By May, however, the wing began losing C-124s as the 6th TCS was transferred to Hickam AFB and the 1502nd ATW. By mid-June, the wing had 17 C-124s remaining.

When MATS became MAC, in June 1966, the 1503rd ATW became the 65th MAG. By 1969, the group's only remaining active C-124 squadron, the 22nd MAS, had transferred to the 61st MAW and the 65th MAG closed down.

1607th ATW/436th MAW

In March 1954, notification was received by the 1607th Air Base Group that its activities were to be terminated and responsibility for Dover AFB, Delaware, was to go to the 1607th ATW, to be activated in June. Wing composition, in July, was two medium transport squadrons and three heavy transport squadrons. One of the heavy airlift squadrons had not received C-124s when its designation changed from medium to heavy, and as the chart below shows, another heavy airlift squadron was in the process of transitioning to the C-124 during the last half of 1954.

	Jul	Aug	Sep	Oct	Nov	Dec
1st ATS (Medium)						
C-54	7	7	7	5	2	1
C-124	0	0	0	3	3	6
21st ATS (Heavy)						
C-54	8	8	8	8	8	6
C-124	0	0	0	0	0	0
39th ATS (Medium)						
C-54	9	9	9	9	9	8
40th ATS (Heavy)						
C-124	7	7	8	8	8	8
45th ATS (Heavy)						
C-124	8	8	8	8	8	8

The units becoming operational with the new C-124s received credit for achieving several firsts. The achievements were not viewed as speed or distance records. Rather, they were looked upon as accom-

plishments indicative of routine operations that would be the norm once the units became fully operational with the new airplanes.

1 December: A C-124 left Kindley AFB, Bermuda with 5,000 pounds of cargo and flew non-stop to Burtonwood, England, in just under 14 hours.

6 December: A 45th ATS C-124 flew non-stop from Dover AFB to Burtonwood, England, and completed the 3,550 mile flight, carrying 12 tons of cargo, in 13.5 hours.

29 December: A 45th ATS C-124 flew from Nouasseur, French Morocco, to Dover AFB, a total of 4,000 miles, in just under 19 hours.

30 December: Another 45th ATS C-124 made the first non-stop flight from Burtonwood, England, to Dover AFB, against prevailing headwinds, in just over 16 hours.

These "high points" set the stage for what follows. Again, looking through wing historical records, I found that they were divided into three distinct categories:

1.) Chronology of Wing Organization Actions.

2.) Chronology of Major Exercises.

3.) Global Operations and Chronology of Significant Events

Rather than attempting to mesh information from all three categories, let's take each category separately and view the information in the light of what it represents.

Chronology Of Wing Organization Actions

1 January 1954: The 1607th Air Transport Wing (ATW) was designated and organized at Dover AFB, Delaware. The 1607th Air Transport Group (ATG) was designated and organized under the 1607th ATW. The 1st and 21st Air Transport Squadrons (ATSs), Medium, were reassigned from the 1607th Air Base Group to the 1607th ATG.

15 February 1954: The 39th ATS and 45th ATS were activated at Dover AFB and assigned to the 1607th ATG (MATS General Order 211, dated 16 November 1953).

16 February 1954: The 39th Air Transport Squadron was designated as a "Medium" squadron while the 45th Air Transport Squadron was designated as a "Heavy" squadron.

8 March 1954: The 40th Air Transport Squadron was activated as a "Heavy" airlift squadron at Dover AFB.

8 September 1954: The 1st and 21st Air Transport Squadrons, Medium, were redesignated as 1st and 21st Air Transport Squadrons, Heavy, and reorganized with an authorized strength of 46 officers and 228 airmen each.

20 September 1954: The 1607th Air Transport Wing was redesignated as the 1607th Air Transport Wing, Heavy.

20 April 1955: The 15th Air Transport Squadron, Heavy, was reassigned from the 1600th Air Transport Group, Heavy, Westover AFB, Massachusetts, to the 1607th ATW. Records indicate the actual transfer was implemented on 15 April, 12 C-124 aircraft being taken on strength.

20 May 1955: The 20th Air Transport Squadron, Heavy, was reassigned from the 1600th Air Transport Group, Heavy, Westover AFB, Massachusetts. The squadron arrived in mid-May with 8 C-124 aircraft.

20 June 1955: The 31st Air Transport Squadron, Heavy, was reassigned from the 1600th Air Transport Group, Heavy. The unit arrived at Dover AFB around mid-June with 12 C-124 aircraft.

1 July 1955: The 21st and 45th Air Transport Squadrons were inactivated. Personnel of the 21st were phased into the 1st Air Transport Squadron while the 20th and 40th Air Transport Squadrons absorbed personnel from the 45th Air Transport Squadron.

8 September 1957: The 39th Air Transport Squadron, Medium, was redesignated the 39th Air Transport Squadron, Heavy (MATS General Order 87, dated 20 Aug 57).

8 December 1960: The 40th Air Transport Squadron was discontinued and its personnel were absorbed by the other ATSs.

1 January 1965: The 15th Air Transport Squadon, Heavy, was discontinued at Dover AFB and reverted to the control of the Department of the Air Force. The 20th Air Transport Squadron, Heavy, was redesignated as the 20th Troop Carrier Squadron (TCS), Heavy, with no change of assignment at Dover.

1 June 1965: The 31st Air Transport Squadron, Heavy, was redesignated the 31st Troop Carrier Squadron, Heavy, and reorganized at Dover AFB.

1 July 1965: The 20th Troop Carrier Squadron, Heavy, was redesignated the 20th Air Transport Squadron, Heavy, with no change of assignment.

Chronology Of Major Exercises And Global Operations

March 1960: BIG SLAM/PUERTO PINE: This exercise joined forces from MATS and the Strategic Army Corps (STRAC) for the deployment of approximately 22,000 combat troops and 12,000 tons of equipment from stateside sites to Ramey Air Force Base and Roosevelt Roads Naval Air Station in Puerto Rico. Dover

AFB aircraft and crews flew 9,073 C-124 hours and 1,232 C-133 hours during the exercise.

July 1960 - 1964: CONGO AIRLIFT: On 16 July 1960, MATS entered the airlift of United Nations troops and equipment into the strife torn Belgian Congo. This operation, under the direction of United States Air Forces Europe (USAFE), was known as NEW TAPE and was history's longest airlift. From the beginning of the operation until December 1961, the major portion of the Congo airlift support was provided by the Dover wing. During that period, entire squadrons from the wing were deployed overseas to man Provisional Squadrons that had formed at Chateauroux Air Station, France, which had been activated to support this operation. Requirements for Congo missions slowly decreased, but the wing continued to support the airlift on a special mission basis. By the end of June 1963, the wing had flown nearly 28,000 hours in support of the United Nations effort.

13 - 28 August 1960: BRIGHT STAR/PINE CONE III: This exercise was conducted with elements of STRAC. Ten of the wing's C-124 aircraft, 16 aircrews, and maintenance personnel participated in the airlift of 8,600 troops and 3,500 tons of equipment of the 101st Airborne Division from Campbell Army Air Field, Kentucky, to base in North and South Carolina.

October 1960: TIP TOP: This exercise was conducted in support of Air Force-Army joint airborne operations. Four C-133s and 8 C-124s from the wing, their crews and members of the Movement Control Team were involved.

Above, 1607th ATW C-124C 52-1003, at Fort Worth, TX, on 9 August 1958. (L. Paul via Williams) Below, 52-1067 with da-glo nose and tail stripes. (via Williams)

October - November 1960: SOUTH WIND: Eleven Dover-based C-124 aircraft and their crews, plus over 40 support personnel were involved with the airlift of more than 10,000 troops and their equipment from various stateside locations to an area in the southeastern part of the country.

February 1961: LONG PASS: This exercise was conducted by units of the United States Armed Forces in the Clark Air Base - Stotsenberg Training Area in the Philippines. The wing furnished 23 C-124s and 13 C-133s and crews which airlifted approximately 6,000 Army and Air Force personnel and tons of supplies and combat gear to a simulated battle in the Philippines. The C-124s flew 2,337+ hours and the C-133s flew 1,035+ hours during the operation.

August 1961: SWIFT STRIKE I: This was one of the largest full scale joint peacetime field training exercises held in the United States to date. Troops and equipment were airlifted from Campbell AAF to North and South Carolina, where the exercise was conducted. The wing was committed to provide 20 C-124 aircraft and crews and flew 1,180 hours.

September 1961: CHECK MATE II: The exercise consisted of deployment and redeployment of elements of the 301st Airborne Division from Campbell AAF to Europe for a series of training exercises. The wing was committed to provide 24 C-124s and 23 C-133s which flew 1,689 and 1,153 hours respectively.

January - February 1962: GREAT SHELF: This exercise was a joint EASTAF/WESTAF operation involving the airlift of more than 2,300 Army troops and over 1,100 tons of combat equipment from the United States to an area in the Pacific for training exercises. The Dover-based wing contributed 3 C-133s and 17 C-124s to the effort. 20 C-133 missions and 26 C-124 missions were flown.

May 1962: QUICK KICK/LONG BASE: This was a major Atlantic Command exercise conducted in the Camp LeJeune-Cherry Point area of North Carolina. The exercise, aside from being a training function, was designed to test the latest methods and weapons of warfare employed by the U.S. Armed Forces (other than the Coast Guard). The Dover wing flew 31 C-124 missions in support of the exercise.

July - August 1962: SWIFT STRIKE II: This exercise was conducted by USSTRICOM forces in the North and South Carolina areas. The wing provided 17 C-124s and 5 C-133s in direct support of the exercise.

September - October 1962: THREE PAIRS: This was a joint training exercise conducted in the Fort Hood, Texas, area. The wing flew 12 C-124 and 22 C-133 missions which logged 192 and 438 airframe hours, respectively.

4 -14 October 1962: SOUTHERN EXPRESS: This NATO exercise involved airlift of troops and equipment from central Europe to northern Greece for training exercises. The wing flew 14 C-124 missions in support of the operation.

October 1962: CUBAN MISSILE CRISIS: MATS was called on to support the build-up of U.S. forces in the southeastern part of the United States, as a result of President Kennedy's decision to blockade Cuba. 1607th ATW C-124s and C-133s, along with MATS aircraft from other wings, worked at peak capacity to meet the airlift requirements of U.S. forces, throughout the crisis. Many of the wing's personnel, from maintenance and support units, were dispatched to other locations during the emergency.

November 1962: INDIAN AIRLIFT: MATS airlifted arms for India to stem the Communist Chinese invasion. The mission was given to the 322d Air Division in Europe. On November 21, the 15th ATS (12 aircraft) was deployed to Chateauroux, France, to man the 1st Air Transport Squadron (Provisional) which had been activated to support the 322d's efforts during this emergency.

April - May 1963: COULEE CREST: This was one of the largest joint training exercises to be conducted in the United States to date. USSTRICOM forces from the central and eastern Continental United States (CONUS) were airlifted to the Yakima, Washington, area. Wing C-124s, C-133s and personnel were involved, some of the personnel being sent to four separate bases as support team members.

May - June - July 1963: TIDAL WAVE: CONARC and AFSTRIKE units from the United States were deployed to Korat and Tahkie, Thailand, for participation in the joint SEATO exercise and returned to their home stations upon completion. The wing provided C-124s, C-133s and support teams in support of the exercise.

June 1963: SUNDAY PUNCH: This was a USCINEUR (U.S. Commander in Chief, Europe) Airborne Brigade exercise conducted in the Sennelager area in Germany. Wing C-124s and aircrews supported the deployment and redeployment phases of the operation.

July - August 1963: SWIFT STRIKE III: The wing participated in the MATS stateside airlift of U.S. STRICOM elements in the largest peacetime airlift ever attempted in the United States to date. During the three phases of the exercise, wing C-124 and C-133 aircraft flew just over 9,000 hours. Nearly 1,500 wing personnel were deployed to five separate locations to support aircraft transiting these stations.

October - November 1963: BIG LIFT: The exercise was MATS' first movement of an entire Army Division overseas. 236 missions moved 14,666 troops and 423 tons of battle equipment from Texas to Germany in 63 hours, five minutes. The wing provided 31 C-124 and 40 C-133 aircraft and their crews, logging over 3,400 hours. Over 450 wing personnel were deployed to 11 different locations, stateside and overseas, to the transiting aircraft.

April 1964 DELAWAR: (A Persian word that means "courage") This exercise involved ground, sea and air forces in maneuvers in Iran. MATS airlifted 2,250 combat troops and 425 tons of battle equipment from Fort Cambell, Kentucky, to Iran. The wing provided 14 C-133 and 4 C-124 aircraft. Combined flying time logged was 1,510.5 hours. Over 400 wing personnel were deployed to stateside and overseas locations to support the airlift operations.

April - May - June 1964 DESERT STRIKE: In the largest Army-Air Force exercise since World War II, MATS airlifted nearly 30,000 troops and more than 20,000 tons of equipment to the Mojave Desert area in California, Nevada and Arizona. In airlifting elements of the 101st Airborne Division, STRICOM and the XVIII Airborne Corps, wing C-124 and C-133 aircraft flew a total of 6,164 hours. Over 750 wing personnel were deployed to six stateside bases to support the airlift operations.

June - September 1964 INDIAN RIVER: This three-phase joint exercise was conducted within the Eglin AFB complex. Wing C-124s flew

Below, 1607th ATW C-124C 53-0043, during operation Swift Strike III in July 1963. (USAF via Craig Kaston)

34

more than 1,600 hours, while wing C-133s flew 641 hours, in support of the exercise.

27 August 1964: A Dover C-124 from the 31st ATS flew a mercy mission to Guadaloupe Island to airlift emergency supplies to the inhabitants after the island was hit by hurricane Cleo.

October - November 1964 GOLD FIRE I: MATS flew 1,400 missions in seven days, air-lifting 10,000 men and 20,000 tons of equipment between bases in the southeastern United States. The exercise was a test of the new joint Army-Air Force battlefield logistics concepts and was conducted near Fort Leonard Wood, Missouri. Wing C-124s and C-133s supported the exercise, flying more than 4,900 hours spread over the deployment and redeployment phases. Interestingly, more than two thirds of the hours were flown during the deployment phase.

6 - 8 December 1964 AYACUCHO: This was a multi-nation Latin American Defense exercise, conducted in Peru. Wing C-124 and C-133 aircraft flew a total of 762 hours in support of the operation.

January - March 1965 POLAR STRIKE: This exercise evaluated USSTRICOM's ability to reinforce the Alaskan Command while cold weather testing all exercise components. MATS moved Army units from various United States posts to McChord AFB and Fort Lewis, Washington, and then on to Alaska. The wing provided 15 C-124s during the deployment phase and 9 C-124s during the redeployment phase, for a total of 1,165 hours flown.
April - May 1965

SILVER HAND: This was a joint training exercise conducted in the Fort Hood, Texas, area during May. MATS provided airlift for deployment and redeployment of CINCSTRIKE, CIN-CARSTRIKE, and CINCAFSTRIKE forces. The

---

Below, 1607th ATW C-124C 53-0025. (via S. Nicolaou)

wing's contribution to the exercise was 6 prime and 2 backup C-124 aircraft, 460 hours being logged.

Chronology of Significant Events

12 June 1954: The wing's first heavy transport mission was flown when cargo was flown to Newfoundland on a 45th ATS C-124.

6 December 1954: A 45th ATS C-124 and crew flew non-stop from Dover AFB to Burtonwood, England, carrying 24,000 pounds of priority cargo. This trip, lasting 13.5 hours, was a first for the wing.

29 December 1954: A 45th ATS C-124 and crew flew non-stop from Nousasseur, French Morocco, to Dover AFB. The 4,000 mile trip was completed in 18 hours, 50 minutes.

3 September 1955: A 1st ATS C-124, on a routine mission to Goose Bay, Labrador, was temporarily assigned to the 54th Air Rescue Squadron (ARS) at Goose Bay. The airplane and crew aided in the rescue of 26 passengers and 6 crew members of the Norwegien vessel JOPETER, which was icebound off the coast of Greenland.

15 March 1956: A C-124 from the 1st ATS departed Dover AFB carrying 22,000 pounds of emergency polio equipment and supplies to Buenos Aires, Argentina, to assist in combatting a polio epidemic.

September 1957: Six of the wing's C-124 aircraft and crews participated in Operation GOOD HOPE, involving the airlift of arms to Jordan.

23 March 1958: A C-124 and crew from the 15th ATS was diverted from a scheduled flight to Iceland to airlift a helicopter and crew to Mestersvig, Greenland. The helicopter was needed to evacuate a critically injured crewman from the Norwegian vessel DROTT, which was icebound in the Greenland sea.

July 1958: MATS airlifted 5,500 tons of cargo and 5,400 troops to the Middle East in support of the government of Lebanon. Wing C-124s,

enroute to destinations in the European area, were diverted to Rhein Main AB to joint MATS forces already in position there. Three additional C-124s were dispatched direct from Dover to support the aircraft pool assembled at Rhein Main. On 12 August, the 31st ATS, with 12 C-124s and personnel, began deployment to Rhein Main for a 90 day TDY. The Middle East operation was known as BLUE BAT.

August - September 1959: In support of the U.S. response to a request from Laos for assistance in resisting Communist invasion from neighboring North Vietnam, the wing provided 16 C-124 trips totaling over1,045 hours flying time.

November 1959: Thirty-one C-124 aircraft from the wing flew 1,018 hours in support of Operation SPEARHEAD, which involved the deployment to Europe of a Tactical Air Command (TAC) Composite Air Strike Force.

7 February 1960: A C-124 from the 15th ATS flew non-stop from Hickam AFB, Hawaii, to Dover AFB, the first such trip for a Dover based C-124. The flight lasted 18 hours and 40 minutes.

May - June 1950: MATS flew 77 mercy missions to Chile after earthquakes practically destroyed parts of the country. The first Dover based C-124 departed on 25 May and 33 Globemaster IIs had departed to Zone of Interior onload bases within the following 88 hours. Each C-124 was loaded with an average of 13 tons of supplies and emergency equipment and the wing flew an estimated 1,700 hours in support of the operation.

12 - 13 August 1961: Two wing C-124 aircraft airlift insecticide to Cairo, Egypt, where a battle against army worm infestation of the nation's cotton crop was taking place.

8 - 25 November 1961: 1607th ATW aircraft and crews participated in Mission MERCY. This involved the airlift of relief equipment and supplies to British Honduras after Hurricane Hattie devastated the country.

18 April - 6 August 1962: FRIENDSHIP VII:

The wing was chosen to airlift FRIENDSHIP VII, Lt Col John Glenn's space capsule, on a global tour of the major cities of the free world. The trip, divided into three parts, was flown by each of the wing's C-124 squadrons, each squadron flying a different part. The 31st ATS flew the capsule through Central and South America; the 20th ATS took the capsule through Europe and Africa; the 15th ATS flew the last part of the trip, touring Asia and Australia before terminating the trip at the Seattle World's Fair on 6 August. More than 284 flying hours were logged in support of this mission.

8 May - 26 July 1962: The wing flew 56 C-124 and 21 C-133 missions in support of Operation BACK PORCH, an airlift of high priority electrical and mechanical equipment to South Vietnam for use in a communications network. Also participating in the airlift were C-47 aircraft from the 133rd Air Transport Wing of the Air National Guard. Just under three million pounds of cargo, associated with this project, were processed through the 1607th ATW Air Terminal during this operation.

September 1962: Dover-based C-124 and C-133 aircraft and crews joined other units in Europe in flying emergency food and medical supplies to earthquake stricken Iran, where thousands had been killed and many left homeless.

31 October 1962: C-124 aircraft from the Dover-based wing made their first paradrop at Campbell AAF, Kentucky. Six Dover aircraft made 12 drops each day in an exercise that qualified 82 pilots for day formation flying and another 62 pilots for night formation flying. The exercise was conducted without accident.

January 1963: The wing's 15th ATS, on TDY at

Chateauroux, France, assisted in flying aid to flood victims in the Rabat Province of Morocco.

February 1963: Still at Chateauroux, the 15th ATS assisted in flying aid to victims of an earthquake that struck in the vicinity of Barce, Libya.

February 1964: The 15th ATS delivered a telespectograph to the Ascension Islands in support of space project FIRE. The delivery was believed to be the first such airlift in which the instrument was delivered as a complete unit.

11 May 1964: A mercy mission was flown by a C-124 and crew of the 20th ATS; the emergency evacuation of a Danish boy, who had been mauled by Husky dogs, from a remote site in Greenland. The C-124 flew a helicopter to Kulusk where it was assembled and flown to the boy's home village. The boy was transported to the hospital by the helicopter.

22 - 28 May 1964: Two C-133s from the 1st and 39th Air Transport Squadrons and one C-124 from the 15th Air Transport Squadron were dispatched, carrying emergency fllood control equipment, on a mission to Costa Rica. The equipment was used to prevent loss of lives in the flooded area.

This ends the historical data recorded for the 1607th ATW under

Above, 436th MAW C-124C 52-1028 makes an emergency landing on a Honolulu International foamed runway on 31 January 1968. (Nick Williams)

the three headings previously mentioned.

Dover C-124 Serves As A Control Tower

In February 1966, a Dover C-124 was given the unusual assignment of being pressed into service as a control tower at Tan Son Nhut AB, Vietnam. A 40-minute base power failure left the tower without radio contact with airborne traffic and the field without runway or taxiway lights, wind indicators or altimeters. The C-124 was used because the observer's hatch is so high above the ground and is equipped with auxiliary power. Approximately 35 landings and take-

Below, C-124C 52-1007 in 1968. MAC has replaced the MATS lettering on the tail, fuselage and nose doors. The 1607th ATW became the 436th MAW in 1966. Note "436 MAW" painted on the nose gear doors. (Nick Williams)

436 MILITARY AIRLIFT WING

Robustum Auxilium

offs were controlled from the airplane's observer's hatch.

By June 1966, the 1607th ATW had become the 436th Military Airlift Wing and missions continued uninterrupted. The wing's squadrons, formerly Air Transport Squadrons, were now known as Military Airlift Squadrons (MASs), though their

numerical designations didn't change.

31st MAS Flies Difficult Mission To Kulusuk Island

In early June 1966, a hand-picked C-124 crew of the 31st MAS flew a challenging and unique mission by flying over the icecaps of Greenland to deliver equipment to Kulusuk Island. The island is a Danish outpost approximately two miles wide, off the east coast of Greenland. It has a gravel landing strip 3,400 feet long and 100 feet wide. The strip is built on a permafrost layer and is flanked on either side by gullies. In addition, it is flanked on three sides by high terrain.

The crew made two trips to the island from Sondrestrom AB to deliver a much needed truck and truck bed. Visibility at the strip was near Visual Flight Rules (VFR) minimums and there were no published approaches for the field. The trips in and out were accomplished without incident, despite a virtual non-availability of navigation aids, no ground handling equipment and the complex-

ities of utilizing the Globemaster II systems under extremely cold and primitive conditions.

52nd Military Airlift Squadron

The 52nd MAS was transferred from the 63rd Military Airlift Wing, home-based at Hunter AFB, Georgia, and assigned to the 436th MAW, effective on or about 8 January 1967. Though previously assigned to the 63rd MAW, the squadron was organized and functioned under the operational control of the 322d Air Division, High Wycombe, England, and was actually based at Rhein Main AB, Germany. A rotational squadron, the unit got its C-124s from the 31st MAS, a Dover AFB unit. Personnel were augmented by technicians from the 437th MAW, home-based at Charleston AFB, South Carolina.

The squadron participated in Exercise COLD WINTER, which was conducted from 20 February to 15 March 1967. This was a four-nation training exercise held in Northern Norway. Between February 19th and 26th, the squadron flew six missions in the deployment phase to Bodo and

Below, 52-1028 over Hickam in 1968. (Nick Williams)

Bardufoss, Norway. The squadron flew an additional six missions in March during the redeployment phase. The squadron also flew six missions in support of the deployment phase of Exercise GREEN GRASS during the month, as well.

In another exercise called PATHFINDER EXPRESS, the squadron participated in the airlift of approximately 12,066 personnel and 12,429 tons of cargo between Spain and German bases. In-theatre aircraft flew a total of 11,265 hours, out of a total of 11,745 hours flown. The 52nd flew 1,246 hours during May, in support of the exercise.

In July and August 1968, the squadron participated in DEEP FURROW 1968, flying what were called "prepositioning and post positioning" missions. One hundred eighty two C-124 sorties were flown and the squadron overflew its commitments by 18 hours in July and 228 hours in August.

On August 27, 1968, the unit received its first complete extended duty reserve crew from the 349th Military Airlift Wing (Air Force Reserve), home based at Hamilton AFB, California. The squadron continued to receive TDY reserve crews until it was disbanded.

Between 26 August and 16 September 1967, the 436th MAW's 31st MAS and 52nd MAS participated in Exercise SUNSHINE EXPRESS. 48 C-124 missions were flown.

In December 1968, the squadron's C-124 crews flew 53 missions in support of operation PATHFINDER EXPRESS II. In January 1969, 12 Globemaster II missions were flown in support of REFORGER/CRESTED CAP I. The unit disbanded during the same month, the aircraft departing Rhein Main in groups of four and the last aircraft leaving on the 19th.

Inactivation of the 31st Military Airlift Squadron

In early January 1969, interested Congressional delegations were notified by Headquarters, USAF that the 31st MAS would be deactivated within the coming months. The inactivation was part of the MAC modernization program, the C-124s across the command being replaced by newer aircraft.

1608th ATW/437th MAW

Military Air Transport Service General Order Number 49 (21 June 1957) relieved the 1608th Air Transport Wing, Medium of assignment to the Atlantic Division of MATS and reassigned the wing and its inter-

Below, with 436 MAW insignias on the nose and tail, C-124C 52-1041 roars off the runway at Hickam AFB in 1969. (Nick Williams)

nal units to the Continental Division of the command, effective 1 July 1957. A subsequent General Order from Headquarters MATS transferred jurisdiction of Charleston AFB and associated auxiliary locations from MATS Atlantic Division to MATS Continental Division, also effective 1 July 1957.

The 3rd ATS of the 1700th ATG was transferred to the 1608th ATW (General Order Number 105) on 9 October 1957. The squadron came from Brookley AFB, Alabama. The unit remained at Brookley AFB for a while longer, however.

At the beginning of 1958, the Air Transport Squadrons (ATSs) assigned to the wing were as follows: 3rd ATS, 17th ATS, 22nd ATS, 35th ATS, 41st ATS, 76th ATS. On 18 March 1958, General Order Number 102 (30 September 1957) effected the inactivation of the 22nd ATS. On 1 May, the wing was assigned, once again, to Atlantic Division MATS.

In mid-June, 1958, the 35th ATS was inactivated and the 17th ATS, 1608th ATW and 1608th ATG were all designated as heavy units. The 3rd ATS had arrived at Charleston, from Brookley AFB, at this time and the

17th ATS converted to C-124C aircraft to complete the month's activities. The wing now had four active ATSs: the 3rd, the 17th, the 41st and the 76th.

In the last half of 1964, the wing is found preparing for delivery of the first C-141A Starlifter aircraft. The 3rd ATS is announced as the first unit to receive the new turbofan-powered airlifter. The first C-141A was scheduled to arrive during the first quarter of FY 1966, with the 3rd ATS's C-124s scheduled to be phased out by the second quarter of the year. By the

Above, 1608th ATW C-124C 52-1042 with upper white fuselage and extensive red tail and wing trim. (Nick Williams collection)

third quarter, the squadron was expected to have its full complement of 16 C-141A aircraft.

By 1965, the 41st ATS and 76th ATS were flying C-130E aircraft. C-124s were being operated by the 3rd and 17th Air Transport Squadrons. By 1967, the only squadron still flying

At right, 1608th ATW C-14C 52-1060 in May 1961 with da-glo orange nose and tail stripe and upper white fuselage. (Jack M. Friell) Below, 437th MAW C-124C 53-0051 on its way to support the troops in Vietnam in 1969. (Nick Williams)

the C-124 was the 17th, the other three squadrons having equipped with the newer Starlifter.

By 1968, the unit was deeply involved in providing airlift support for the U.S. involvement in the Vietnam conflict. During the last half of the year, the C-124s of the 17th ATS were flying more hours in support of the Vietnam conflict than they did during the first six months; C-141As were flying fewer hours in support of the conflict than they did during the first half of the year.

The unit history doesn't reflect when the last C-124 left the wing, though it's likely the mighty Globemasters didn't stay much longer, as the C-5A Galaxy's entry into service was just around the corner and the C-124's long service with the Air National Guard and Air Force Reserve was about to begin.

1700th ATG

Historical records for the 1700th Air Transport Group appear to be sparse, though they show the arrival of the first C-124 aircraft to be accept-

ed by the 1291st ATS in the November/December time frame. By 1952, the 1291st and its sister squadron, the 1280th, were both equipped with the C-124s. The huge Globemaster IIs apparently created a problem for the group, there not being sufficient ramp facilities to accommodate the larger airplanes. As a result, both squadrons were transferred to the 1705th Air Transport Group, McChord AFB, Washington. They were replaced by two new squadrons, both C-54 equipped, the 1286th and 1289th Air Transport Squadrons.

The history of the group skips to 1957 and the reassignment of the 3rd ATS, located at Brookley AFB, Alabama, to the group on 18 June. The squadron was later transferred to the 1608th ATW, Medium, though it remained at Brookley AFB for a while longer, and the 1700th ATG was disbanded.

1703rd ATG

For our purposes, we pick up the history of the 1703rd Air Transport Group in 1946. The first C-74 Globemaster was assigned to the

group and the unit was the testing agency for the new airplane. Previously, the group had been the 1601st ATG and, prior to that, the 521st ATG. All three units were associated with testing the C-74, since the only real change was in unit numerical designation and a shift from Altantic Division to Continental Division.

The group received its first C-124 aircraft, an "A" model, on 6 October 1951. The unit flew the C-124A on a regularly scheduled mission to Ramey AB, Puerto Rico, until 11 October 1953.

The unit acted as a testing agency again, beginning in April, 1953, when the first C-124C versions of the Globemaster II arrived. Familiarization tests were completed by 11 June.

In November 1955, the C-74s were put into flyable storage at Brookley, as mentioned in Chapter 1. These same airplanes were flown to Davis-Monthan AFB in 1956, the last departing Brookley AFB in April.

On 30 June 1957, the group was inactivated and the 3rd ATS, which remained at Brookley, was assigned to the 1700th ATG. Within months, the squadron was assigned to the 1608th ATW.

1705th ATG/443rd MAW

The group's history is picked up in January 1952 as orders are issued to activate the 1705th ATG at McChord AFB, Washington. The unit was to be activated on 24 January. The new unit would have as its flying squadrons the 1286th and 1289th ATSs. Assignment of the 1740th ATS to the group was contemplated. This assignment was not to be, however, as plans were in hand to transfer the squadron to West Palm Beach

Above, C-124A 51-0120 from the 6th TCS in the early '50s. (via C. Kaston) At left, 1705th ATG, 34th ATS C-124A in July 1953 with red tail and wing trim. (W. J. Balogh, Sr. via Earl Berlin)

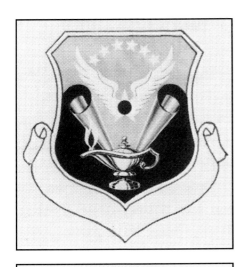

443rd MAW

International Airport, proposed to be the future MATS training center.

The 1286th and 1289th ATSs were reassigned to Kelly AFB during March. The squadrons, equipped with C-54 Cargomasters, were exchanged for the 1280th and 1291st ATSs, both of which were C-124-equipped. It appears that the moves didn't alter the assignment of the the affected squadrons; all apparently came under the control of the group, though some of the squadrons were geographically separated from group headquarters.

During the second half of the year, the group received the newly activated 77th ATS. The unit was equipped with C-124 aircraft.

The group suffered a serious loss when one of its C-124s (51-107) crashed in Alaska, killing all on board. This too took place during the second half of 1952.

General Order Number 99, dated 11 July 1952, redesignated the 1280th, 1284th and 1291st ATSs as the 32nd, 33rd and 34th ATSs, respectively. Where and when the unit picked up the 1284th ATS isn't clear.

Unit historical records for the first half of 1954 show the 33rd ATS as a C-54 unit. These same records indicate the 32nd ATS transitioned to the C-124C at this time. The 77th ATS was transferred from the 1705th to the 1501st ATG during this period.

By the January - June 1959 time frame, the 32nd ATS was still flying the C-124 but the 33rd had transitioned to the C-118A. The 34th ATS was deactivated in 1955.

Unit history is picked up again in the July - December 1966 time frame, by which time the group had become the 443rd MAW. The 56th MAS, formerly the 1740th ATS, is still flying the C-124 but its operations are about to come to a close. The unit is to be moved to Altus AFB, along with the rest of the 443rd MAW, where it will assume the responsibility for training C-5A Galaxy aircrews. Training of C-124 aircrews is being turned over to the 937 MAG, an Air Force Reserve unit.

With the termination of C-124 training operations and the subsequent move to Altus AFB, Oklahoma, the 443rd found itself conducting jet transport training only. The 57th MAS, responsible for training C-141A (later C-141B) aircrews, moved to Altus as a C-141 unit. It appears the 56th MAS moved as a "paper" unit, acquiring personnel and aircraft upon arrival at Altus.

1707th ATG

Historical records indicate the 1707th ATG was activated and organized in mid-summer 1952, and the first students attended the C-124 class in August of the same year. The group was organized at Palm Beach International Airport, Florida.

The 1740th ATS, the group's C-97 and C-124 aircrew conversion

Above, 1705th ATG C-124C assigned to the Continental Division had artic red tail and outer wings and a white cabin roof. (via Craig Kaston)

unit, gained an additional tasking in January 1956, when it was reorganized to include the training of TB-50 Superfortress aircrew members. By July, the same year, the squadron found itself training only C-124 crews as the 1742nd ATS had been activated to train crews for the C-97 and TB-50 aircraft types. C-118 aircrew conversion was conducted by the 1741st ATS.

Unit records, gathered at the Air Force Historical Research Center, indicate the 1707th continued training operations until at least 1964. When C-124 training operations ceased wasn't specified.

1740th ATS

EARLY MATS C-124s

Above, early Continental Division C-124A 51-136 in flight on 22 February 1956. Early MATS markings consisted of artic red tail and wing markings, a blue tail stripe bordered in yellow with Continental Division in yellow. The MATS markings on the forward fuselage were yellow outlined by blue. Engine exhaust area stripes that run across the wings were black. (Douglas) At left, C-124A 50-083 shows unusal MATS wing markings where MATS are outlined by natural metal where it enters the artic red wing panel. (Douglas via S. Nicolaou) Below, Continental Division C-124A 50-117 at Thule, Greenland, flanked by two C-54s. The C-124 brought in a 29,000 pound snow shovel as well as other equipment. (USAF via S. Nicolaou)

62nd TCW/ATW/MAW

MATS AND MAC SERVICE

On 1 July 1957, the 62nd Troop Carrier Wing (see page 49 for the wing's history prior to 1 July 1957) was transferred to the Military Air Transport Service (MATS), but retained its designation as a Troop Carrier Wing until 1 January 1965, when it became the 62nd Air Transport Wing. At that time the 62nd ATW was composed of the the 4th ATA, 7th TCS, 8th ATS at McChord AFB. Aircraft assigned were: C-124As; 50-0099, 50-0102-0103, 0109, 50-1262-1263, 50-1268, 51-0074, 51-0076, 51-0092, 51-0094-0100, 51-0159, 51-0161, 51-0178. C-124Cs; 50-0083, 50-0101, 50-0104-0105, 50-0108, 50-0110, 50-0112, 50-0112, 50-0118, 50-1264-1267, 51-0073, 51-0075, 51-0077-0078, 51-0084, 51-0086, 51-0090-0091, 51-0093, 51-0108, 51-0158, 51-0163-

0164, 51-0166, 51-0172-0173, 51-0175, 51-0182 at McChord AFB, WA. The 19th ATS stationed at Kelly AFB, TX, was equipped with C-124Cs; 52-0973-0979, 52-0984-0989, 52-1006, 52-1013, 52-1016, 52-1018-1020.

On 8 January 1966, the 62nd was redesignated a Military Airlift Wing when MATS became MAC.

The 62nd was stationed at Larson AFB, Washington, when it was reassigned to MATS and transferred to McChord AFB on 13 June 1960, where it remained until C-124 operations within the wing were suspended.

During the International Geophysical Year 1957-58, the wing supported scientific stations in the arctic Ocean, by landing on the ice and often airdropping supplies as needed. These activities continued through

Above, 62nd ATW C-124A 50-109 taxis out for take-off. 62 ATW is painted on the nose gear doors. (via Earl Berlin)

1962.

In 1960, the wing transported United Nations troops to the Congo. Then in 1963, the unit assumed the responsibility for the worldwide airlift of nuclear weapons and associated equipment. The Wing continued this mission long after the C-124 was no longer assigned to the wing.

Below, 62nd TCW C-124A 50-0103 taxis in at Tan Son Nhut Air Base in April 1964. Note RF-101 in the background. (via Craig Kaston)

Above, C-124C 52-0998 of the 62nd MAW. Nose gear writing says 62nd Military Airlift Wg instead 62nd MAW. (USAF via Craig Kaston) At left, 62nd MAW C-124C 53-0025 at Elmendorf AFB, Alaska, on 24 May 1969. (Norm Taylor via Earl Berlin) Below, 62nd MAW C-124C 51-0099 at Shemya AFS, Alaska, on 27 January 1967. Nose ramp was down as was elevator aft of the wing. Pallets of supplies are stacked in the foreground next to the snow. (Norm Taylor via Earl Berlin)

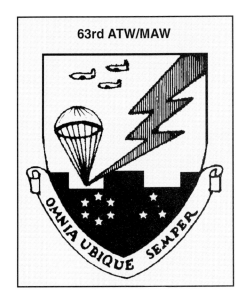

63rd ATW/MAW

OMNIA UBIQUE SEMPER

Above, 52nd ATS C-124C with white fuselage roof and squadron insignia on the forward fuselage in 1957. Some squadrons retained their original markings when the TCWs became MATS ATWs in 1957. (via Nick Williams)

On 1 July 1957, the 63rd Troop Carrier Wing was transferred to the Military Air Transport Service as a Troop Carrier Wing (see page 49 for the wing's history prior to its service in MATS). The wing was never redesignated as an Air Transport Wing (ATW) but was redesignated as a Military Airlift Wing on 8 January 1966.

The wing was stationed at Donaldson AFB, SC, when assigned to MATS on 1 July 1957 and remained there until 1 June 1963 when it transferred to Hunter AFB, GA. The wing moved to Norton AFB,

Above, 9th ATS C-124C 52-0956 at Harewood, New Zealand, on 11 November 1958 was used in the South Polar Expedition. (via Nick Williams) Below, another 63rd ATW MATS C-124C used to support the South Polar Expedition was 53-0040, seen here on the ice in early 1958. (USAF)

At right, C-124C 52-0950 with ramp down waits for Air Force personnel to board. (Clyde Gerdes collection via Nick Williams) At right middle, C-124C 52-0950 taxis with its clam shell doors open. (via S. Nicolaou) At right bottom, up-close and personel view of C-124C 53-0024 on 21 January 1968 at Hickham AFB, Hawaii. (Nick Williams)

At top, 53rd ATS C-124C 51-5174 on a foggy morning. The 53rd was originally assigned to the 61st TCW before being assigned to the 63rd TCW/ATW. (via Nick Williams) Above, 63rd ATW C-124C 53-0052 at Harewood, New Zealand, in November 1961. (via Jack M. Friel) Below, C-124C 52-0976 leaving Hickham Field, Hawaii on 2 January 1968. (Nick Williams)

CA, on 1 April 1967.

Beginning in 1957 the wing helped support the Navys Operation Deep Freeze with airlift and airdrop missions. The C-124s supported the Arctic operations through 1966. From April 1967 the wings primary aircraft was the Lockheed C-141A Starlifter.

The 63rd had the following C-124As assigned on 1 January 1965; 49-0250, 50-0085, and 51-0168. C-124Cs assigned were: 49-0248, 49-0252, 49-0255-0256, 49-0259, 50-0084, 50-0090-0091, 50-0093-0096, 50-0113, 50-0117, 50-1261, 51-0155, 50-0160, 51-0169-0171, 51-5174-5175, 51-5177-5179, 51-5181, 51-5184-5186, 51-5189, 51-5191, 51-5193-5195, 51-5199-5200, 51-5207-5208, 51-5211, 51-5213, 51-7273, 51-7276-7277, 51-7284, 52-0940, 52-0950, 52-0952, 52-0955, 52-0957-0958, 52-0983, 52-1046, 52-1066, 52-1077, 52-1085-1086, 53-0024, 53-0028, 53-0031, 53-0036, 53-0040, 53-0048 and 53-0052.

TACTICAL AIR COMMAND

Tactical Air Command (TAC) operated C-124s from 1951 to July 1957. After that period, its C-124s were taken over by the Military Air Transport Service. While the C-124 appeared to be too large and cumbersome to be a good airplane for formation flying and paratroop drops, that's just what the units in TAC used it for, and they did a superior job of it. The experience gained was later put to good use when the command picked up C-130s, but that's a totally different story.

Above right, parachute brigade marches into waiting TAC C-124A. (Douglas) Below, six C-124As of the 8th TCS in formation. Nose markings were black outlined in white. Outer wings and tail were in signia red. (Douglas)

Tactical Air Command C-124 Units (As of December 1956)

UNIT		LOCATION	ASSIGNED TO
3rd	Troop Carrier Squadron (Heavy)	Donaldson AFB, S. C.	63rd Troop Carrier Group (Heavy)
4th	Troop Carrier Squadron (Heavy)	Larson AFB, Washington	62nd Troop Carrier Group (Heavy)
7th	Troop Carrier Squadron (Heavy)	Larson AFB, Washington	62nd Troop Carrier Group (Heavy)
8th	Troop Carrier Squadron (Heavy)	Larson AFB, Washington	62nd Troop Carrier Group (Heavy)
9th	Troop Carrier Squadron (Heavy)	Donaldson AFB, S. C.	63rd Troop Carrier Group (Heavy)
14th	Troop Carrier Squadron (Heavy)	Donaldson AFB, S. C.	61st Troop Carrier Group (Heavy)
15th	Troop Carrier Squadron (Heavy)	Donaldson AFB, S. C.	61st Troop Carrier Group (Heavy)
52nd	Troop Carrier Squadron (Heavy)	Donaldson AFB, S. C.	63rd Troop Carrier Group (Heavy)
53rd	Troop Carrier Squadron (Heavy)	Donaldson AFB, S. C.	61st Troop Carrier Group (Heavy)
54th	Troop Carrier Squadron (Heavy)	Donaldson AFB, S. C.	Eighteenth Air Force
61st	Troop Carrier Group (Heavy)	Donaldson AFB, S. C.	Eighteenth Air Force
62nd	Troop Carrier Wing (Heavy)	Larson AFB, Washington	Eighteenth Air Force
62nd	Troop Carrier Group (Heavy)	Larson AFB, Washington	62nd Troop Carrier Wing (Heavy)
63rd	Troop Carrier Wing (Heavy)	Donaldson AFB, S. C.	Eighteenth Air Force
63rd	Troop Carrier Group (Heavy)	Donaldson AFB, S. C.	63rd Troop Carrier Wing (Heavy)

48

THE C-124 IN THE TACTICAL AIR COMMAND

17 September 1951

The 62nd TCW (Heavy) was assigned to the Eighteenth Air Force, and activated at McChord AFB, Washington. This was the first C-124 unit assigned to Eighteenth Air Force, and was TAC's first C-124-equipped organization.

1 October 1951

The 61st and 62nd Troop Carrier Groups (TCGs) were assigned to the Eighteenth Air Force. The 61st TCG remained attached to FEAF (Far East Air Force) for administration, operational control and logistical support. The 62nd TCG was assigned to the 62nd Troop Carrier Wing (Heavy) (TCW-H).

December 1951

Operation FRUITCAKE: A series of missions to the Far East, flown by C-124 aircraft from the 62nd TCW-H.

January 1952

Operation BACKBREAKER: Emergency airlift to FEAF of 1,200 F-86 Sabre drop-tanks and shackles, flown by the 62nd TCW-H in 21 flights.

February - March 1952

Service-testing of the C-124A air-craft. For the first time, live jumps were made from this aircraft at Fort Bragg, North Carolina.

14 March 1952

In an air transportability test, an Army T-41 tank was successfully airlifted by a C-124 aircraft at Camp Campbell, Kentucky.

April 1952

Two C-124s participated in airlifting 674,000 lbs. of emergency equipment during the Mississippi River Flood Emergency.

1 April 1952

The 62nd TCW-H assumed command of Larson AFB, Moses Lake, Washington; however, the 62nd TCG-H remained at McChord AFB during the month of April to support Exercise LONG HORN.

September 1952

Non-stop flight of a C-124 aircraft from Iceland to McChord AFB, a distance of 3,800 miles in 19 hours.

September - December 1952

Project REDHEAD: Flying 17 trips monthly, the 62nd TCW-H provided logistic support to SAC units in the United Kingdom.

November 1952

The 8th TCS-H of the 62nd TCW-H made a record equipment drop of 360,000 lbs. within 8-10 seconds on Drop Zone "Holland" at Fort Bragg, North Carolina.

27 November 1952

After returning from its deployment at Tachikawa, Japan, the 61st TCG-H was attached to the 62nd TCW-H at Larson AFB, and began transition from the C-54 to C-124 aircraft.

31 December 1952

The 63rd TCW-H was activated and assigned to the Eighteenth Air Force at Donaldson AFB.

8 January 1953

Headquarters 63rd TCW-H became operational at Altus AFB, Oklahoma. [Its tactical group - the 63rd - wasn't activated until 20 June 1953.] Altus AFB was assigned to the jurisdiction of the Eighteenth Air Force at this time.

7 May 1953

The 63rd TCW-H received its first C-124 aircraft.

31 May - 6 June 1953

Operation BRUSH BAY: Eleven C-124 aircraft from the 62nd TCW-H airlifted 938 personnel of the 82nd Airborne Division from France AFB, Canal Zone, to Pope AFB.

June/July/August 1953

Project DOG SLED: During this NEAC project, the 62nd TCW-H airlifted approximately 800 tons of

---

Below, the 8th TCS insignia was a blue disc with white clouds, edged in black. The horse was yellow with a red cross on its hip, wearing a tan holster and cartridge belt, and carrying a machine gun and green box. A black figure and white parachute are seen in the lower right. (Craig Kaston)

Below, 8th TCS C-124C 52-1014. (Balogh via Menard)

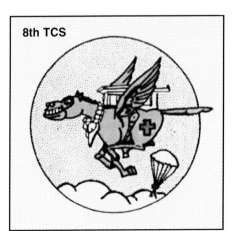

8th TCS

49

63rd TCW

54th TCS

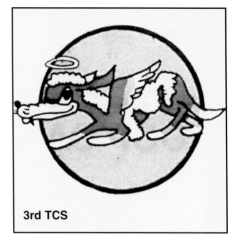
3rd TCS

Above, the insignia of the 63rd Troop Carrier Group is divided into two sections. Upon the upper blue section is a red lightning bolt, a white parachute with black detail, and three black and white cargo aircraft. Upon the lower section are sets of three white stars, signifying the unit's numerical designation. The motto "Omnia Ubique Semper" translates to Anything, Anywhere, Anytime. (Craig Kaston)

Above, the Eager Beaver in the 54th TCS insignia is brown with a beige belly. It carries two white aircraft engines under its arms while carrying brown and white soldiers and cargo on its back. Behind the beaver is a turquoise blue disc with dark brown speed marks. (Craig Kaston)

Above, the 3rd TCS squadron insignia consists of a brown, beige, and white wolf draped in sheep's skin (clothing), superimposed upon a golden orange disc. The disc was surrounded with a black border except where crossed by a white halo. (Craig Kaston)

equipment to Thule Air Force Base, Greenland. It marked the first time a C-124 aircraft landed on an ice-island (T-3, located in the Arctic Ocean).

20 June 1953

The 63rd TCG-H was reactivated and assigned to the 63rd TCW-H at Donaldson AFB.

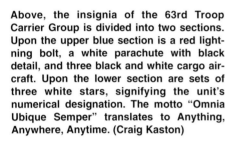
Below, 54th TCS aircraft in the foreground, followed by five 3rd TCS aircraft in 1957. The 54th TCS nose flash was red with the design aft of the squadron insignia in dark blue. The 3rd TCS design aft of the squadron insignia was red. (S. Parker collection via Earl Berlin)

15 October 1953

Altus AFB was transferred from the jurisdiction of TAC to SAC, and the 63rd TCW-H moved from Altus AFB to Donaldson AFB.

Note: In later years, Altus AFB would revert to being a home base for an airlift organization, though it would be the Military Airlift Command, and not TAC.

February 1954

Three C-124 aircraft from the 53rd TCS-H, 61st TCG-H, participated in an airborne operation at Colorado Springs, Colorado. During this operation, paratroopers were dropped from the highest altitude ever attempted in the history of air-

borne operations.

23 February - 4 March 1954

The 62nd TCW-H airlifted the 479th Fighter-Bomber Wing (Ninth Air Force) from George AFB, California, to and from Ladd AFB, Alaska, for its participation in a joint defense maneuver, Exercise NORTH STAR.

12 - 17 March 1954

Operation WINDCHILL (TACAIR 54-3): Airlift of the 11th Airborne Division to NEAC by the 62nd TCW-H, and paradrop of men and equipment at Thule AFB, Greenland. This was the northernmost maneuver to date, and involved a mock airborne invasion of three installations.

April - May 1954

Operation BALI HAI: After receiving a warning order on 8 April, 13 C-124 aircraft from the 62nd TCW-H airlifted, on 29 April, French airborne troops from France to Dien Bien Phu in Indo-China by way of the Middle East.

8 - 15 April 1954

Operation BOXKITE (Phase I): Airlift of the 21st Fighter-Bomber Wing (Ninth Air Force) from George AFB, California, to North Field, South Carolina. Nineteen aircraft from the 61st TCG-H airlifted over 600 personnel and 350,000 pounds of equipment and cargo. In Phase II of the operation, which began on 8 May 1954, the fighter-bomber wing was returned to George AFB.

20 April 1954

TACAIR 54-7: The 62nd and 63rd TCW-H airlifted the 145th Regimental Combat Team from Alexandria, Louisiana, to Pope AFB as a prelude to Operation FLASHBURN, the Army's first simulated atomic maneuver. 80 C-124 aircraft were used for the airlift. Of special significance was the paradrop of 216,000 pounds of equipment in nine seconds into the designated drop zone by the 61st TCG-H.

July - August 1954

Operation RIDGE RUNNER: Airlift of 1,700 tons of cargo to Thule AFB, Greenland, by 17 C-124s for supply of rehabilitation and construction programs in the Far North.

August 1954

Seven C-124s from the 62nd TCW-H airlifted 150,000 pounds of medical supplies to Pakistan for flood relief.

25 August 1954

The 61st TCG-H was relieved from attachment to the 62nd TCW-H and attached to the 63rd TCW-H at Donaldson AFB.

At right, 4th TCS C-124A 51-096 with dark blue nose flash and insignia red tail and wing markings. (W. J. Balogh, Sr. via Earl Berlin)

19 September - 1 October 1954

Ten aircraft from the 61st TCG-H airlifted the 389th Fighter-Bomber Squadron (Ninth Air Force) from Alexandria, Louisiana, to Toul Air Base, France.

February 1955

Operation TEAPOT: This involved support of atomic tests in Nevada. Late in January, during the preparation phase, the 63rd TCW-H airlifted more than 300 tons of equipment and 200 personnel to the testing areas.

5 - 17 February 1955

Operation SNOWBIRD (TACAIR 55-3): This involved the airlift of the 503rd Regimental Combat Team to its maneuver site at Anchorage, Alaska. 50 C-124 aircraft from the 62nd and 63rd TCWs-H were used in the airlift and paradrop at Talkeetna, Alaska.

1 - 10 May 1955

Exercise APPLE JACK (TACAIR 55-4): A joint Army-Air Force operation designed to train tactical air units in control of the air, isolation of the battlefield, and close support of ground troops. The 62nd TCW-H provided logistical support for the operation.

3 - 6 May 1955

Operation JUNGLE JIM (TACAIR 55-5): This was a joint Army-Navy-Air Force operation in the Caribbean area; the airlift role (Exercise BARRACUDA) was performed by the 62nd and 463rd TCWs. In this operation, which marked the first time a C-124 was used to drop paratroops outside the continental United States —

4th TCS

Above, the insignia of the 4th TCS was a blue disc with white clouds edged in black. The Army mule was brown with a green box on his back and is secured by what is believed to be a black belt..

1,100 paratroops of the 11th Airborne Division were dropped on the Rio Hato airstrip in Panama.

July 1955

A C-124 from the 61st TCG airlifted a replica of the "Spirit of St. Louis" to Europe in support of the Warner Brothers Studio movie, "The Lindberg Story." The motion picture crew and aircraft were returned in August.

1 - 20 July 1955

Operation GYROSCOPE (TACAIR 56-4): The 508th Regimental Combat Team was airlifted from Fort Campbell, Kentucky, to Japan, and the 187th Regimental Combat Team was returned to Camp MacKall, North Carolina, by the 62nd and 63rd TCW-H in one the of the most extensive peace-time missions to date. There were 3,850 men airlift-

7th TCS

Above, the 7th TCS insignia was a light blue disc marked in dark blue. A gold hand clasping a gold double-edge sword, which has a red handle, and a white pommel and hilt. Green olive branches with central yellow banding are below the sword, and a white lightning bolt cut across the emblem. (Craig Kaston)

ed over 63 million passenger miles in the round-the-clock operation.

16 August 1955

Operation LODESTAR (TACAIR 56-2): Aircraft from the 62nd TCG-H participated in aerial resupply drops to personnel of the Army's 77th Mountain and Cold Weather Command in Leadville, Colorado.

Above, 7th TCS C-124C at Larson AFB, Washington. Nose flash was yellow outlined in black. Tail was insignia red. (S. Parker collection via Earl Berlin)

Below, the Douglas modification line with a 7th TCS aircraft in the foreground. Note white upper forward cabin area and insignia red tail markings. (Douglas via Harry Gann)

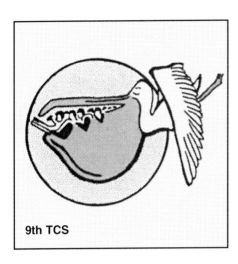

9th TCS

Above, the emblem of the 9th TCS consisted of a stylized white Pelican on a blue disc. The Pelican with orange beak and feet was carrying a group of soldiers in black and white. (Craig Kaston)

The first drop occurred on 16 August, and periodic drops continued through 16 February 1956.

19 September 1955

H-21 helicopters were successfully loaded on C-124 aircraft.

21 September 1955

C-124s from the 63rd TCW-H airlifted the 401st Fighter-Bomber

Below, 9th TCS C-124C 51-5190 at Scott AFB on 17 May 1958. The design aft of the squadron insignia is believed to be colored orange. (Dave Ostrowski)

Group from England AFB, Louisiana, to Chaumont Air Base, France.

23 October 1955

The 63rd TCW-H airlifted 31,000 pounds of cargo from Albrook AFB, Canal Zone, to Galeao Air Field, Rio de Janerio, and Carrosco Air Field, Uruguay.

20 November 1955 - 28 February 1956

Operation DEEP FREEZE (TACAIR 57-1): An Eighteenth Air Force survey party went to New Zealand and Antarctica for this operation. It involved eight C-124s from the 63rd TCW-H which provided logistical and airdrop support to Naval Task Force 43 during the establishment of scientific research stations in Antarctica in preparation for the International Geophysical Year Program, 1957 - 58.

1 December 1955

Fourteen C-124s from the 63rd TCW-H transported the 390th Fighter-Bomber Squadron from England AFB, Louisiana, to Aviano, Italy.

10 January 1956

The 3rd TCS-H of the 63rd TCW-H made a 30-day tour through the USAFE theater of operations to assist in reducing backlog cargo. A total of 764 tons of cargo was moved in flights to bases in Denmark, Greece, France, Italy, Turkey, England, French Morocco and Libya.

16 - 18 January 1956

Operation ROCKLIFT: A joint mobility training maneuver during which the 62nd TCW-H airlifted 2,115 infantrymen and equipment of the 38th Regimental Combat Team at Fort Lewis, Washington, from McChord AFB to Larson AFB.

1 -18 March 1956

Exercise ARCTIC NIGHT (TACAIR 56-5): An airborne troop carrier training mission in the NEAC area. C-124s from the 63rd TCW-H airlifted 664 Army personnel and 24,000 pounds of equipment during the exercise.

6 - 14 March 1956

A C-124 from the 14th TCS-H airlifted iron lungs from Boston to Buenos Aires, Argentina, on a mercy mission to aid in the struggle against a polio epidemic.

1 April 1956

Operation CROSS SWITCH: Nine C-124s from the 63rd TCG-H airlifted the 430th Fighter-Bomber Squadron from Clovis AFB, New Mexico, to Toul, France; it then returned the 612th Fighter-Bomber Squadron from Chaumont Air Base, France, to England AFB, Louisiana.

12 June 1956

C-124s from the 63rd TCW-H airlifted the 614th Fighter-Bomber Group from England AFB, Louisiana, to Aviano, Italy, to replace the 390th Fighter-Bomber Group.

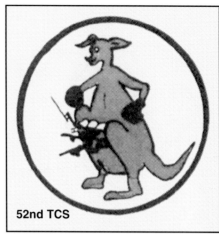

52nd TCS

Above, 52nd TCS C-124C 52-983 had a blue design aft of the squadron insignia and insignia red tail and wing markings. (LT. Col. C. Cook via Dave Menard)

17 June 1956

Operation FALCON: The 62nd TCW-H airlifted a group of cadets from the United States Air Force Academy to Grandview, Barksdale, and Langley Air Force Bases.

Below, 52nd TCS C-124C "State of Washington'. Note electrical power plug location next to the nose gear door. (AAHS via Craig Kaston)

23 July 1956

The 54th TCS-H returned from Elmendorf AFB, Alaska, and was assigned to the 63rd TCW-H at Donaldson AFB. The 62nd TCW-H assumed all Alaskan airlift commitments formerly performed by the 54th TCS.

19 September - October 1956

Operation MOBILE BAKER: C-124s from the 63rd TCW-H provided airlift support for a composite strike force of Ninth Air Force units, deploying to Germany and Italy on a training mission.

October 1956 - February 1957

Operation DEEP FREEZE: (TACAIR 57-1): Eight C-124s from the 63rd TCW-H airdropped 500 tons

Above, the insignia of the 52nd TCS centers upon a brown kangaroo wearing black boxing gloves. It carries three young kangaroos in its pouch wearing green helmets, armed with a rifle with fixed bayonet, a revolver, and a "Tommy" gun. Encircled by a green line, the disc is either white or the base color on which the insignia was painted (natural metal). (Craig Kaston)

of equipment in the South Polar regions. The first supply drop over the South Pole occurred on 26 October 1956.

31 October 1956

One C-124 aircraft from the 63rd TCW-H airlifted emergency Red Cross supplies from Andrews AFB, Maryland, to Vienna for subsequent

shipments to the Hungarian patriots in revolt.

6 December 1956

Eighteenth Air Force C-124s replaced MATS scheduled flights to Europe. MATS flights were diverted to Austria for airlift of Hungarian refugees. Thirteen C-124s from the 62nd TCW-H and 38 C-124s from the 63rd TCW-H flew a total of 7 sorties to North Africa, 8 sorties to Libya, 11 sorties to India, and 25 sorties to France.

1 July 1957

TAC lost all of its C-124s to the Military Air Transport Service

61ST TROOP CARRIER GROUP

The history of the 61st TCG is picked up in January 1952. The group's headquarters was in Ashiya, Japan, as were the group's 15th and 53rd TCSs. The 14th TCS was assigned to Tachikawa AB, Japan at this time, under the control of the 374th TCW-H. All three squadrons operated the C-54 Skymaster.

In March 1952, the 61st TCG Headquarters and the 15th TCS moved to Tachikawa AB. The 53rd TCS remained at Ashiya AB and was reassigned to the 403rd TCW-M.

Some time in 1952, the group received its first C-124s. It appears the first C-124s arrived while the group was still in Japan, but the group moved to the continental United States (Larson AFB, Washington) in December. Transition to the C-124 was completed at Larson AFB.

All three squadrons had their full complement of C-124s by July 1953. The 14th and 15th TCSs received C-124Cs, while the 53rd TCS received the earlier C-124A. The squadrons received their transition training from the 62d TCW at McChord AFB, Washington.

In August 1954, the group moved to Donaldson AFB, South Carolina, and was integrated into the 63rd TCW-H. When the Korean Conflict broke out in mid-1950 and became critical later in the year, the 4th TCS (from the 62nd TCW) was sent on temporary assignment to the Far Eastern Air Forces, and was assigned to the 61st TCW. Some time between October and December 1951, the 61st and 62nd TCWs were realigned: the 4th TCS remaining in Japan, assigned to the 61st TCW, and being redesignated as the 14th TCS, until November, at which time it was again redesignated the 4th TCS and returned to the 62nd TCW in the United States.

Author's Note: The history of the 62d TCW reflects that the 14th TCS, which had been at McChord AFB and "attached" to the 62d, was redesignated the 4th TCS and permanently assigned to the 62d wing. Reference documents for that unit make no reference to the 14th TCS in Japan, being redesignated the 4th TCS and being returned to McChord AFB.

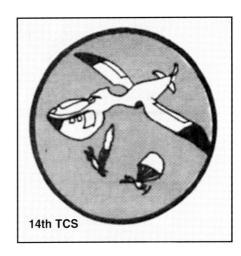

14th TCS

Above, the insignia of the 14th TCS is displayed on a medium blue disc bordered with orange and white on which a white Pelican trimmed in blue is presented. The Pelican's beak was orange. The figures were in brown with white parachutes lined in black. (Craig Kaston)

62ND TROOP CARRIER WING

Our history of the 62nd TCW is picked up, for our purposes, on 1 June 1950, when the components of the wing, with the exception of the 62nd TCG, are inactivated. Prior to deactivation, the wing was assigned to the 4th AF. Upon deactivation, the 62nd TCG was reassigned to the 12th AF, Continental Air Command.

Below, C-124C 51-5192 of the 14th TCS. The nose markings were red outlined in black. (via S. Nicolaou)

15th TCS

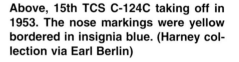

Above, the 15th TCS insignia is overall light blue with white longitude and latitude lines superimposed. All land masses are yellow. There were three eight-pointed stars on the globe which are in white with red borders. They signify the three major air lifts supported by the 15th TCS, and they represent the actions in Berlin, the Pacific and Korea. The eagle on the globe is in natural colors (assumed to be white and brown) with gold beak and claws, highlighted in black. The sphere was bordered in red and dark blue. (Craig Kaston)

On the first of July, the group was reassigned to the 14th AF. The change left the unit under the control and jurisdiction of Continental Air Command, but two weeks later the unit was assigned to Continental Division, Military Air Transport Service. Unit components (squadrons) that were stationed at Kelly AFB, Texas, were returned to McChord AFB on 27 July and, on that same day, the group was attached to the Northern Pacific Air Transport Wing, a Provisional unit.

The attachment was short lived.

On August 24, the group was assigned to the 1705th Air Transport Wing, still under Continental Division, MATS. The temporary change of station from Kelly AFB, Texas, to McChord AFB, Washington, became permanent on 19 February 1951.

From April to October 1951, the group's two C-124s were engaged in the execution of Operation BLUEJAY, the transportation of personnel, construction materials and supplies from Westover AFB to Thule, Greenland. The two C-124s were apparently the only such aircraft in the group, the majority of the unit's planes being C-54s.

The 62nd TCW was activated again (under the 18th AF, Tactical Air Command) in September 1951, and the group was assigned to that wing in October. As noted in the history of the 61st TCG, the 4th TCS (H), on temporary assignment to the 61st TCG, was redesignated the 14th TCS and assigned to the 61st TCG. At the same time, the 14th TCS, assigned to McChord AFB, was redesignated the

Above, 15th TCS C-124C taking off in 1953. The nose markings were yellow bordered in insignia blue. (Harney collection via Earl Berlin)

4th TCS (H) and assigned to the 62d TCW.

The wing provided transition training for the 61st TCG during the first half of 1953, and provided similar training for the 63rd TCG during the second half of the year.

As noted earlier, the wing was very active in various exercises up to the first of July 1957, when all TAC airlift units were reassigned to the Military Airlift Command. The history reflected above, exercise descriptions left out, is provided to illustrate unit assignments and organizational changes.

63RD TROOP CARRIER WING

The 63rd TCG was activated (with the 3rd, 9th and 52nd TCSs) at Altus AFB, Oklahoma, in January 1953. The group received its first C-124s, "C" models, there. By the end of June, the group had 21 Globemaster II's assigned. In October, the group moved to Donaldson AFB, South Carolina, where it joined the 63rd TCW, which would soon have the 61st TCG and 309th TCS assigned.

At left, 15th TCS C-124C 51-5188 in 1957. Note the yellow forward fuselage markings have been re-positioned. (via S. Nicolaou)

The wing was heavily involved in supporting the construction of the Distant Early Warning Radar network, most commonly known as the DEW Line. The wing's contribution to the construction project was such that, in 1955, it received the Air Force Outstanding Unit Award for its efforts.

The airlift efforts in support of DEW Line construction weren't without accidents. A C-124C (Serial No. 52-991) crashed at Frobisher Bay, Canada, on 27 April 1955. A wing broke and an outboard engine, its control cable severed, continued to run for 24 hours!

The 9th TCS began its part of the DEW Line support in February 1956, in a program known as "Operation Ice Cube." Flights were made from Dover AFB to individual air strips at the DEW Line sites, all being located in Northern Canada. These flights were conducted until the early 1970s under a program called "Cool Mule."

In July, the 54th TCS joined the wing. It had previously been assigned to the 5039th ATG at Elmendorf AFB, Alaska.

Eight of the wing's C-124s were specially equipped to support "Operation DEEP FREEZE", beginning in September 1956. All eight planes were named for particular states or cities and were operated from Christchurch, New Zealand. They flew to McMurdo Sound to pick up their cargoes and air dropped them at the South Pole. The first drop took place on November 2, and was accomplished from a 52nd TCS Globemaster II named "State of Oregon" (Serial No. 52-1015). Among the items dropped during these support flights was a 7-ton Caterpillar tractor, which landed intact and allowed the tractor to be put to immediate good use.

The "Operation DEEP FREEZE" support flights weren't without their share of accidents, but there were no lives lost. The first accident involved a C-124C named the "State of Washington" (Serial No. 52-982). It suffered a nose landing gear failure while attempting to land on rough surfaces. In addition to the landing gear damage, three engines had to be repaired as a result of the accident. A second accident, involving another 52nd TCS Globemaster II, also caused landing gear damage, this time to a main landing gear unit. Damage was repaired and the plane flew again, but not without cost.

53rd TCS

Above, 53rd TCS C-124C 51-5184 while assigned to Continental Division. (via Nick Williams)

JANUARY 1955 C-124 BASES

Above, 53rd TCS insignia's outer ring was yellow with black writing and the Jack and Ace of Spades were on an insignia blue field.

A third plane, dispatched with maintenance personnel, equipment and parts to repair the first two, landed and suffered serious damage, the plane catching fire and subsequently being destroyed. The maintenance and air crew got out alive and the other two C-124s were put back into operational service. The destroyed airplane was the "State of Oregon", the C-124 that made the first air drop over the South Pole.

Below, 53rd TCS C-124C 51-5173 at Philadelphia, PA, in 1955. Nose markings were insignia blue bordered in white. The squadron insignia consisted of an Ace of Spades covered by a Jack of Spades on an insignia blue field bordered by yellow. (via Williams)

Barksdale AFB, Shreveport, Louisiana (SAC)

Biggs AFB, El Paso, Texas (SAC)

Brookley AFB, Mobile, Alabama (MATS)

Castle AFB, Merced, California (SAC)

Donaldson AFB, Greenville, South Carolina (TAC)

Dover AFB, Dover, Delaware (MATS)

Ellsworth AFB, Rapid City, South Dakota (SAC)

Elmendorf AFB, Anchorage, Alaska (AAC)

Hickam AFB, Honolulu, Hawaii (MATS)

Hill AFB, Ogden, Utah (MATS)

Kelly AFB, San Antonio, Texas (AMC)

Kirtland AFB, New Mexico (SAC)

Larson AFB, Moses Lake, Washington

(TAC)

McChord AFB, Tacoma, Washington (MATS)

Norton AFB, San Bernadino, California (AMC)

Robins AFB, Macon, Georgia (AMC)

Tachikawa AB, Tachikawa, Japan (FEAF)

Travis AFB, Fairfield, California (MATS)

Westover AFB, Chicopee Falls, Massachusetts (MATS)

Palm Beach AFB, Palm Beach, Florida (MATS)

Wright-Patterson AFB, Dayton, Ohio (AMC)

Above, 14th TCS C-124C 52-7276 at Thule, Greenland. Nose markings were red and the bar design forward of the squadron insignia was the Air Force Outstanding Unit Award. Nose radar unit was faded to a dirty brown color. (via Craig Kaston)
Below, 8th TCS C-124A 51-091 was assigned to Larson AFB, Washington, in August 1952. (Douglas)

Strategic Air Command

Not surprisingly, but probably not well known, is the fact that the Strategic Air Command, not the Military Air Transport Service, got the very first operational C-124s and put them into service. The reason this should come as no surprise should be obvious. In the early 1950s, the Strategic Air Command (SAC) was the Air Force's strong arm in the sky. The possibility of a Russian attack over the North Pole was a constant threat, and the only way to dissuade them from making such a move was to have a counter-punch that could do as much or more to them than what they could do to us.

Below, SAC C-124A flightline on 3-17-1956. All seven aircraft have insignia red tails and outer wing panels; five out of seven have the SAC fuselage stripes. (S. Parker via Earl Berlin)

In those early years, what SAC wanted, to meet its mission, SAC got! New bombers were bigger, faster, more effective ... and more expensive. Nuclear weapons hadn't been developed to the extent they have since then, and it took a big airplane with a large bomb bay to lift the atomic and hydrogen bombs SAC kept in its arsenal. Naturally, SAC needed a means to move these weapons from depot to base and back to depot again, as well as moving other equipment, parts and personnel whenever and wherever needed.

SAC sent its representative to the board that reviewed the design specifications for the C-124. That representative was Colonel Avery J. Ladd. SAC was commanded by Curtis LeMay at the time and he wanted an airplane that could carry SAC's "weapons" in a fully assembled condition. He got exactly what he wanted in the C-124.

Colonel Ladd accepted the first C-124 for the Air Force and SAC on 17 July 1950, and flew it to its home base at Walker AFB, Roswell, New Mexico, where it joined the 2nd Strategic Support Squadron. That first airplane, Serial No. 49-235, was named "Apache Chieftain", and the other C-124s in the squadron received similar Indian names.

Not long after, Colonel Ladd took that first airplane on a worldwide tour of bases the command's C-124s would be hauling "weapons" to. The idea of the tour was to check facilities,

security and storage areas at those bases where the "weapons" would be located. Not surprisingly, Colonel Ladd became the first pilot in the Air Force to log 1,000 hours in the C-124.

For all of its size and importance, SAC had only four Strategic Support Squadrons that flew the C-124. Perhaps the reason is that its KC-97s, especially the "G" models, could carry cargo and personnel as well as act as airborne filling stations.

1st Strategic Support Squadron

The 1st SSS gained its designation when General Order No. 1, dated 14 January 1949, was published. Issued by Headquarters 97th Bombardment Wing, the general order changed the squadron's name from 1st Strategic Support Unit (1st SSU). The squadron was operating 12 C-97 aircraft at this time and was stationed at Biggs AFB, El Paso, Texas. It was shortly thereafter joined by the 2nd SSS, which was activated and equipped with C-54 Skymasters.

On 18 January 1951, the squadron took delivery of its first C-124A, and shortly thereafter some of the unit's crews went to Walker AFB, New Mexico, to transition to the new airplane, training being provided by the 2nd SSS, which had moved to Walker and had received SAC's first

1st SSS insignia was yellow with white clouds and a dark green earth, all bordered in black. The hornet was green and white with black gloves & boots.

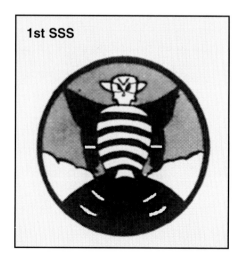

1st SSS

At right, 1st SSS C-124C 50-0088 crashed at Cooks Inlet, Anchorage, Alaska, in January 1957. The plane was carrying a cargo of engines, which were salvaged after boats attached lines to bulldozers and the craft was pulled ashore. (Norm Taylor collection via Earl Berlin)

C-124 on 17 July 1950.

Conversion from the C-97 to the C-124 continued through February, and further deliveries of new C-124s were expected in March. By the end of March, five additional Globemaster IIs had arrived.

April 1951 brought something of a setback to the squadron as it was forced to utilize five of its reconditioned C-97s (the aircraft had been reconditioned and inspected in preparation for acceptance by MATS inspection and acceptance crews) plus three C-124s to complete a maximum effort mission. The C-97s had to be to be reserviced, reconditioned and reinspected upon completion of the mission. Subsequently, all of the squadron's C-97s were turned over to Lockheed Aircraft Corporation at Burbank, California, for final inspections and necessary reconditioning prior to handover to MATS. This transfer of responsibility took a huge load off the squadron.

By the end of April, the squadron had a total of eight C-124s. All the aircraft were "A" models. The last of the squadron's C-97s were flown to Lockheed's Burbank facility at the end of May. In June, the squadron operated for the first time as a "C-124 only" squadron.

As of July 1951 the squadron was equipped with C-124As serial numbers 50-086 through 50-089 and 50-091, 50-092 and 50-094 through 50-098. All these aircraft are believed to have been decorated with the squadron's "Green Hornet" insignia. The C-124Cs that replaced the C-124As did not carry the Green Hornets insignia. The first C-124C, 52-0973, was received by the squadron on 12 August 1953.

In what's believed to be the year 1951, in September, the 1st SSS suffered its first major C-124 accident.

2nd SSS insignia was green bordered in yellow. The running indian was yellow with a brown tomahawk and loin cloth. (Craig Kaston)

Below, 2nd SSS C-124A 49-241 with its distinctive green fuselage and nose stripe. The triangle beneath and in front of the the squadron insignia was burnished metal. The tail and outer wings were arctic red. (Doug Olson via Nick Williams)

2nd SSS

The pinto was dark brown and white with gray shading. The indian features bronze skin with tan and black highlights, wearing bright tan pants with dark brown shadows. Moccasins were tan and the war bonnet is believed to be in white with red tips. The dust cloud below the pinto was tan with a black outline. The words "Apache Chieftain" are believed to be in black with white outlines around all letters.

Below, the first aircraft accepted by the Air Force for operational use was C-124A 49-235, which was assigned to the 2nd Strategic Support Squadron (SAC). It was named the Apache Chieftain. (Harry Gann)

The airplane was performing a practice Ground Controlled Approach (GCA) and was on final to the runway when a severe downdraft was encountered. The crew applied full power and fought with the controls but the airplane continued to settle and struck a rock wall short of the runway. Both main landing gears and the right wing spar were severely damaged, though the gear supported the airplane after landing, without additional damage. There were no reported deaths or injuries.

In January 1954, the unit is reported to have performed five general types of missions. These were:

1. Ferrying four new C-124Cs, assigned to the squadron, from the Douglas Plant at Long Beach, California, to Biggs AFB.

2. Ferrying two aircraft from Biggs AFB to Norton AFB for inspection and repair.

3. Participating, with the Air Force Special Weapons Center, in trial loads of experimental equipment.

4. Unit participation in an exercise with the Atomic Energy Commission.

A chronological rundown for 1955 shows the unit continued to operate C-124As alongside its newer C-124Cs. Of significance is the transfer of the squadron from assignment to the 8th AF to 15th AF on 1 April.

At this point, records at the Air Force Historical Research Center, applicable to the squadron, appear to end.

2nd Strategic Support Squadron

We pick up the history of the 2nd SSS in July 1950, as the unit is preparing for the arrival of its first C-124A. At the time, the unit was equipped with C-54 Skymasters and was stationed at Biggs AFB. The squadron was redeployed to Walker AFB, Roswell, New Mexico, and nicknamed the "Globe Girdlers".

C-124A, Serial No. 49-235, arrived at Walker AFB at 15:04, Mountain Standard Time, on 17 July. It was the first C-124A delivered to the Air Force for operational purposes. The airplane was, at this time,

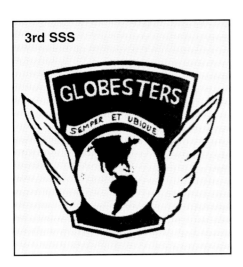

3rd SSS "Globesters" insignia was yellow over a black field. The globe was medium blue. (Craig Kaston)

also being operated by the 1703rd ATG, but in the service test capacity.

The squadron received four additional C-124As during August. By this time, a training syllabus had been set up. Pilots were given 19 hours of "dual" and 5 additional hours of "solo" time in the airplane before being cleared for cross-country flights. Nonetheless, the squadron flew three missions in the Zone of Interior during the month.

In September, seven additional C-124As arrived at the unit. This brought the squadron to its full complement of 12 Globemaster IIs. However, the unit's C-54s, or at least some of them, were still flying and performing regular missions with the squadron at this time, as evidenced by the 31 missions flown by Skymasters during the month.

Apparently, in October the squadron received a tasking to train C-124 crews in response to the activation of the 3rd Strategic Support

Above, close up of nose of 3rd SSS C-124A 49-247. Forward cabin was white. The stylized Eagle was yellow and dark blue as was the fuselage speed stripe. The prop spinners were also yellow. (E. Van Houten via Dave Menard and Earl Berlin)

Below, side view of upgraded 49-247 with radar nose shows the remainder of the blue and yellow fuselage speed stripe. The aircraft did not have the standard insignia red tail and outer wings. (via SDAM)

Above, 3rd SSS C-124C 49-259 from Barksdale AFB, during an open house at Pease AFB in May 1959. Aircraft is overall natural metal with a SAC fuselage stripe of blue with white stars and the SAC insignia. (Jim Burridge)

Squadron. The specific tasking is to train four crews, but the squadron's intent is to train as many crews as possible, if time allows.

The squadron's C-124s were grounded in November due to severe nose wheel shimmy problems. Corrective action was taken by Douglas Aircraft Corporation and 2nd SSS maintenance personnel, and the first airplane was back in the air on the 19th. Between the 19th and 23rd all aircraft were modified and released for operational commitments.

In December, some of the squadron's personnel, including aircrews, were transferred to the newly organized 3rd SSS. In January, replacement personnel, all pilots, arrived in the squadron. Of the six pilots received, three had a high level of experience, though the history doesn't indicate it was in C-124s.

In May 1951, the squadron moved to Castle AFB, Merced, California, where it remained until reassigned to the Air Material Command as a Logistics Support Squadron.

3rd Strategic Support Squadron

The 3rd SSS was activated, in accordance with General Order No. 75, on 16 November 1950 at Hunter AFB, Georgia, and nicknamed the "Globesters". By the beginning of January 1951, the squadron had seven C-124s on strength, and by the end of February a full complement of 13 aircraft were on hand. The squadron was transferred to Barksdale AFB, Louisiana in 1953 and remained there until it was disbanded in 1961.

4th Strategic Support Squadron

The 4th SSS was activated at Rapid City AFB on 18 February 1953. The unit was assigned to the 8th AF and attached to the 28th Strategic Reconnaissance Wing (SRW) for administrative and logistical support. The unit was scheduled to be equipped with C-124C aircraft. To help get the squadron on its feet, three experienced C-124 crews from each of the existing Strategic Support Squadrons, for a total of nine crews, were transferred to the unit.

Completion of squadron manning was expected not later than 1 August. Six C-124s were expected in August, with six more arriving in September. From the 15th to the 26th of August, five 4th SSS crews ferried six brand-new C-124Cs to the squadron. The new airplanes were used to provide transition training for aircrews who, though qualified on the C-124A, had not been qualified on the "C" model Globemaster II. The base, meanwhile, had been renamed Ellsworth AFB.

In September, the squadron received its last six C-124Cs. They were aircraft Serial Nos. 52-984 through 52-989.

"The mission of the 4th Strategic Support Squadron is to:

a. Maintain the unit in a state of readiness so that the squadron will at all times be capable of conducting:

(1) World-wide airlift operations in support of Strategic Air Command units. This logistic support must be capable of instantaneous reaction and capable of airlifting personnel, spares, and equipment of any nature, thus providing the command with a capability to launch an immediate offensive with a prime portion of the strategic force from any location.

(2) Specialized airlift of nuclear weapons and experimental or high priority cargo during peacetime in support of this or other commands to insure that aircrews maintain a high degree of proficiency in wartime operational requirements.

(3) Operations individually or in conjunction with other agencies in disaster relief or other domestic emergencies.

b. Conduct continuous ground and flying training to insure that a high level of proficiency is maintained by the flight and maintenance crews.

c. Conduct other special support missions as may be directed."

William L. Farrar, offered the following information about flying for SAC and provided a comparison by writing a piece about flying the C-124 for the Air Force Reserve. I'd written to Bill and told him I'd run up against a wall, of sorts, in that much of the information about SAC C-124 operations was still classified at the time I made my request. His response makes wonderful reading:

"SAC: It doesn't surprise me, and in fact amuses me some that the SAC history office states that most of the SSS information is still classified. They had a fetish for classifying everything, and probably have several tons of paper buried in some warehouse that no one wants to wade through.

I don't know exactly when the support squadrons first started. Their official names were 1st (through 4th) Strategic Support Squadron, very clever. The First was at Biggs AFB (El Paso), and started with other equipment, such as C-54s, YC-97, and later some 124s. I believe the 2nd SSS (commonly called triple-S), formed at Castle, got the first Shakeys from Douglas that SAC had. The 3rd, at Barksdale, and 1st, all then received early models, 49's and early 50's. These were of course, all A-models, slick wings (without the wing-tip heater). The 1st later got some C models, and flew both until deactivated in the late 1950's; the 4th got its C models, and the A's were divided between the 2nd and 3rd. The 2nd moved later to what became McCoy AFB (at Orlando). The 3rd always was at Barksdale.

The 4th SSS was formed at Ellsworth in the early 50s, with new late 52 models out of the factory. I went to this unit in Jan. '57 right out of flying school. That summer the squadron moved to Dyess, where it remained until deactivation in early '61. At that time its planes were re-assigned to the three squadrons operated by the old Air Material Command, stationed at Robins, Kelly, and Hill (did you know these existed?). The 2nd and 3rd also deactivated later that year, and their planes were the first given to the Reserves (the unit I later went into got some of them).

General LeMay at one time apparently wanted to have a force as independent as possible from the rest of the Air Force, and thus was able to form the transport units. SAC even had its own fighter wings at one time, using F-84s. Every base also had a mish-mash of support aircraft, ranging from B-25s to H-19s and various small transports. Originally the 124s were used for the famous SAC deployments, supporting the Bomb Wings as they would fly off to the UK, Guam, Thule, Goose, etc. for 90-day TDYs. This apparently did not last long, as MATS (now MAC) assumed this mission, until today. The primary mission became the airlifting of special weapons for the bomb wings, i.e. we carried around atomic bombs from one place to another. The primary mission was to airlift weapons to forward bases being used by the bombers in time of war; this was never done of course, and was classified at the time TOP SECRET, so no one ever spoke of it. We all had to have a TS clearance to be a crew member. The secondary mission, performed regularly, was to airlift weapons between various bases and/or depots as the bomb wings changed targets, or the units were due for modifications, or had just been modified, and were ready for a location. These missions, always classified SECRET, were closely choreographed operations, of-one to-five or six planes, often lasting up to a week, rotating back and forth, usually three units per plane. As you would expect, there was a lot of stress and tension during one of these, as the units would be brought to, and picked up from, the planes by the weapons depot people, the couriers signing for them (as co-pilot I was the courier in flight, and carried a two-inch barrel .38 revolver to protect them), and AP security acting profoundly officious. This was probably the most professional mission anyone in the SS outfits ever performed, as the regs governing these missions were strict, detailed and lengthy.

SAC however, tried to run the SS units like bombers and tankers. Everyone was formed into a crew, AC, CP, nav, engineer (one only), and loadmaster. Early in the outfits each crew also had a radio operator, but these were phased out as the SSB radios were installed (1958 or so). The AC, N, and FE were primary crew members, meaning that two of the three at least had to be

involved with each mission. This restriction was ludicrous, as MAC has proven with thousands of flights. It also restricted the upgrading of CPs to ACs, as each squadron could only have so many crews, and if there was not an AC slot, no upgrading was performed. (So much for the morale of the young pilots). Some missions would add loadmasters, or even other crewmembers if unusually long legs, or extra loads were involved. Every flight, even locals, carried maintenance people, two, and three on x-countries. They performed scanning and other in-flight jobs done by the second engineer on MAC flights.

Every x-country was classified CONFIDENTIAL, or above. This even included flights to other bases for static-display purposes, at air shows. Why, I never knew, nor I doubt did anyone else.

SAC, who invented standardization boards, included this in the SS units. Each squadron had 2 or 3 stand-board crews, who terrorized everyone else on check rides. Every crew received two flights annually, one formal (scheduled, and sometimes lasting several days on a x-country mission) and one no-notice, which could be done locally. Interestingly enough, there was no one in any higher headquarters (15th AF, SAC) qualified on the C-124, so the chief of the standboard was pretty much the highest flying authority in the unit. Crews (pilots and FEs) started to go to the simulators in about 58 or so; we went to Dover. The MATS instructors made it plain that the SAC crews needed some serious retraining. This was mainly ignored.

Other than the weapons missions as I mentioned, professionalism in SAC 124s was not impressive (my experiences in the reserves are my yardstick, where it was profoundly higher). Crew-rest times were ignored, IFR restrictions ignored, tricks performed (full-flap takeoff for instance), carelessness was allowed (an engineer on a flight I was on over the North Atlantic, at night, allowed all four engines to quit with carburetor ice; we only lost a couple of thousand feet before getting them started); maintenance deficiencies were played with to either get home, or stay away, depending on the AC's whims; and petty regs were fol-

Above, 321st BW C-124A 49-0245 in April 1959 at an open house at McCoy AFB, FL. Note the insignia red tail and the SAC fuselage stripe. (Norm Taylor via Earl Berlin)

lowed to the letter. For instance, parachute harnesses had to be worn on all flights (unless specifically exempted, as happened on rare passenger missions); this meant for passengers too if any. Thus, I have seen emergency leave space-A passengers left at terminals because the plane didn't have enough chutes. All in all, SAC was not a command to operate transport planes.

I separated and came back to Kansas City about the time the 4th SSS broke up. The other personnel were shipped to the LSS units (AMC), and those were shortly thereafter absorbed into MATS. A lot of the old-timers did not cope.

Surprisingly enough, their safety record was fairly good. There were some accidents. The 1st had the only successful ditching of a Shakey, off the south coast of Alaska, but they landed partially on an ice flow. All other known ditchings lost several crewmen each, as the clam-shell doors would collapse, causing fast sinking. The 4th bellied in one off the runway at the old Gray AFB, located within Fort Hood, TX. Contaminated ADI was the cause, with all engines stopping more or less simultaneously. It was jacked up, the engines changed, and flown out, after a bunch of tanks ran around in the field making enough of a runway for it. I remember flying through some thunderstorms, however, that scared me witless, though we made it (some of the ACs thought it was fun). Engine changes on trips were common, and delays were the norm. No one hardly ever offered any support, even SAC bases, and we were often referred to as a 'bastard' outfit, with good reason.

Do not get the idea, by any means, that the 4th SS was a totally incompetent outfit. There were many, the majority in fact, of highly skilled and professional airmen assigned. It just seemed that the few otherwise were allowed to persist in their

habits."

As previously mentioned, SAC ultimately deactivated its Strategic Support Squadrons, many of the C-124s going to Air Force Reserve units. Bear in mind the transfer of SAC's Shakys didn't leave it without airlift capability. By 1961, SAC had a huge force of KC-135A tankers, each airplane fully capable of being used in the airlift capacity. The KC-135 carries all of its fuel in the wing and lower fuselage tanks; the upper half of the fuselage interior being clear except for the auxiliary power unit (APU) on the left side, toward the rear of the airplane. A goodly amount of cargo and/or passengers could be carried, quickly and smoothly. For passengers, it wasn't the most comfortable way to fly, but it certainly got you there.

Before pressing on to the particulars of the Logistic Support Squadrons of the Air Materiel Command, the following two stories are worth sharing. The first reflects Shaky's sturdiness. The second reflects some of the aspects of depot level maintenance on the C-124, as well as some of the testing done in cooperation with the depot personnel.

Durward L. Matthews was a flight examiner navigator on the C-124 and shared this story which reflects that, in this instance at least, Shaky was a lot tougher than her human handlers.

"As the flight examiner Navigator we left Dover AFB on April 27, 1956, for Upper Heyford, England, via Harmon AB in Newfoundland. I was giving a routine flight check to another Navigator on this flight. He was an experienced line navigator and required little or no supervision. However, as we approached the British Isles, I noticed that we were off course and if we continued on that heading we would have made a landfall over Ireland. We corrected course and flew on to Upper Heyford without further incident.

The return flight was via Lajes, and when we filed our flight plan from Lajes to Dover AFB, Delaware, we found that we couldn't make it to Dover with the fuel load we could carry. So we filed for Kindly AB in Bermuda and took off. Halfway between Lajes and Kindley, the US Coast Guard had a vessel on a fixed station, code name Ocean Station Vessel ECHO, which was used for weather reports and position reports in addition to emergency assistance. When we approached ECHO we called in and were informed that we could not land at Bermuda because of a frontal passage [which] was estimated to arrive at about the same time as our ETA. We immediately altered course to Dover AFB and revised our flight plan accordingly.

Shortly thereafter, we started picking up radar indications of cumulus buildups associated with the cold front. The navigator was busily recomputing distances, course, etc, but the C-124 radar (which I think was the APS 42) could not determine the tops of the buildups and of course, ol' Shakey was best flying at about 10,000 feet.

All of a sudden, we hit a downdraft, and dropped about 1500 feet, then we were lifted back up about 1000 feet in a matter of seconds and then we bounced around for about 3 or 4 minutes but it seemed like a lifetime. I was standing alongside the navigators table and was able to grasp a corner of the table with one hand and the back of the navigators seat with the other and ride out the turbulence. The flight deck was covered with all sorts of things like tools from the flight engineer's tool box, coffee cups, etc.

Meantime, down below in the main cargo compartment, the Loadmasters and some passengers were being tossed about like dead leaves in a hurricane. One loadmaster was unfortunate in that he was lifted to the top of the cargo compartment and slammed down across the tie-down equipment box and received three broken ribs. Two other crew members received minor injuries and were admitted to the hospital upon landing at DAFB.

Shortly after entering clear air, I readjusted the radar and discovered the navigator did not have the set fine-tuned for weather penetration, and as a result it was necessary to give him a failing grade on his flight. Upon examination of the C-124 upon landing it was determined that the plane was completely airworthy. The plane hadn't even popped a rivet.

Incidentally, the hospital at Dover AFB had become operational at 0001 on 1 May 1956, and the plane we were flying landed at 0600."

Here's another story.

"I first flew the C-124 in Nov 1955 while stationed at Norton AFB, CA, with the San Bernadino Air Materiel Area - I had been doing desk duty and was returned to the cockpit per AF policy.

Two missions at SBAMA involved the C-124. SBAMA was the 'prime' AMA for the C-124 and operated an IRAN line on the base where C-124s went thru at the rate of 12 per month. The Directorate of Maintenance at SBAMA consisted of some 6,000 civilian employees and 25 officers, led by Col. Arthur C. Perry.

The second mission involved C-124A #51-048*. This aircraft came to Norton from Kirtland AFB, NM. The mission was to transport the SNARK (Northrup) missile from Los Angeles International Airport to Cape Canaveral and the Navaho (North American) missile and booster from Long Beach Municipal Airport to the Cape. These missions involved precision loading since each load 'barely' fit. In fact, 51-048 had been modified so that the loads had about a four inch clearance on each side.

Additional ramps were added to those at the nose of the C-124 to elongate the ramp and thereby decrease the grade into the C-124. Each load was filmed. Took 6-12 hours to complete. SLOWLY!!!

Then we staged to Kelly AFB for a RON [Rest Overnight]. Departed Kelly so as to arrive at the Cape after 1700 ET, and landed on the skid strip. Then we parked in one of the revetments. The cargo was unloaded between 1700 & 0700 the next day. We usually departed for Patrick at 0600 where we refueled.

Much care was taken to avoid any rough air, as 'old Shakey' didn't like it, and the cargo would 'wallow' some even though chained down.

Back to the first mission, IRAN, Inspection and Repair as Necessary. Many T.O. compliances were done; control cables were untwisted to look for corrosion or deterioration and then retensioned per T.O. Engines, wheels, generators, pumps, etc., were

7th LSS

removed & tested & replaced when necessary or economically prudent.

The business grew! By June 1956, SBAMA contracted with Douglas Aircraft Company for IRAN of C-124s. I delivered the first on June 30 from Hill AFB, UT. The 'aluminum balloon' had a crash landing somewhere in Alaska after which it got a one-time flight to Hill. Another one-time flight to Long Beach. The nose gear was inoperative, bolted in the down position. Needless to say, there was severe damage to the nose of the aircraft. Other temporary fixes were duly recorded on the Form 1. A slow, leisurely flight was made from Hill to Long Beach and this 'Old Shaky' was back home again.

Then Douglas Aircraft Company learned the difference between building new aircraft and 'keeping 'em flying!' It cost the taxpayer a buck or two. How nice it was to collect a gaggle of parts and assemble them! The real work is in disassembly, test, repair, and successful test flight followed by another tour of duty."

Air Materiel Command

Air MateriEl Command (AMC), now Air Force Logistics Command (AFLC), had three C-124 squadrons assigned before MATS took them over around 1957.

7th Logistic Support Squadron (LSS)

The 7th LSS was activated at Robins Air Force Base on 18 October 1954. Its first C-124, Serial No. 53-011, was delivered five days later. One more airplane was delivered in October, five in November and three in December, for a total of ten machines.

The squadron was named the Pack Rats and was characterized by a large fuselage insignia of a mouse swinging a log. The 7th was also known as the "Loggers" and became notorious for "zapping" every transient aircraft and barracks they came in contact with on their globe-hopping assignments with their squadron stickers. In early 1955, the unit was administratively transferred, without change of station, from Warner-Robins Air Material Area to the 3079th Aviation Depot Wing (ADW) at Wright-Patterson AFB.

The 7th LSS was redesignated

the 58th Military Airlift Squadron in early 1966. Then, in early 1967, the squadron converted to C-141 Starlifters. The squadron was deactivated on 15 August 1971.

19th Logistic Support Squadron (LSS)

The 19th LSS was activated at Kelly AFB on 24 September 1952. On 24 November 1952, the squadron was assigned to the Air Materiel Command and the San Antonio Air Materiel Area (SAAMA) at Kelly AFB. The squadron is recorded in historical records as being the first of its kind in the Air Force.

Effective 6 February 1955, the 19th LSS was removed from the jurisdiction of the San Antonio Air Materiel Area and assigned to the 3079th Aviation Depot Wing at Wright-Patterson AFB, Ohio. The 7th LSS and 28th LSS were assigned to the 3079th on this same date. For logistical support, the squadron was attached to the 2851st Air Base Wing at Kelly AFB.

During the first half of 1957, the squadron participated, under AMC Operations Orders, in "Rear Door", "Down Beat", "Leap Frog", "Boot Heel", "Dum Dum", "Rat Tail", "Hop Toad", "Low Tide", and "Total Rest".

At left, 7th LSS C-124C 53-0023 at Norton AFB, CA, on 19 May 1962. Nose and tail stripes and wing tip heaters were insignia red. (William Swisher)

Above, 7th LSS loads a Thor rocket section at the Douglas Plant in December 1958. (via Harry Gann)

The last half of 1957 saw the squadron participating in several other AMC Operations Orders, details of which were still classified when the historical data were written. The only information given other than the names of the Operations, was the fact that all were completed without incident.

The first half of 1958 saw the squadron participate in AMC Operations "Big Dog", "Blow Out", and "Pony Boy". Once again, the details were classified at the time the history was documented. All were completed without incident.

In late 1960, the squadron traded its 13 C-124A aircraft for "C" models, the first arriving from the 28th LSS on 15 November. The change from 13 to 18 airplanes complicated operations somewhat in that the unit didn't have

as much ramp space as it needed to accommodate the airplanes. Nonetheless, it accomplished its missions.

On 1 July 1962, the squadron was reassigned from the 3079th Aviation Depot Wing to the 39th Logistic Support Group at Kelly AFB.

Below, 19th LSS C-124A loading a logistic support trailer for Project Sightline. (Douglas via Earl Berlin)

28th LSS

An annual Air Force Logistics Command (AFLC) inspection was conducted in November; no major discrepancies being recorded.

The squadron received the Air Force Outstanding Unit Award, for its participation in the Cuban Missile Crisis, in April 1963. This was followed by a letter of appreciation from the Secretary of Defense for the squadron's efforts during Project Dominic. No further historical data is recorded.

Below, 28th LSS C-124C 52-0968 undergoing maintenance at Norton AFB, CA, in 1957. (Douglas via Nicolaou)

28th Logistic Support Squadron (LSS)

The primary mission of the 28th LSS was to provide air transportation in direct worldwide support of special weapons activities through the airlift of special weapons and related equipment. Its secondary mission was the airlift of other Department of Defense cargo as required when space was available.

The 28th LSS was activated at Hill AFB on 8 July 1953 and, on 4 January 1954, the squadron was declared operational. LtCol Robert L. Foley was the squadron's first Commanding Officer. The second Comanding Officer was LtCol James

Above, 28th LSS C-124C 52-0970 in 1957. Tail and outer wings were red, upper fuselage was white, and the Materiel Air Command insignia is positioned high on the tail. (via Nicolaou)

L Harcrow, who took over on 4 August 1955. LtCol James S. Van Epps took over on 25 May 1958, and LtCol Woodland M. Styron took command on 1 January 1962.

On 6 February 1962, the 28th LSS was transferred from the AFLC to MATS. The unit remained at Hill AFB, UT, but was administratively assigned to the 1501st Air Transport Wing at Travis AFB, CA. (see page 15).

Pacific Air Forces (PACAF)

The 374th TCW was activated at Harmon Air Force Base, Guam, Marianas Air Materiel Area (Provisional) in August 1948. In February 1949, the wing was transferred from Harmon AFB to Tachikawa AB, Japan. The unit remained there, under the 20th Air Force, until 14 August. At the time, the unit's 21st TCS, flying C-54s, was the only squadron in PACAF equipped with four-engine cargo planes.

On 15 January 1950, the wing was assigned to the 315th Air Division (Combat Cargo), by order of Far East Air Force (FEAF) Headquarters. The wing didn't change home station or radius of operations.

The wing received its first C-124A (S/N 51-111) in May 1952. The airplane was assigned to what was then called the "C-124 training unit". Subsequent aircraft, arriving throughout June, were assigned to either the C-124 training unit or the 6th TCS-H. Wing operations with C-47D and C-54D aircraft continued.

In July, the first cargo flight to Korea was made by Gen McCarty and members of the 315th headquarters staff. The cargo on the inaugural flight consisted of five J-33 F-86 engines for the 5th Air Force and about thirty crew member observers and photographers.

In August, the 6th TCS suffered a major accident at Komaki Air Base. At just after 1 o'clock in the afternoon,

on the 24th, the C-124 crashed while landing. There were no crew injuries or deaths.

The C-124's airlift missions to Korea steadily increased and in

Above, three mail trucks were part of the cargo sent to Korea in the C-124s. (USAF) Below, Another C-124A carried two fire trucks to Korea. (USAF) Bottom, giant construction equipment was yet another delivery. (USAF)

At left, five 374th C-124As and one C-54 await loading for missions to Korea. (USAF) Below left, 6th TCS C-124A was used to transport Indian Gurkas to Korea. (USAF) Below left, two ambulances await evacuees from a 374th C-124A (USAF) Bottom, good interior view of the C-124's nose compartment including the ladder required to access the flight deck. (USAF)

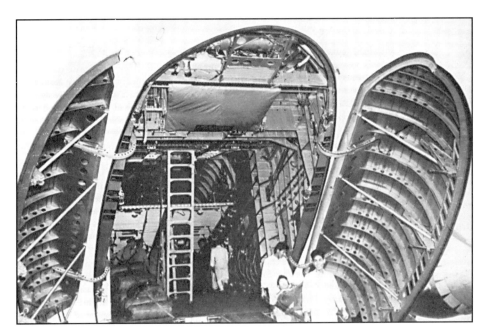

September 240 flights were made. The 374th carried 11,000 passengers, 2,400 tons of cargo and 590 evacuees. In October, the flights increased to 330, in November they increased again to 380. The wing peaked out in December with 400 sorties carrying 48,000 passengers, 4,700 tons of cargo and 450 evacuees.

Records indicate that the 6th and 22nd TCSs received the C-124A but that those assigned to the 22nd were grounded somewhere around January 1953, due to fuel leaks. Those assigned to the 6th apparently weren't affected. The problem was solved in the wing's maintenance shops, but crews from the 22nd flew alongside 6th TCS crews, in 6th TCS aircraft, until those of the 22nd were removed from grounded status. The first modified 22nd TCS aircraft returned from the base shops in mid-January, and all of the squadron's planes had been modified by the end of February.

In April 1953, the wing transported repatriated prisoners from Korea to Japan during Operation Little Switch. This was followed by Operation Big Switch, in which United Nations prisoners were transported from Korea to Japan.

In June 1953, the unit suffered another major accident, this one having tragic consequences. A C-124 loaded with 120 passengers took off from Tachikawa AB, Japan, returning to Korea. After the plane was airborne, the pilot reported that he had a generator fire in one engine and was shutting down the engine and feathering the prop. He would land back at Tachikawa as soon as he had gained enough altitude [apparently to manuever in]. He reported everything

else on the airplane was fine and the bird was in a steady climb. A few minutes later, the plane crashed and caught fire. Firemen from Tachikawa had to battle the flames before passengers and crew could be reached. All on board the airplane were killed in the crash. The wing's C-124s were grounded, pending an investigation. When it was found that pilot error had caused the crash, the C-124s went back into service.

After the Korean War, the wing resumed its normal troop carrier and airlift operations in the Far East and the Pacific area. In 1954, they started supporting operations into Indo-China (Vietnam). On 1 July 1957 the wing was inactivated.

One final unit, actually two, bears commenting on before we close our review of Shaky's service with the active duty Air Force. The 17th Tactical Airlift Squadron (TAS), assigned to Alaskan Air Command, was flying Lockheed C-130 Hercules aircraft in late 1969 when, on December 1, the squadron took on strength two C-124 Globemaster IIs. Used to airlift outsize cargo to remote Alaskan radar sites, the C-124s could do what the unit's C-130s couldn't. Often, the giant planes landed on incredibly short runways and did it in perfect safety. So effective were the C-124s, that the squadron continued flying them until October 1, 1971, at which time the airplanes were turned over to the 5041st Tactical Operations Squadron. How long that unit flew the airplanes isn't recorded.

At right, 51-0075 from the 5041 TOS Squadron. (Nrom Taylor)

At top, C-124C 51-0099 after assignment to the 17th TAS at Elmendorf AFB, AK, on 1 February 1970. (Norm Taylor) Above, C-124C 51-0098 from the 17th TAS at Elmendorf AFB, AK, on 2 December 1969. (Norm Taylor) Below, C-124C 51-0132 was assigned to the 5041st Tactical Operations Squadron, 21st Composite Wing at Elmendorf on 29 July 1972. (Norm Taylor)

THE C-124 AIRCRAFT DESCRIBED

General

The C-124 is a long range, low wing monoplane of semi-monocoque construction. It is powered by four Pratt & Whitney Wasp Major (R4360) engines and has fully retractable landing gear. Propellers, depending on aircraft series, are made by Curtiss Electric or Hamilton Standard. A crew of six is standard; members being the pilot, co-pilot, loadmaster, flight engineer, radio operator and navigator. A relief crew of three can be carried for very long-range missions. 200 troops or 136 litter patients can be accommodated.

Above, late in it's career witn nose radome and wing-tip heaters, the first C-124 prepares to taxi out from the Douglas plant for a test flight. It was tested with four bladed props, which were not used on production C-124s. (Boeing)

COMPARTMENTS AND AREAS

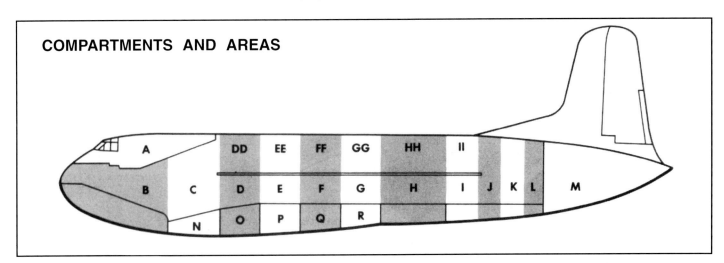

CREW MOVEMENT DIAGRAM

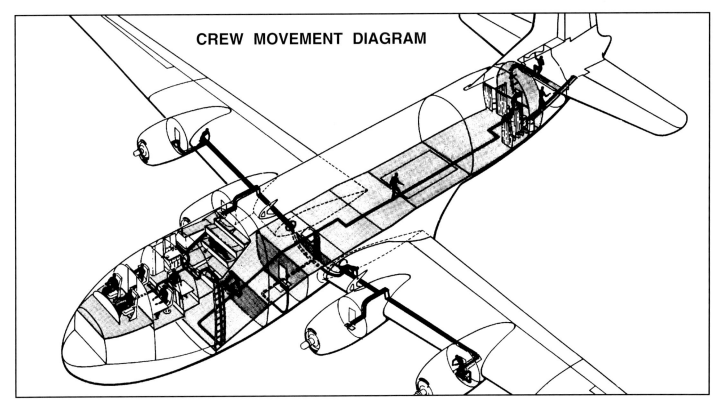

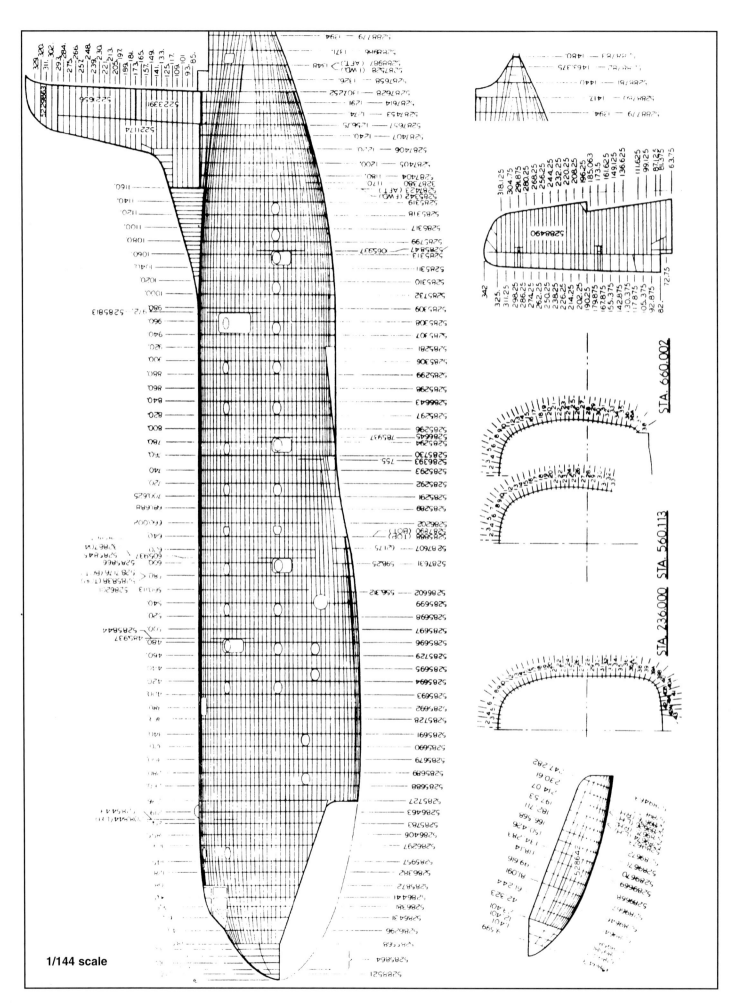

1/144 scale

STATIONS DIAGRAM

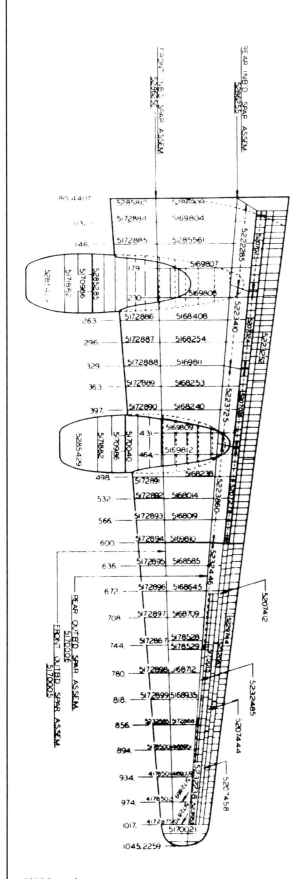

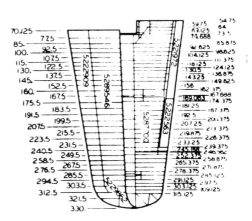

AIRCRAFT SERIAL NUMBERS AND MAIN DIFFERENCES
(at production roll-out)

AIRCRAFT C-124A 48-795 through 50-1268 features:
R-4360-20W engine, individual refueling, internal heaters, windshield de-icing (hot-air), fuel system (six-tank), cowling (removable section type), wing flaps (full span), front facing engineer, two single-phase inverters, two auxiliary power plants.

AIRCRAFT C-124A 51-073 through 51-132 feature changes:
Single point refueling, external wing tip heater pods added, windshield de-icing (nesa glass), cowling (orange peel type).

AIRCRAFT C-124A 51-133 through 51-157 feature changes:
Fuel system (twelve-tank).

AIRCRAFT C-124A 51-158 through 51-182 feature changes:
Radome.

AIRCRAFT C-124A 51-5173 through 51-5187 feature changes:
Wing flaps (partial span).

AIRCRAFT C-124C 51-5188 through 51-5197 feature changes:
R-4360-63A engine.

AIRCRAFT C-124C 51-5198 through 51-7285 feature changes:
Side facing engineer.

AIRCRAFT C-124C 52-939 through 52-1021 feature changes:
Two single-phase inverters and three 3-phase inverters.

AIRCRAFT C-124C 52-1022 through 52-1033:
One auxiliary power unit.

AIRCRAFT C-124C 52-1034 and subsequent:
Two single-phase inverters and two 3-phase inverters.

NOTE: Most C-124s were upgraded with radomes & C-124C R-4360-63A engines.

1/144 scale

GENERAL THREE VIEWS AND DIMENSIONS

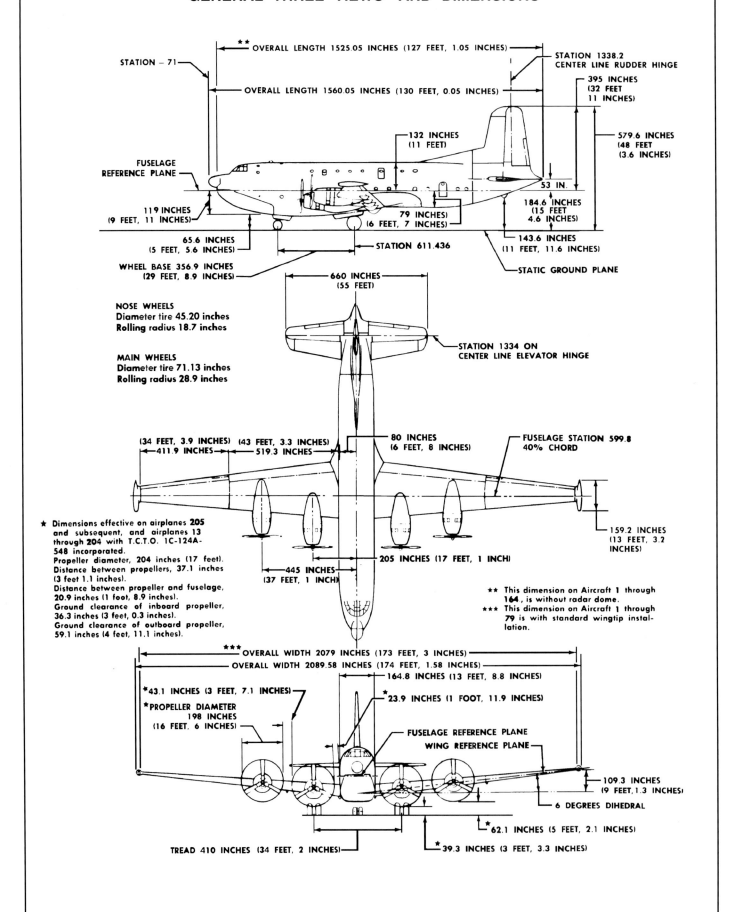

STATION – 71

** OVERALL LENGTH 1525.05 INCHES (127 FEET, 1.05 INCHES)

OVERALL LENGTH 1560.05 INCHES (130 FEET, 0.05 INCHES)

STATION 1338.2
CENTER LINE RUDDER HINGE

395 INCHES
(32 FEET
11 INCHES)

579.6 INCHES
(48 FEET
(3.6 INCHES)

132 INCHES
(11 FEET)

FUSELAGE
REFERENCE PLANE

53 IN.

184.6 INCHES
(15 FEET
4.6 INCHES)

119 INCHES
(9 FEET, 11 INCHES)

79 INCHES)
(6 FEET, 7 INCHES)

143.6 INCHES
(11 FEET, 11.6 INCHES)

65.6 INCHES
(5 FEET, 5.6 INCHES)

STATION 611.436

STATIC GROUND PLANE

WHEEL BASE 356.9 INCHES
(29 FEET, 8.9 INCHES)

660 INCHES
(55 FEET)

NOSE WHEELS
Diameter tire 45.20 inches
Rolling radius 18.7 inches

STATION 1334 ON
CENTER LINE ELEVATOR HINGE

MAIN WHEELS
Diameter tire 71.13 inches
Rolling radius 28.9 inches

(34 FEET, 3.9 INCHES)
411.9 INCHES

(43 FEET, 3.3 INCHES)
519.3 INCHES

80 INCHES
(6 FEET, 8 INCHES)

FUSELAGE STATION 599.8
40% CHORD

★ Dimensions effective on airplanes 205
and subsequent, and airplanes 13
through 204 with T.C.T.O. 1C-124A-
548 incorporated.
Propeller diameter, 204 inches (17 feet).
Distance between propellers, 37.1 inches
(3 feet 1.1 inches).
Distance between propeller and fuselage,
20.9 inches (1 foot, 8.9 inches).
Ground clearance of inboard propeller,
36.3 inches (3 feet, 0.3 inches).
Ground clearance of outboard propeller,
59.1 inches (4 feet, 11.1 inches).

159.2 INCHES
(13 FEET, 3.2
INCHES)

445 INCHES
(37 FEET, 1 INCH)

205 INCHES (17 FEET, 1 INCH)

** This dimension on Aircraft 1 through
164, is without radar dome.
*** This dimension on Aircraft 1 through
79 is with standard wingtip installation.

*** OVERALL WIDTH 2079 INCHES (173 FEET, 3 INCHES)

OVERALL WIDTH 2089.58 INCHES (174 FEET, 1.58 INCHES)

164.8 INCHES (13 FEET, 8.8 INCHES)

*43.1 INCHES (3 FEET, 7.1 INCHES)

*23.9 INCHES (1 FOOT, 11.9 INCHES)

*PROPELLER DIAMETER
198 INCHES
(16 FEET, 6 INCHES)

FUSELAGE REFERENCE PLANE
WING REFERENCE PLANE

109.3 INCHES
(9 FEET, 1.3 INCHES)

6 DEGREES DIHEDRAL

*62.1 INCHES (5 FEET, 2.1 INCHES)

TREAD 410 INCHES (34 FEET, 2 INCHES)

*39.3 INCHES (3 FEET, 3.3 INCHES)

Wing Description

The wing is a full-cantilever, stress-ed-skin type composed of the following sections: the center section, which supports the four nacelles and contains the integral fuel tanks, two detachable wing outer panels, and two detachable tips. On aircraft 80 and subsequent, pods for housing the wing heaters are installed, forming the tip of each outer panel. The wing center section and the wing outer panels have a continuous two-spar central section. Flush-type rivets are used on the outer surfaces. The wing upper covering is reinforced by span-wise 75S-T rolled-hat-section stiffeners. The heavy solid spars consist of 14S-T or 75S-T caps and stiffeners and 24S-TAL or 75 S-T webs. Between the spars and extending chordwise are 24S-TAL sheet ribs (formers) with lightening holes. The ribs are attached to the skin reinforcing stringers, but not to the skin. Also extending chordwise at areas of high stress are heavy solid bulkheads of 24S-TAL sheet that are attached to both the skin and the reinforcing stringers. The covering joints are of the butt and joggle lap-type. The leading edge of the wing between the nacelles and extending from the outboard side of the outboard nacelles to the wing tips is of double-skin construction. A web in the leading edge of the wing forms a D-shaped duct to carry thermal and anti-icing air to the leading edge. Access doors are provided in the wing for maintenance, and, in flight, a walkway in the wing, just forward of the forward spar, gives access to each nacelle. The wing trailing edge incorporates a full-length flap that is supported by heavy hinges and fairings.

Empennage Description

The empennage consists of the dorsal fin, a vertical stabilizer, a rudder and the rudder tab, two horizontal stabilizers, and two elevators and elevator tabs. The all-metal and full-cantilever fixed surfaces are attached to the fuselage stubs by tension bolts at the spars. The fixed surfaces are of the two-spar type, with covering that is reinforced by chord-wise ribs only. The spars are of the flat-webbed type,

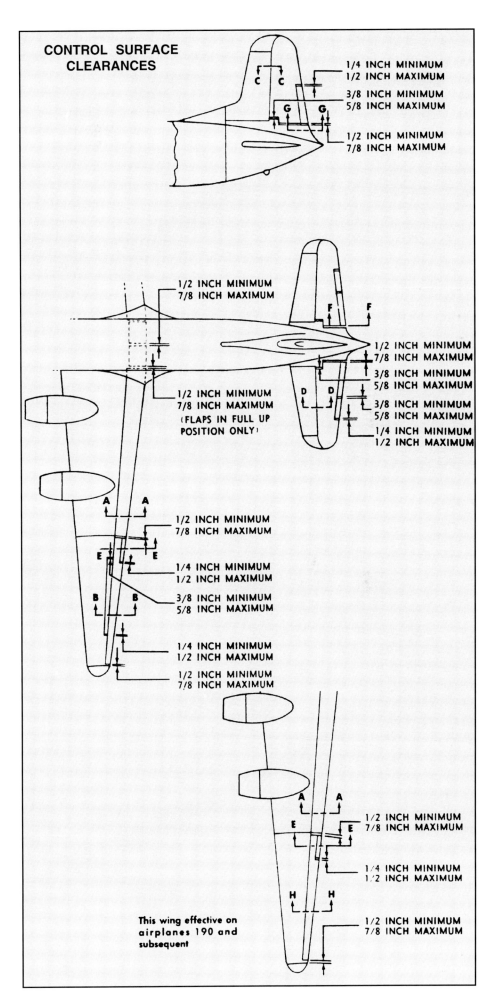

CONTROL SURFACE CLEARANCES

1/4 INCH MINIMUM
1/2 INCH MAXIMUM

3/8 INCH MINIMUM
5/8 INCH MAXIMUM

1/2 INCH MINIMUM
7/8 INCH MAXIMUM

1/2 INCH MINIMUM
7/8 INCH MAXIMUM

1/2 INCH MINIMUM
7/8 INCH MAXIMUM

1/2 INCH MINIMUM
7/8 INCH MAXIMUM
(FLAPS IN FULL UP POSITION ONLY)

1/2 INCH MINIMUM
7/8 INCH MAXIMUM

3/8 INCH MINIMUM
5/8 INCH MAXIMUM

3/8 INCH MINIMUM
5/8 INCH MAXIMUM

1/4 INCH MINIMUM
1/2 INCH MAXIMUM

1/2 INCH MINIMUM
7/8 INCH MAXIMUM

1/4 INCH MINIMUM
1/2 INCH MAXIMUM

3/8 INCH MINIMUM
5/8 INCH MAXIMUM

1/4 INCH MINIMUM
1/2 INCH MAXIMUM

1/2 INCH MINIMUM
7/8 INCH MAXIMUM

1/2 INCH MINIMUM
7/8 INCH MAXIMUM

1/4 INCH MINIMUM
1/2 INCH MAXIMUM

1/2 INCH MINIMUM
7/8 INCH MAXIMUM

This wing effective on airplanes 190 and subsequent

AILERON FLAP OPERATION

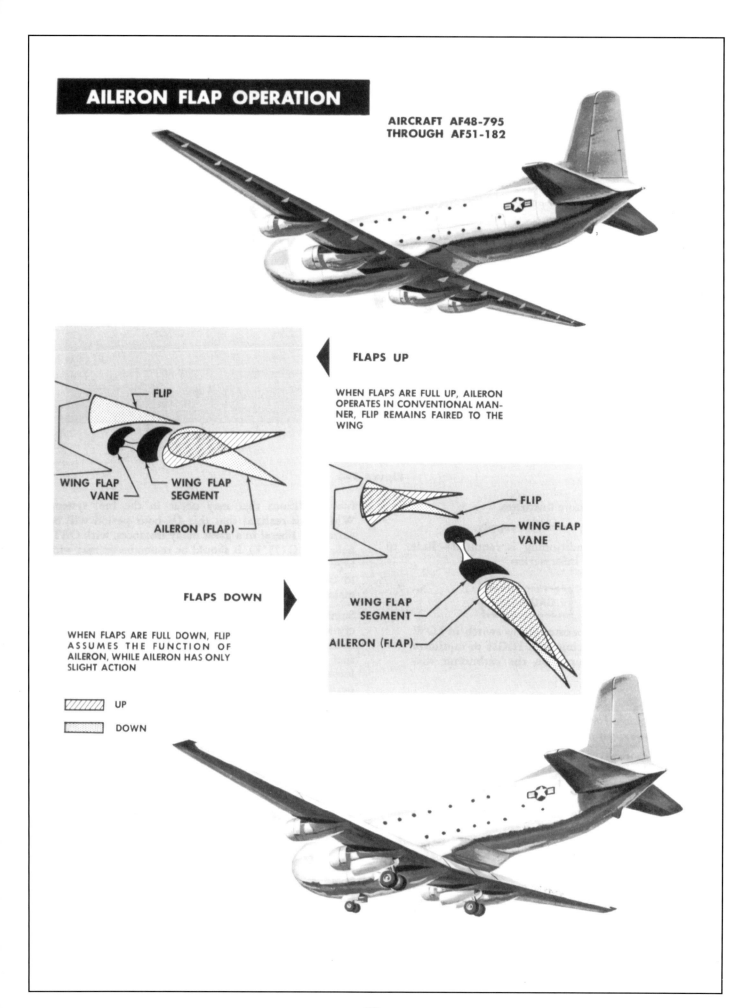

AIRCRAFT AF48-795
THROUGH AF51-182

FLIP

WING FLAP
VANE

WING FLAP
SEGMENT

AILERON (FLAP)

FLAPS UP

WHEN FLAPS ARE FULL UP, AILERON
OPERATES IN CONVENTIONAL MAN-
NER, FLIP REMAINS FAIRED TO THE
WING

FLIP

WING FLAP
VANE

WING FLAP
SEGMENT

AILERON (FLAP)

FLAPS DOWN

WHEN FLAPS ARE FULL DOWN, FLIP
ASSUMES THE FUNCTION OF
AILERON, WHILE AILERON HAS ONLY
SLIGHT ACTION

UP

DOWN

having 24S-TAL webs, extruded or formed stiffeners, and 24S-T or 14S-T caps. The covering material is 24S-TAL. The movable surfaces consist of 24 S-TAL framework with 24S-TAL covering. The brackets that support the movable surfaces are made of 14S-T forgings into which suitable anti-friction bearings are pressed.

Surface Controls Description

... The control surfaces consist of wing flaps; the ailerons and aileron trim tabs; the elevators, elevator flying tabs and elevator trim tabs; rudder, rudder flying tab and rudder trim tab. The control surfaces are essentially operated by direct drive cable systems. Aerodynamic boost of the control surfaces is obtained by using flying tabs on the rudder and elevators. The ailerons are controlled by [a] conventional cable-operated system which also incorporates a hydraulic boost system to reduce the pilot's efforts in handling the aileron control. The elevator is trimmed by a conventional trim tab system with a control wheel, located on each side of the control pedestal, accessible to both the pilot and co-pilot. The rudder is trimmed by a spring force applied to the rudder flying tab by means of a spring trim mechanism. The aileron is trimmed by an electrically operated actuator located within the aileron and attached to the trim tab. A cable-operated control-surface-lock-throttle-interlock system is installed on aircraft A through 164. On aircraft 165 and subsequent, a hydraulically operated snubber is installed for the aileron to dampen out possible sudden motion of the surfaces during buffeting conditions and when the propellers are in reverse pitch while the aircraft is on the ground. A hydraulically-operated snubber is installed for the rudder and elevators on all aircraft. In addition to the cable-operated surfaces controlled by the pilot and co-pilot, an automatic pilot system is installed. A manually-operated shut-off valve is provided to release the rudder and elevator snubbers on aircraft A through 164. A cable-operated emergency release system is provided to disengage all the snubbers on aircraft 165 and subsequent.

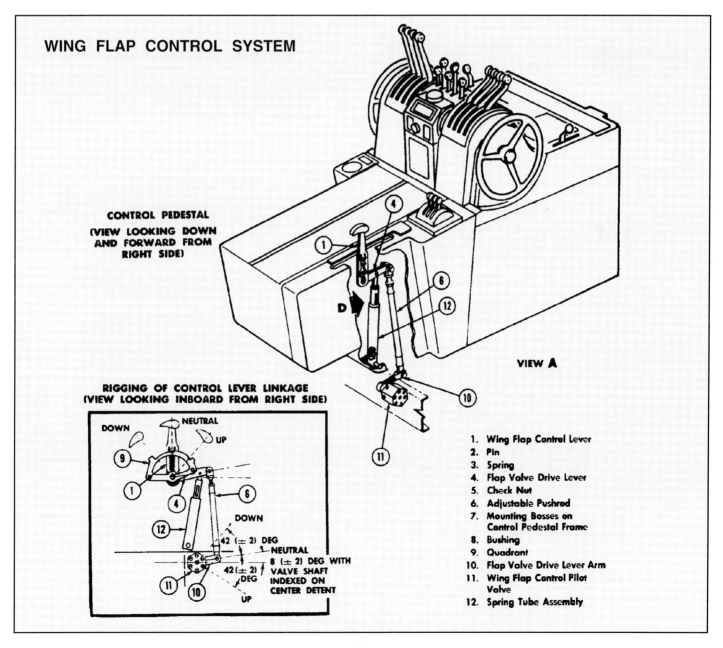

WING FLAP CONTROL SYSTEM

CONTROL PEDESTAL
(VIEW LOOKING DOWN AND FORWARD FROM RIGHT SIDE)

VIEW A

RIGGING OF CONTROL LEVER LINKAGE
(VIEW LOOKING INBOARD FROM RIGHT SIDE)

DOWN   NEUTRAL   UP

DOWN

42 (± 2) DEG
NEUTRAL
42 (± 2) DEG
8 (± 2) DEG WITH VALVE SHAFT INDEXED ON CENTER DETENT
UP

1. Wing Flap Control Lever
2. Pin
3. Spring
4. Flap Valve Drive Lever
5. Check Nut
6. Adjustable Pushrod
7. Mounting Bosses on Control Pedestal Frame
8. Bushing
9. Quadrant
10. Flap Valve Drive Lever Arm
11. Wing Flap Control Pilot Valve
12. Spring Tube Assembly

SERVICING DIAGRAM

AIRCRAFT AF48-795 THROUGH AF51-132

1. LEFT OUTBOARD FUEL TANK FILLER NECK
2. LEFT INBOARD FUEL TANK FILLER NECK
3. LEFT AUXILIARY FUEL TANK FILLER NECK
4. RIGHT AUXILIARY FUEL TANK FILLER NECK
5. RIGHT INBOARD FUEL TANK FILLER NECK
6. RIGHT OUTBOARD FUEL TANK FILLER NECK
7. LEFT AUXILIARY POWER PLANT OIL TANK FILLER NECK
8. LEFT OUTBOARD OIL TANK FILLER NECK AND DIP STICK
9. LEFT WATER INJECTION SYSTEM TANK FILLER NECK
10. LEFT INBOARD OIL TANK FILLER NECK AND DIP STICK
11. SINGLE-POINT REFUELING CONNECTION POINT
12. HYDRAULIC FLUID RESERVOIR FILLER NECK
13. OXYGEN SYSTEM FILLER VALVE
14. FLIGHT COMPARTMENT WATER SUPPLY TANK FILLER NECK
15. ALCOHOL DE-ICER TANK FILLER NECK

16. RIGHT INBOARD OIL TANK FILLER NECK AND DIP STICK
17. RIGHT WATER INJECTION SYSTEM TANK FILLER NECK
18. RIGHT OUTBOARD OIL TANK FILLER NECK AND DIP STICK
19. RIGHT AUXILIARY POWER PLANT OIL TANK FILLER NECK

Note:
Gray areas on wing and empennage indicate walkways.

FLUID SPECIFICATIONS

	NO. OF TANKS	FLUID SPECIFICATION
ENGINE OIL	4	MIL-L-6082 GRADE 1100 (WINTER & SUMMER)
WATER — ALCOHOL	2	O-M-232 GRADE A (ALTERNATE MIL-A-6091)
HYDRAULIC FLUID	1	MIL-O-5606
DE-ICER ALCOHOL	1	MIL-A-6091
AUXILIARY POWER PLANT OIL	2	MIL-L-8383
FUEL	12	MIL-F-5572 *GRADE 115/145
CREW WATER	1	
*ALTERNATE FUEL GRADE 100/130 PERMISSIBLE		

11.677

Fuselage General

The semielliptical, semimonocoque fuselage is constructed of longitudinal floor beams, floor panels, longitudinal stiffeners, traverse frames, and flush-riveted stressed skin. The fuselage is composed of two major sections: The main cabin section, extending from station -36 to station 1160, incorporates the nose loading ramp and the loading platform, and the fuselage tail section extending from station 1160 to station 1480. The wing center section is permanently joined to the fuselage between fuselage stations 560 and 660. The maximum width of the fuselage is 13 feet, 9 inches; the maximum height is 20 feet, 11 inches. Ice protection strips reinforce the fuselage skin in the plane of rotation of the inboard propellers.

Materials for construction are mainly 24S-TAL for such items as skins, frames and stringers that are

At right, head-on view of a C-124C with ramps fully extended. (Douglas)

LOADING RAMPS RETRACTED

LOADING RAMP RETRACTING CABLE

LOADING RAMPS EXTENDED

LOADING RAMP HINGED TOE SECTION

fabricated from flat stock; 24S-T for extrusions and plate stock fittings; 14S-T for forged fittings, and 75S-T for certain construction in the forward spar and in the fuselage main bulkheads.

Two rows of oval-shaped Plexiglas windows, each equipped with a blackout curtain, are spaced approximately 60 inches from center to center along each side of the main cabin. Windows are also provided adjacent to the radio operator's, flight engineer's, and navigator's stations, and two in the relief crew's quarters, one on each side.

On aircraft A thru 16, ten emergency escape hatches are installed in the sides of the main cabin, five on each side, of which three on each side are accessible from the main cabin floor and two from the auxiliary floor. Two of the hatches accessible from the main cabin floor on each side are located over the wing area. On aircraft 17 and subsequent, eight emergency escape hatches are installed in the sides of the main cabin, four on each side, of which two on each side are accessible from the main cabin floor and two from the auxiliary floor. One of the hatches, accessible from the main cabin floor on each side, is located over the wing area.

Note From Author: Provision is made for four alternate means of emergency escape. These come in the form of floor panels, windshield panels, and inward opening astrodome and an auxiliary exit on the flight deck.

Above right, as an air ambulance with 127 litters fitted, the C-124 uses the upper deck to increase capacity. At right center, with troop carrier seats installed, 200 troops can be carried on the upper & lower decks. At right, simulated maximum cargo load illustrated.

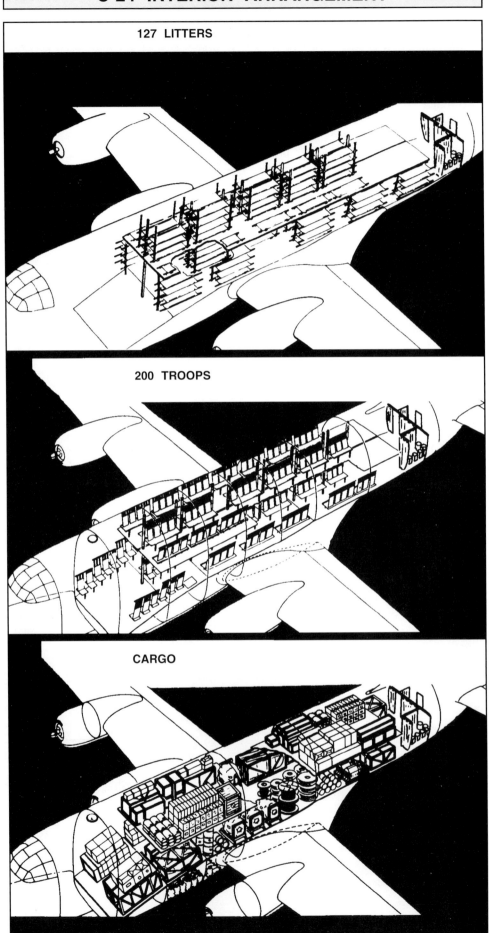

C-24 INTERIOR ARRANGEMENT

127 LITTERS

200 TROOPS

CARGO

C-124 DOLLY LOADING SEQUENCE

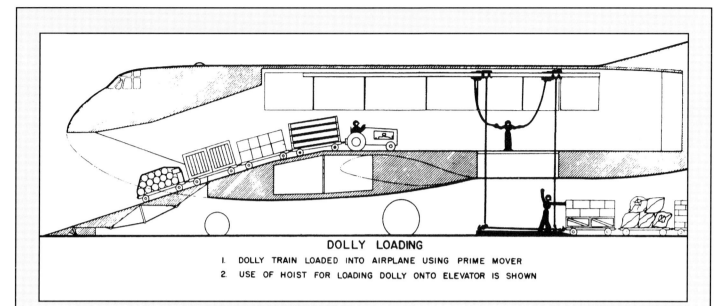

DOLLY LOADING

1. DOLLY TRAIN LOADED INTO AIRPLANE USING PRIME MOVER
2. USE OF HOIST FOR LOADING DOLLY ONTO ELEVATOR IS SHOWN

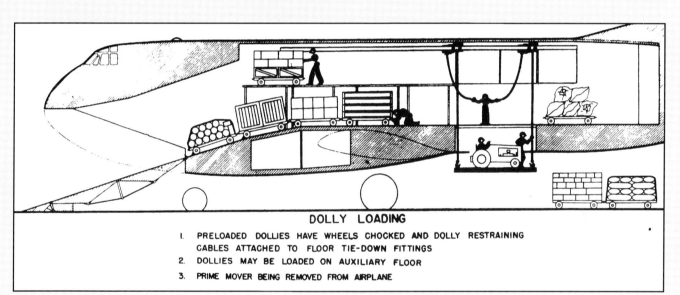

DOLLY LOADING

1. PRELOADED DOLLIES HAVE WHEELS CHOCKED AND DOLLY RESTRAINING CABLES ATTACHED TO FLOOR TIE-DOWN FITTINGS
2. DOLLIES MAY BE LOADED ON AUXILIARY FLOOR
3. PRIME MOVER BEING REMOVED FROM AIRPLANE

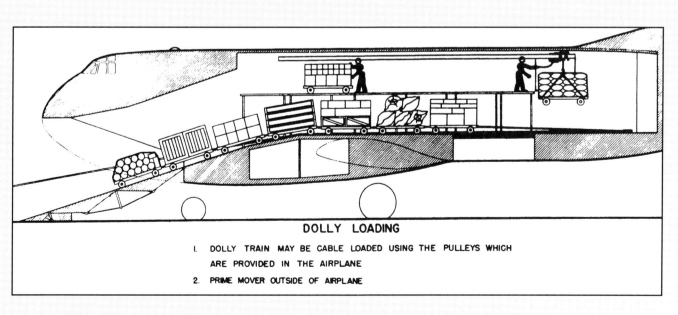

DOLLY LOADING

1. DOLLY TRAIN MAY BE CABLE LOADED USING THE PULLEYS WHICH ARE PROVIDED IN THE AIRPLANE
2. PRIME MOVER OUTSIDE OF AIRPLANE

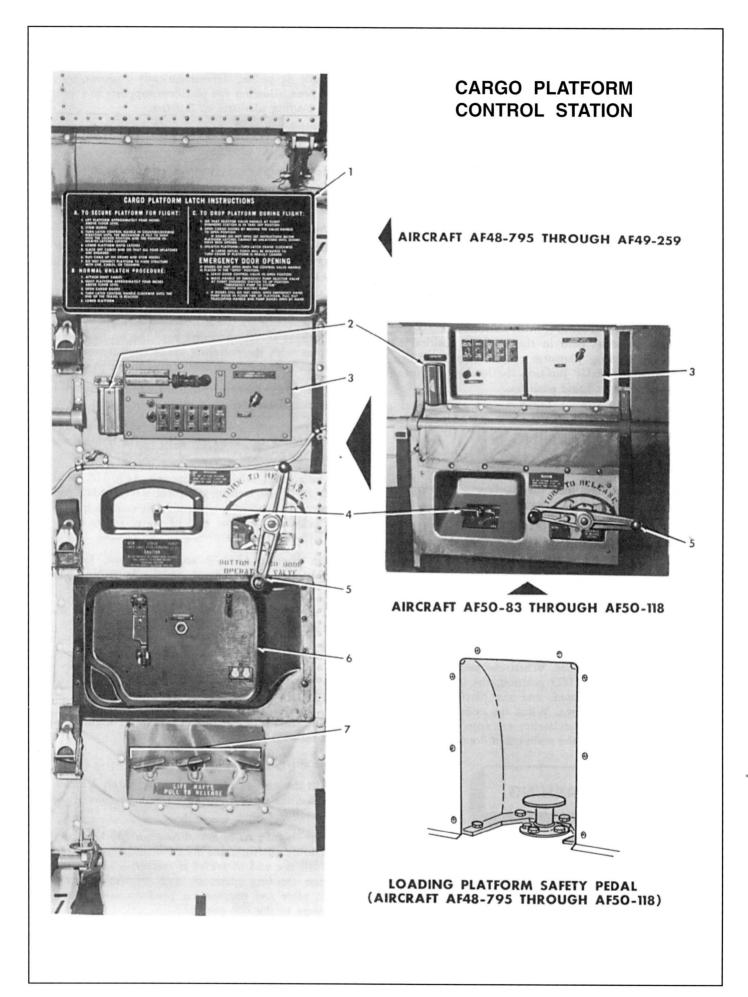

CARGO PLATFORM
CONTROL STATION

◀ **AIRCRAFT AF48-795 THROUGH AF49-259**

AIRCRAFT AF50-83 THROUGH AF50-118

**LOADING PLATFORM SAFETY PEDAL
(AIRCRAFT AF48-795 THROUGH AF50-118)**

CARGO PLATFORM
CONTROL STATION

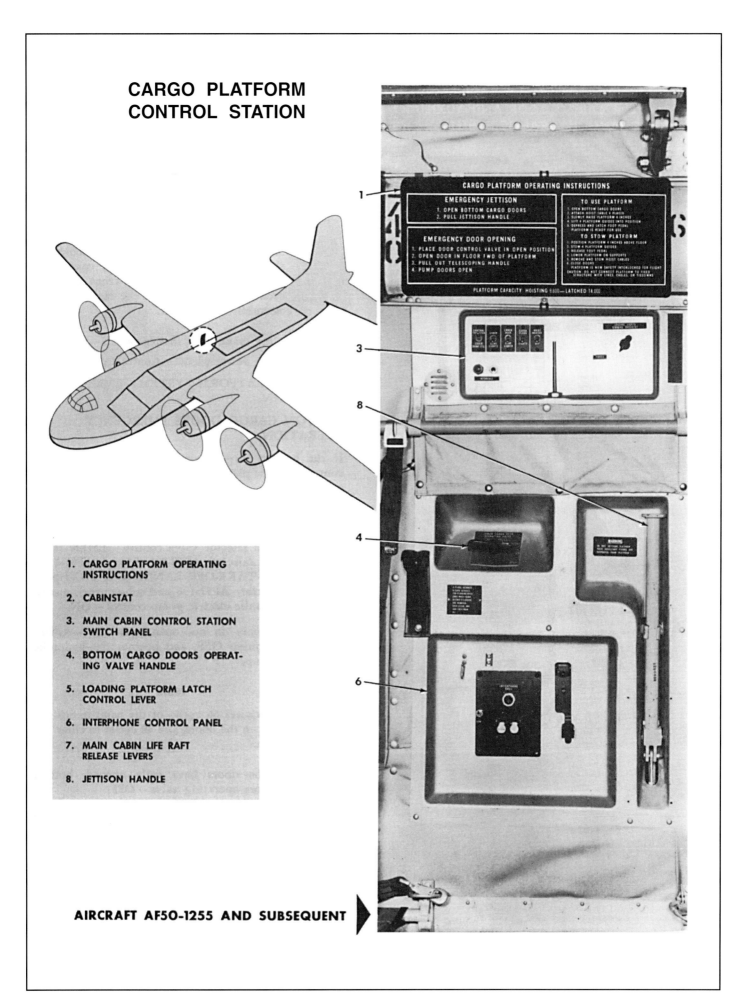

1. CARGO PLATFORM OPERATING INSTRUCTIONS

2. CABINSTAT

3. MAIN CABIN CONTROL STATION SWITCH PANEL

4. BOTTOM CARGO DOORS OPERATING VALVE HANDLE

5. LOADING PLATFORM LATCH CONTROL LEVER

6. INTERPHONE CONTROL PANEL

7. MAIN CABIN LIFE RAFT RELEASE LEVERS

8. JETTISON HANDLE

AIRCRAFT AF50-1255 AND SUBSEQUENT

LOADING PLATFORM LATCH CONTROL PEDAL

IRCRAFT AF 50-1255 AND SUBSEQUENT

Below, C-124 cargo hold with upper deck folded up and traveling crane hoist positioned aft. Troop carrier seats are stowed in the upright position. (Boeing via Pat McGinnis)

GAINING ENTRANCE TO AIRCRAFT

1. Nose Loading Door Access Ladder
2. Flight Compartment Retractable Ladder
3. Fixed Auxiliary Ladder
4. Bottom Fuselage Door
   (Ladder is Field Equipment)

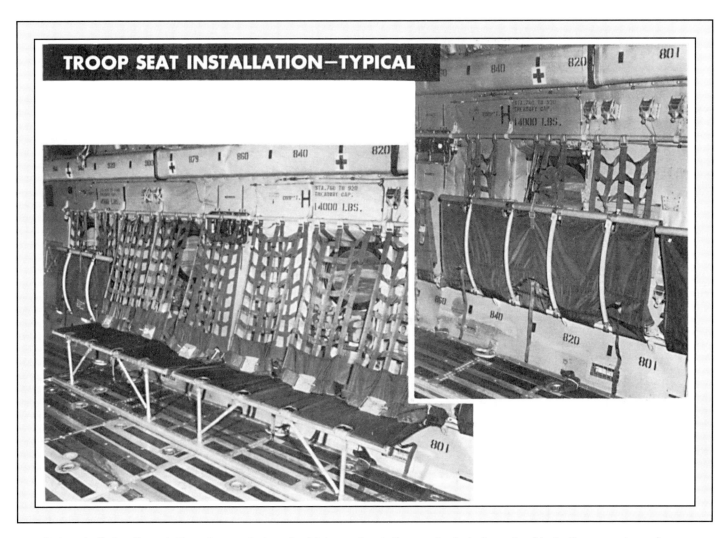

TROOP SEAT INSTALLATION—TYPICAL

Below, belly loading platform lowered. Jeep is driving onto platform prior to being raised in to the cargo bay of a C-74. The C-124 platform was almost identical. (Douglas via Harry Gann)

CARGO CONFIGURATION WITH NETTING AND ROLLERS

Cargo nets are strung to protect the fuselage and roller floor boards are
installed to facilitate the loading of pallets. (Boeing via Pat McGinnis)

OPENING THE ASTRODOME

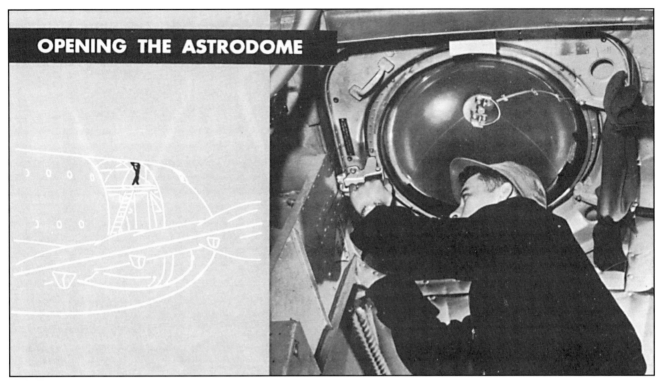

EMERGENCY EXITS AIRCRAFT
48-795 THROUGH 49-245

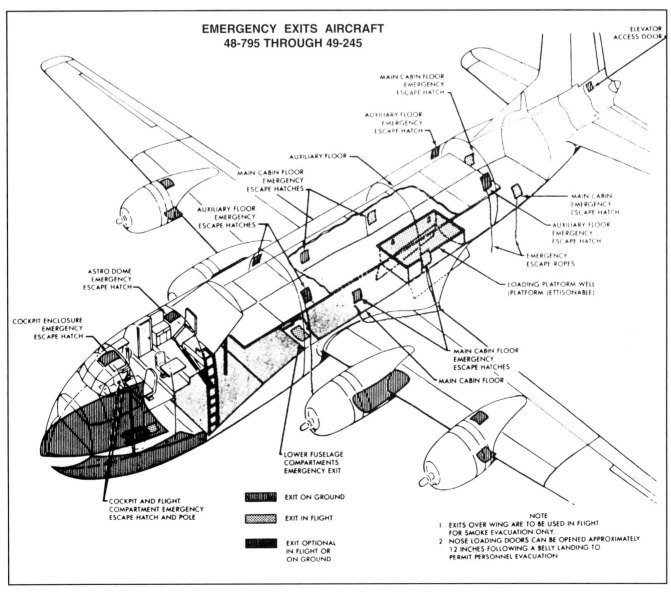

ELEVATOR ACCESS DOOR

MAIN CABIN FLOOR EMERGENCY ESCAPE HATCH

AUXILIARY FLOOR EMERGENCY ESCAPE HATCH

AUXILIARY FLOOR

MAIN CABIN FLOOR EMERGENCY ESCAPE HATCHES

AUXILIARY FLOOR EMERGENCY ESCAPE HATCHES

MAIN CABIN EMERGENCY ESCAPE HATCH

AUXILIARY FLOOR EMERGENCY ESCAPE HATCH

EMERGENCY ESCAPE ROPES

ASTRO DOME EMERGENCY ESCAPE HATCH

LOADING PLATFORM WELL (PLATFORM JETTISONABLE)

COCKPIT ENCLOSURE EMERGENCY ESCAPE HATCH

MAIN CABIN FLOOR EMERGENCY ESCAPE HATCHES

MAIN CABIN FLOOR

COCKPIT AND FLIGHT COMPARTMENT EMERGENCY ESCAPE HATCH AND POLE

LOWER FUSELAGE COMPARTMENTS EMERGENCY EXIT

EXIT ON GROUND

EXIT IN FLIGHT

EXIT OPTIONAL IN FLIGHT OR ON GROUND

NOTE

1 EXITS OVER WING ARE TO BE USED IN FLIGHT FOR SMOKE EVACUATION ONLY.

2 NOSE LOADING DOORS CAN BE OPENED APPROXIMATELY 12 INCHES FOLLOWING A BELLY LANDING TO PERMIT PERSONNEL EVACUATION

REMOVING NOSE LOADING DOOR SAFETY PINS

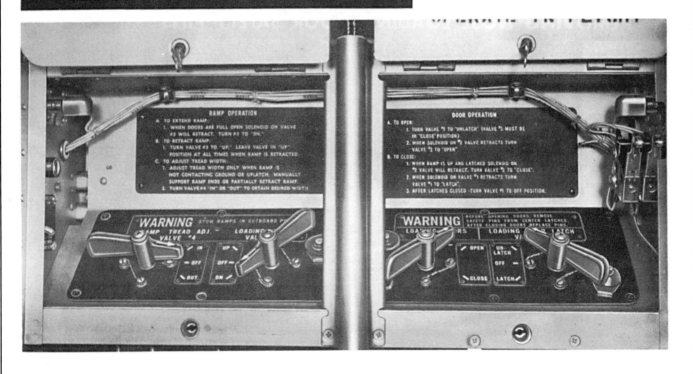

NOSE LOADING CONTROL PANEL

1. PILOT'S AUXILIARY CONTROL PANEL	9. CONTROL SURFACE SNUBBER SWITCH
2. RADAR SCOPE	10. CO-PILOT'S CONTROL COLUMN
3. PILOT'S MICROPHONE SWITCH	11. CO-PILOT'S AUTOMATIC PILOT ELECTRICAL RELEASE BUTTON
4. PILOT'S AUTOMATIC PILOT ELECTRICAL RELEASE BUTTON	12. CO-PILOT'S MICROPHONE SWITCH
5. PILOT'S CONTROL COLUMN	13. CO-PILOT'S SIDE PANEL
6. PILOT'S MAIN INSTRUMENT PANEL	14. CO-PILOT'S AUXILIARY CONTROL PANEL
7. PILOT'S OVERHEAD ELECTRICAL PANEL	15. CO-PILOT'S RUDDER PEDALS
8. RUDDER TRIM TAB CONTROL WHEEL	16. CONTROL PEDESTAL
	17. PILOT'S RUDDER PEDALS

Page 94 top, YC-124B pilot's instrument panel on 14 December 1953. (Douglas via Bruce Cunningham) bottom, pilot and copilot prepare for takeoff from Hickam AFB, Hawaii. (via Craig Kaston)

PILOTS' MAIN INSTRUMENT AND SIDE PANELS

AIRCRAFT AF48-795
THROUGH AF49-259

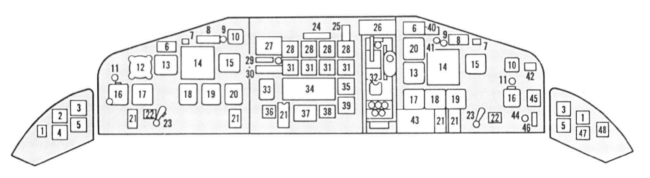

1. FOOTWARMER CONTROL KNOB (2)

2. EMERGENCY AIR BRAKE PRESSURE INDICATOR

3. OXYGEN PRESSURE GAGE (2)

4. HYDRAULIC SYSTEM PRESSURE INDICATOR

5. OXYGEN FLOW INDICATOR (2)

6. MAXIMUM AIRSPEED PLACARD (2)

7. RADIO CALL PLACARD (2)

8. TAKE-OFF WARNING PLACARD (2)

9. TAKE-OFF WARNING LIGHT (2)

10. CLOCK (2)

11. MARKER BEACON INDICATOR LIGHT (2)

12. GLIDE PATH INDICATOR

13. AIRSPEED INDICATOR (2)

14. DIRECTIONAL GYRO (2)

15. GYRO HORIZON (2)

16. AUTOMATIC RADIO COMPASS (2)

17. ALTIMETER (2)

18. TURN-AND-BANK INDICATOR (2)

19. RATE-OF-CLIMB INDICATOR (2)

20. REMOTE INDICATOR COMPASS (2)

21. CARD HOLDER (5)

22. RUDDER PEDAL ADJUSTMENT PLACARD

23. RUDDER PEDAL ADJUSTMENT HAND CRANK

24. MANIFOLD PRESSURE LIMITS PLACARD

25. LANDING GEAR RED WARNING LIGHT TEST SWITCH

26. LANDING GEAR OPERATION PLACARD

27. WATER INJECTION SYSTEM FLOW LIGHT AND READY LIGHT

28. MANIFOLD PRESSURE GAGES

29. AUTOMATIC PILOT POWER-OFF WARNING LIGHT

30. ENGINE FIRE WARNING LIGHTS

31. TACHOMETERS

32. LANDING GEAR CONTROL PANEL

33. COVER PLATE

34. COVER PLATE

35. WING FLAP POSITION INDICATOR

36. FREE AIR TEMPERATURE INDICATOR

37. AIRSPEED—FLAPS AND LANDING GEAR EXTENSION LIMITATIONS

38. TAXI WARNING PLACARD

39. AILERON TAB INDICATOR

40. DOOR OPEN PLACARD

41. DOOR OPEN WARNING LIGHT

42. INTERPHONE SWITCH AND LIGHT

43. EMERGENCY GEAR EXTENSION PLACARD

*44. MASTER CODE SELECTOR INDICATOR LIGHT

*45. MASTER CODE SELECTOR SWITCH

*46. FLASHER CODE CONTROL SWITCH

47. WINDSHIELD ANTI-ICER HEATER CONTROL KNOB

48. VENTILATING AIR SHUTOFF VALVE

*Some aircraft

PILOTS' MAIN INSTRUMENT AND SIDE PANELS

AIRCRAFT AF50-83 THROUGH AF51-157

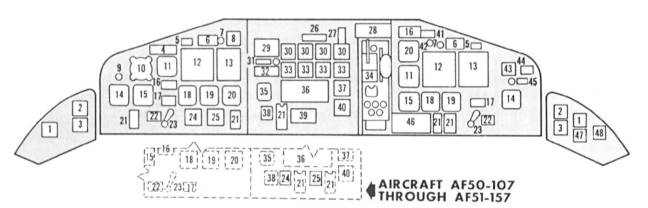

AIRCRAFT AF50-107 THROUGH AF51-157

1. FOOTWARMER CONTROL KNOB (2)
2. OXYGEN PRESSURE GAGE (2)
3. OXYGEN FLOW INDICATOR (2)
4. LIMIT LOAD FACTOR PLACARD
5. RADIO CALL PLACARD (2)
6. TAKE-OFF WARNING PLACARD (2)
7. TAKE-OFF WARNING LIGHT (2)
8. CLOCK
9. MARKER BEACON INDICATOR LIGHT (2)
10. GLIDE PATH INDICATOR
11. AIRSPEED INDICATOR (2)
12. DIRECTIONAL GYRO (2)
13. GYRO HORIZON (2)
14. AUTOMATIC RADIO COMPASS (2)
15. ALTIMETER
16. AIRSPEED WARNING PLACARD (2)
17. RUDDER PEDAL ADJUSTMENT WARNING PLACARD
18. TURN-AND-BANK INDICATOR
19. RATE-OF-CLIMB INDICATOR (2)

20. REMOTE INDICATOR COMPASS (2)
21. CARD HOLDER (5)
22. RUDDER PEDAL ADJUSTMENT PLACARD
23. RUDDER PEDAL ADJUSTMENT HAND CRANK
24. EMERGENCY AIR BRAKE PRESSURE INDICATOR
25. HYDRAULIC PRESSURE INDICATOR
26. MANIFOLD PRESSURE LIMITS PLACARD
27. LANDING GEAR RED WARNING LIGHT TEST SWITCH
28. LANDING GEAR OPERATION PLACARD
29. WATER INJECTION SYSTEM FLOW LIGHTS AND READY LIGHT
30. MANIFOLD PRESSURE GAGES
31. AUTOMATIC PILOT POWER OFF WARNING LIGHTS
32. ENGINE FIRE WARNING LIGHTS
33. TACHOMETERS

34. LANDING GEAR CONTROL PANEL
35. COVER PLATE
36. COVER PLATE
37. WING FLAP POSITION INDICATOR
38. FREE AIR TEMPERATURE INDICATOR
39. AIRSPEED-FLAPS AND LANDING GEAR EXTENSION LIMITATIONS
40. AILERON TAB INDICATOR
41. DOOR-OPEN PLACARD
42. DOOR-OPEN WARNING LIGHT
43. CLOCK
44. INTERPHONE SWITCH AND LIGHT
45. MARKER BEACON INDICATOR LIGHT AND PLACARD
46. EMERGENCY GEAR EXTENSION PLACARD
*47. WINDSHIELD ANTI-ICER HEATER CONTROL KNOB
*48. HEATING AIR SHUTOFF VALVE CONTROL

*Some aircraft

PILOTS' MAIN INSTRUMENT AND SIDE PANELS — AIRCRAFT AF51-158 AND SUBSEQUENT

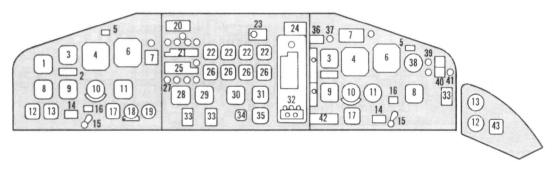

1. ID-249/ARN COURSE INDICATOR
2. MAXIMUM AIRSPEED INDICATOR (2)
3. AIRSPEED INDICATOR (2)
4. DIRECTIONAL GYRO INDICATOR (2)
5. RADIO CALL PLACARD (2)
6. ATTITUDE INDICATOR (2)
7. TAKE-OFF WARNING PLACARD AND LIGHT (2)
8. ID-250/ARN RADIO MAGNETIC INDICATOR (2)
9. ALTIMETER (2)
10. TURN-AND-BANK INDICATOR (2)
11. RATE-OF-CLIMB INDICATOR (2)
12. OXYGEN FLOW INDICATOR (2)
13. OXYGEN CYLINDER PRESSURE INDICATOR (2)
14. RUDDER PEDAL ADJUSTMENT PLACARD (2)
15. RUDDER PEDAL ADJUSTMENT HAND CRANK (2)

16. RUDDER PEDAL ADJUSTMENT WARNING PLACARD (2)
17. CLOCK (2)
18. AIR PRESSURE INDICATOR
19. HYDRAULIC PRESSURE INDICATOR
20. AIRSPEED LIMITATIONS PLACARD
21. WATER INJECTION SYSTEM FLOW LIGHTS, READY LIGHT AND PLACARD
22. MANIFOLD PRESSURE GAGES
23. LANDING GEAR WARNING LIGHT TEST SWITCH AND PLACARD
24. LANDING GEAR OPERATION PLACARD
25. AUTOMATIC PILOT POWER OFF WARNING LIGHTS AND PLACARD
26. TACHOMETERS
27. ENGINE FIRE WARNING LIGHTS
28. DISTANCE MEASURING EQUIPMENT INDICATOR PROVISIONS

29. RADIO ALTIMETER PROVISIONS
30. ALTIMETER SWITCH PROVISIONS
31. WING FLAP POSITION INDICATOR
32. LANDING GEAR CONTROL PANEL
33. CARD HOLDERS
34. AILERON TAB POSITION INDICATOR
35. AIR TEMPERATURE INDICATOR
36. DOOR OPEN PLACARD
37. DOOR OPEN WARNING LIGHT
38. SLAVED GYRO MAGNETIC INDICATOR
39. MARKER BEACON PLACARD AND LIGHT
40. INTERCALL PLACARD AND LIGHT
41. INTERCALL SWITCH
42. EMERGENCY GEAR EXTENSION PLACARD
43. FOOTWARMER CONTROL KNOB

PILOTS' MAIN INSTRUMENT AND SIDE PANELS

1. ID-249/ARN COURSE INDICATOR

2. MAXIMUM AIRSPEED PLACARD (2)

3. AIRSPEED INDICATOR (2)

4. DIRECTIONAL GYRO INDICATOR (2)

5. RADIO CALL PLACARD (2)

6. ATTITUDE INDICATOR (2)

7. TAKE-OFF WARNING PLACARD AND LIGHT (2)

8. ID-250/ARN RADIO MAGNETIC INDICATOR (2) (4 ON AIRCRAFT AF52-1086 AND SUBSEQUENT)

9. ALTIMETER (2)

10. TURN-AND-BANK INDICATOR (2)

11. RATE-OF-CLIMB INDICATOR (2)

12. OXYGEN FLOW INDICATOR (2)

13. OXYGEN CYLINDER PRESSURE GAGE (2)

14. RUDDER PEDAL ADJUSTMENT PLACARD (2)

15. RUDDER PEDAL ADJUSTMENT HAND CRANK (2)

16. RUDDER PEDAL ADJUSTMENT WARNING PLACARD (2)

17. CLOCK (2)

18. EMERGENCY AIRBRAKE PRESSURE INDICATOR

19. HYDRAULIC PRESSURE INDICATOR

20. AIRSPEED LIMITATIONS PLACARD

21. ADI SYSTEM PRESSURE LIGHTS, READY LIGHT AND PLACARD

22. MANIFOLD PRESSURE GAGES

23. LANDING GEAR WARNING LIGHT TEST SWITCH AND PLACARD

24. LANDING GEAR OPERATION PLACARD

25. AUTOPILOT POWER OFF WARNING LIGHTS AND PLACARD

26. TACHOMETERS

27. ENGINE ACCESSORY SECTION FIRE WARNING LIGHTS

28. DISTANCE MEASURING EQUIPMENT INDICATOR PROVISIONS

29. RADIO ALTIMETER PROVISIONS

30. ALTIMETER SWITCH PROVISIONS

31. WING FLAP POSITION INDICATOR

32. LANDING GEAR CONTROL PANEL

33. CARD HOLDERS

34. AILERON TAB POSITION INDICATOR

35. AIR TEMPERATURE INDICATOR

36. DOOR-OPEN PLACARD

37. DOOR-OPEN WARNING LIGHT

38. SLAVED GYRO MAGNETIC INDICATOR

39. MARKER BEACON PLACARD AND LIGHT

40. INTERCALL PLACARD AND LIGHT

41. INTERCALL SWITCH

42. EMERGENCY GEAR EXTENSION PLACARD

43. FOOT-WARMER CONTROL KNOB

**AIRCRAFT AF48-795
THROUGH AF50-94**

CONTROL PEDESTAL

1. PILOT'S THROTTLE CONTROL LEVERS

2. THROTTLE LOCK LEVER

3. PROPELLER MASTER RPM CONTROL LEVER

4. PROPELLER MASTER RPM CONTROL LOCK LEVER

5. MIXTURE CONTROL LEVER

6. MIXTURE CONTROL LOCK LEVER

7. CO-PILOT'S THROTTLE CONTROL LEVERS

8. AILERON BOOST EMERGENCY RELEASE LEVER

9. CO-PILOT'S ELEVATOR TRIM TAB CONTROL WHEEL

10. AUTOMATIC PILOT CONTROLLER

11. AUTOMATIC PILOT MECHANICAL ENGAGING LEVERS

12. AUTOMATIC RADIO COMPASS CONTROL PANEL (TWO)

13. WING FLAP CONTROL LEVER

14. UHF COMMAND RADIO CONTROL PANEL

15. UHF AND VHF COMMAND MICROPHONE SWITCH

16. HF LIAISON RADIO CONTROL PANEL

17. GLIDE PATH AND LOCALIZER CONTROL PANEL

18. RADIO FREQUENCY CARD HOLDER

19. VHF COMMAND RADIO PANEL

20. AUTOMATIC APPROACH SELECTOR CONTROL PANEL

21. AILERON TRIM CONTROL SWITCH

22. THROTTLE REVERSE LOCK MANUAL RELEASE LEVER

23. PILOT'S ELEVATOR TRIM TAB CONTROL WHEEL

24. PARKING BRAKE CONTROL LEVER

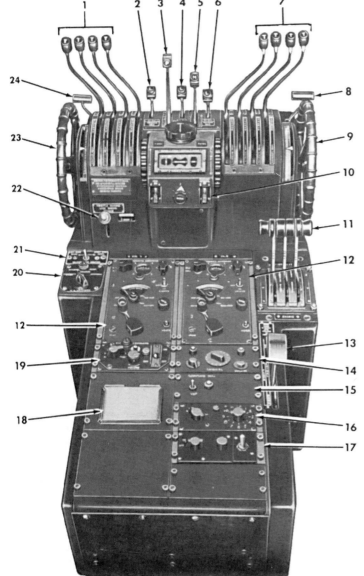

CONTROL PEDESTAL

AIRCRAFT AF50-95 THROUGH AF51-107

1. PILOT'S THROTTLE CONTROL LEVERS.
2. THROTTLE LOCK LEVER.
3. PROPELLER MASTER RPM CONTROL LEVER.
4. PROPELLER MASTER RPM CONTROL LOCK LEVER.
5. MIXTURE CONTROL LEVER.
6. MIXTURE CONTROL LOCK LEVER.
7. CO-PILOT'S THROTTLE CONTROL LEVERS.
8. AILERON BOOST EMERGENCY RELEASE LEVER.
9. CO-PILOT'S ELEVATOR TRIM TAB CONTROL WHEEL.
10. AUTOMATIC PILOT CONTROLLER.
11. AUTOMATIC PILOT MECHANICAL ENGAGING LEVERS.
12. INTERPHONE CONTROL PANEL (2).
13. WING FLAP CONTROL LEVER.
14. AUTOMATIC RADIO COMPASS CONTROL PANEL (2).
15. GLIDE PATH AND LOCALIZER CONTROL PANEL.
16. RADIO FREQUENCY CARD.
17. RANGE FILTER CONTROL (2).
18. VHF COMMAND RADIO CONTROL PANEL.
19. UHF AND VHF COMMAND MICROPHONE SWITCH.
20. HF COMMAND RADIO CONTROL PANEL.
21. PUBLIC ADDRESS SYSTEM CONTROL PANEL.
22. UHF COMMAND RADIO CONTROL PANEL.
23. AUTOMATIC APPROACH SELECTOR CONTROL PANEL.
24. AILERON TRIM CONTROL SWITCH.
25. THROTTLE REVERSE LOCK MANUAL RELEASE LEVER.
26. PILOT'S ELEVATOR TRIM TAB CONTROL WHEEL.
27. PARKING BRAKE CONTROL LEVER.

AIRCRAFT AF50-1255 THROUGH AF50-1261

AIRCRAFT AF50-1262 THROUGH AF51-107

CONTROL PEDESTAL

1. PILOT'S THROTTLE CONTROL LEVERS
2. THROTTLE LOCK LEVER
3. PROPELLER MASTER RPM CONTROL LEVER
4. PROPELLER MASTER RPM CONTROL LOCK LEVER
5. MIXTURE CONTROL LEVER
6. MIXTURE CONTROL LOCK LEVER
7. CO-PILOT'S THROTTLE CONTROL LEVERS
8. AILERON BOOST EMERGENCY RELEASE LEVER
9. CO-PILOT'S ELEVATOR TRIM TAB CONTROL WHEEL
10. AUTOMATIC PILOT CONTROLLER
11. AUTOMATIC PILOT MECHANICAL ENGAGING LEVERS
12. INTERPHONE CONTROL PANEL
13. UHF COMMAND RADIO CONTROL PANEL
14. WING FLAP CONTROL LEVER
15. VHF NAVIGATION RADIO CONTROL PANEL
16. VHF COMMAND RADIO CONTROL PANEL
17. UHF AND VHF COMMAND MICROPHONE SWITCH
18. INSTRUCTION PLACARD
19. RANGE FILTER CONTROL (2)
20. HF LIAISON TRANSMITTER CONTROL PANEL
21. PUBLIC ADDRESS SYSTEM CONTROL PANEL
22. AUTOMATIC COMPASS RADIO CONTROL PANEL
23. AUTOMATIC APPROACH SELECTOR CONTROL PANEL
24. AILERON TRIM CONTROL SWITCH
25. THROTTLE REVERSE LOCK MANUAL RELEASE
26. PILOT'S ELEVATOR TRIM TAB CONTROL WHEEL
27. PARKING BRAKE CONTROL LEVER
28. SURFACE SNUBBER EMERGENCY RELEASE LEVER

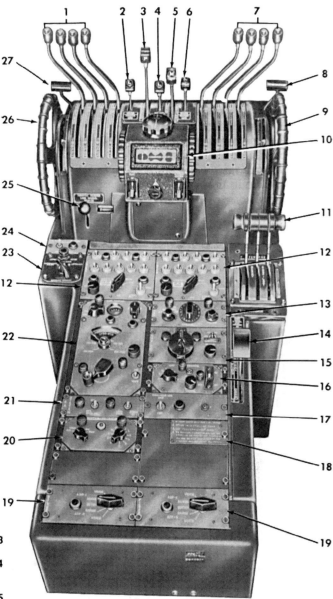

AIRCRAFT AF51-108 AND SUBSEQUENT

AIRCRAFT AF51-108 THROUGH AF51-157

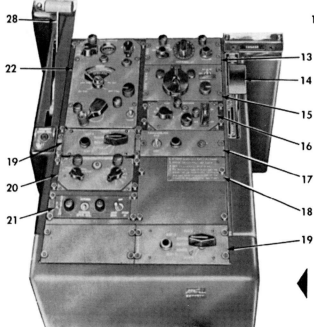

AIRCRAFT AF51-158 AND SUBSEQUENT

CONTROL PEDESTAL—TYPICAL

AIRCRAFT AF51-5188 THROUGH AF51-7285

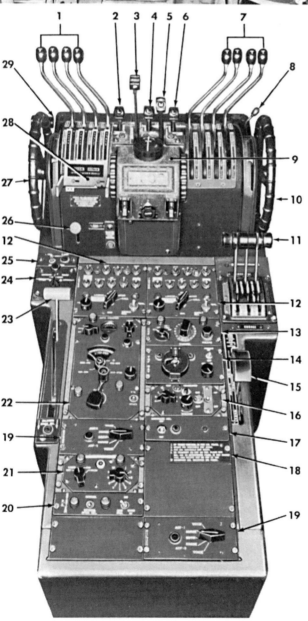

1. PILOT'S THROTTLE LEVERS
2. THROTTLE LOCK LEVER
3. PROPELLER MASTER RPM LEVER
4. PROPELLER MASTER RPM LOCK LEVER
5. MIXTURE CONTROLS
6. MIXTURE CONTROL LOCK
7. CO-PILOT'S THROTTLE LEVERS
8. AILERON BOOST EMERGENCY RELEASE LEVER
9. AUTOMATIC PILOT CONTROLLER
10. CO-PILOT'S ELEVATOR TRIM TAB WHEEL
11. AUTOMATIC PILOT MECHANICAL ENGAGING LEVERS
12. INTERPHONE CONTROL PANEL
13. UHF COMMAND RADIO CONTROL PANEL
14. VHF NAVIGATION RADIO CONTROL PANEL
15. WING FLAP LEVER
16. VHF COMMAND RADIO CONTROL PANEL
17. VHF AND UHF COMMAND MICROPHONE SWITCH
18. INSTRUCTION PLACARD
19. RANGE FILTER CONTROL
20. PUBLIC ADDRESS SYSTEM CONTROL PANEL
21. HF LIAISON TRANSMITTER CONTROL PANEL
22. AUTOMATIC RADIO COMPASS CONTROL PANEL
23. SURFACE SNUBBER EMERGENCY RELEASE LEVER
24. AUTOMATIC APPROACH SELECTOR
25. AILERON TRIM SWITCH
26. THROTTLE REVERSE LOCK MANUAL RELEASE LEVER
27. PILOT'S ELEVATOR TRIM TAB CONTROL WHEEL
28. THROTTLE REVERSE GUARD AND PLACARD
29. PARKING BRAKE LEVER

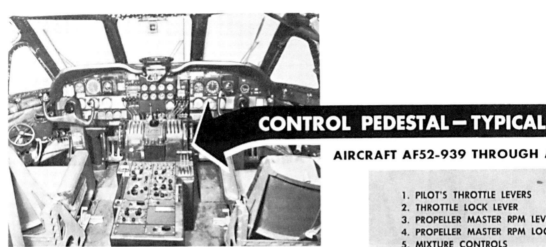

CONTROL PEDESTAL — TYPICAL

AIRCRAFT AF52-939 THROUGH AF52-1085

1. PILOT'S THROTTLE LEVERS
2. THROTTLE LOCK LEVER
3. PROPELLER MASTER RPM LEVER
4. PROPELLER MASTER RPM LOCK LEVER
5. MIXTURE CONTROLS
6. MIXTURE CONTROLS LOCK
7. CO-PILOT'S THROTTLE LEVERS
8. AILERON BOOST EMERGENCY RELEASE LEVER
9. AUTOPILOT CONTROLLER
10. CO-PILOT'S ELEVATOR TRIM TAB WHEEL
11. AUTOPILOT CONTROL SWITCHES
12. INTERPHONE CONTROL PANEL
13. WING FLAP LEVER
14. UHF COMMAND RADIO CONTROL PANEL
15. VHF NAVIGATION RADIO CONTROL PANEL
16. VHF COMMAND RADIO CONTROL PANEL
17. RANGE FILTER CONTROL
18. HF LIAISON TRANSMITTER CONTROL PANEL
19. PUBLIC ADDRESS SYSTEM CONTROL PANEL
20. AUTOMATIC RADIO COMPASS CONTROL PANEL
21. SURFACE SNUBBER EMERGENCY RELEASE LEVER
22. AUTOMATIC APPROACH SELECTOR SWITCH
23. AILERON TRIM SWITCH
24. THROTTLE REVERSE LOCK MANUAL RELEASE LEVER
25. PILOT'S ELEVATOR TRIM TAB WHEEL
26. THROTTLE REVERSE GUARD AND PLACARD
27. PARKING BRAKE LEVER

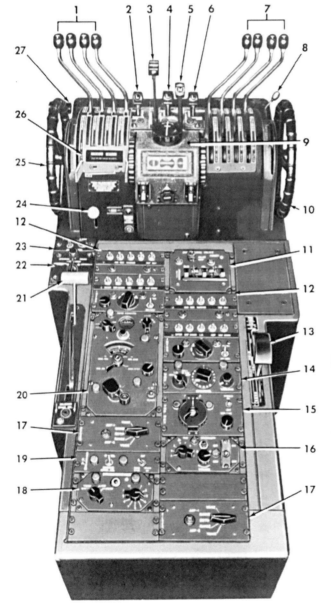

AIRCRAFT AF52-1022 THROUGH AF52-1085

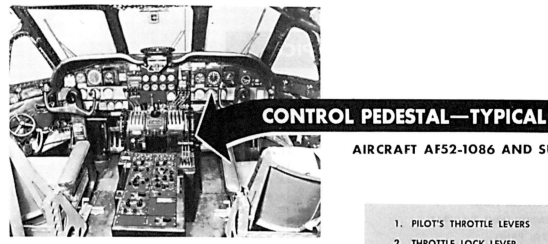

CONTROL PEDESTAL—TYPICAL

AIRCRAFT AF52-1086 AND SUBSEQUENT

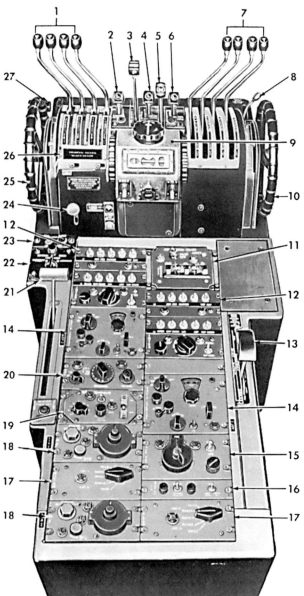

1. PILOT'S THROTTLE LEVERS
2. THROTTLE LOCK LEVER
3. PROPELLER MASTER RPM LEVER
4. PROPELLER MASTER RPM LOCK LEVER
5. MIXTURE CONTROLS
6. MIXTURE CONTROLS LOCK
7. CO-PILOT'S THROTTLE LEVERS
8. AILERON BOOST EMERGENCY RELEASE LEVER
9. AUTOMATIC PILOT CONTROLLER
10. CO-PILOT'S ELEVATOR TRIM TAB WHEEL
11. AUTOMATIC PILOT CONTROL SWITCHES
12. INTERPHONE CONTROL PANEL
13. WING FLAP LEVER
14. AUTOMATIC RADIO COMPASS CONTROL PANEL
15. VHF NAVIGATION RADIO CONTROL PANEL
16. PUBLIC ADDRESS SYSTEM CONTROL PANEL
17. RANGE FILTER CONTROL
18. HF LIAISON TRANSMITTER CONTROL PANEL
19. VHF COMMAND RADIO CONTROL PANEL
20. UHF COMMAND RADIO CONTROL PANEL
21. SURFACE SNUBBER EMERGENCY RELEASE LEVER
22. AUTOMATIC APPROACH SELECTOR SWITCH
23. AILERON TRIM SWITCH
24. THROTTLE REVERSE LOCK MANUAL RELEASE LEVER
25. PILOT'S ELEVATOR TRIM TAB WHEEL
26. THROTTLE REVERSE GUARD AND PLACARD
27. PARKING BRAKE LEVER

PILOTS' SEATS

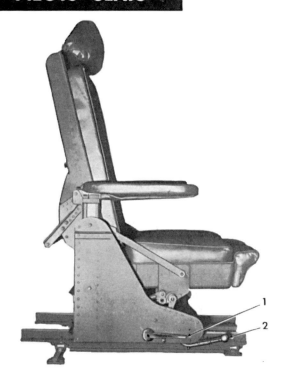

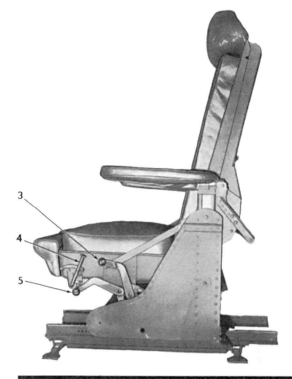

1. TRANSVERSE CONTROL LEVER

2. FORE-AND-AFT CONTROL LEVER

3. RECLINING CONTROL LEVER

4. SHOULDER HARNESS LOCK CONTROL LEVER

5. VERTICAL CONTROL LEVER

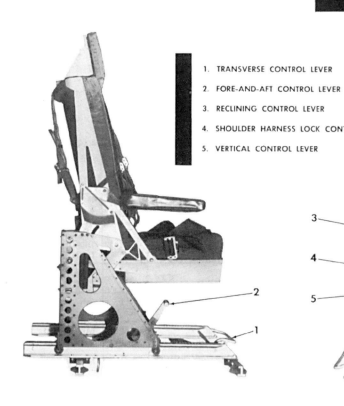

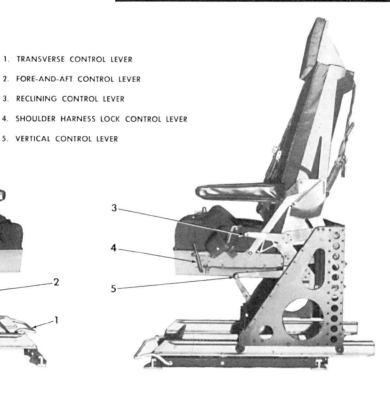

AIRCRAFT AF50-1265 AND SUBSEQUENT

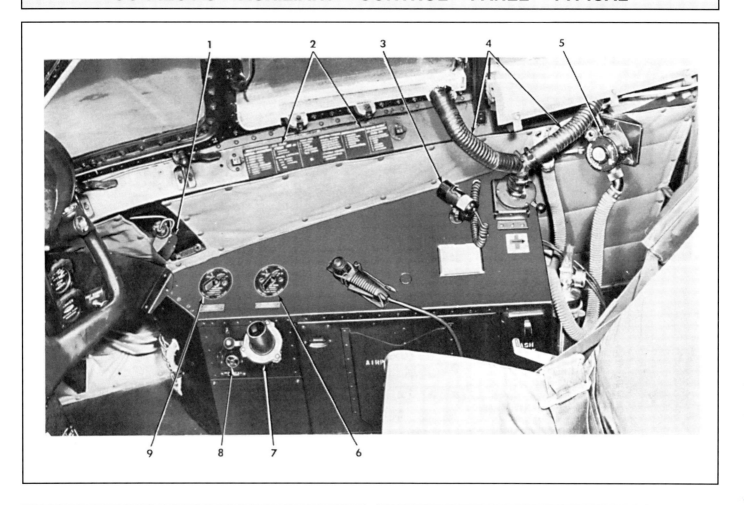

PILOT'S AUXILIARY CONTROL PANEL

1.) OXYGEN REGULATOR
2.) SIDE WINDOW DEFROSTING DUCTS
3.) SPOTLIGHT
4.) FOOTWARMER CONTROL KNOB
5.) PILOT'S CHECK LIST
6.) EMERGENCY AIR BRAKE LEVERS
7.) NOSE WHEEL STEERING WHEEL
8.) APS-42 SCOPE
9.) UTILITY OUTLET
10.) COLD-AIR ORIFICE
11.) LEFT WINDSHIELD WIPER RHEOSTAT
12.) WINDSHIELD WIPER POWER SWITCH
    (Aircraft 51-5188 through 52-1085)
13.) HIGH LATITUDE CUTOUT SWITCH AND PLACARD
14.) ASH TRAY

CO-PILOT'S AUXILIARY CONT. PANEL

1.) RED FLOODLIGHT
2.) CO-PILOT'S CHECK LIST
3.) SPOTLIGHT
4.) SIDE WINDOW DEFROSTING DUCTS
5.) OXYGEN REGULATOR
6.) RIGHT WINDSHIELD WIPER RHEOSTAT
7.) COLD AIR ORIFICE
8.) UTILITY OUTLET
9.) CENTER WINDSHIELD WIPER RHEOSTAT

At left, pilot's right-hand control panel typical. The large three-spoked wheel was the nose gear steering wheel. (USAF via Craig Kaston)

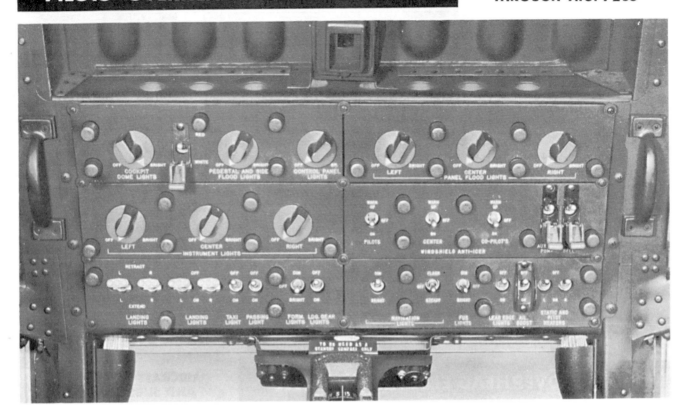

PILOT'S OVERHEAD ELECTRICAL PANEL

AIRCRAFT AF 52-939
AND SUBSEQUENT

1.) Fuel Grade Placard
2.) Fuel Quantity Ind. Test Switches
3.) Door-Open Warning Light
4.) Take-Off Warning Light
5.) Wing Passage Lights and Interphone
6.) Fuel Quantity Indicators
7.) Anti-Icer Heater Temp. Indicator
8.) Water Injection System Pressure Ind.
9.) Water Injection System Quantity Ind.
10.) Hydraulic System Pressure Ind. (late)
11.) Auxiliary Power Plant Oil Press. Ind.
12.) Heater Fuel Pressure Indicator
13.) Free-Air Temperature Indicator

AIRCRAFT AF48-795 THROUGH AF51-132

25.) "Main Inverter Out" Light
26.) Inverter Switch
27.) Battery Switches
28.) Clock
29.) Airspeed Indicator
30.) Tachometer Indicators
31.) Cyl. Head Temp. Gages
32.) Ammeters (four engines); Two Auxiliary Power Plants

Control Switch
51.) Water Injection System Ready Light
52.) Cowl Flap Control Switches
53.) Fire Detector Test Switch
54.) CO_2 Cyl. Bank Sel. Switch
55.) Left Auxiliary Power Plant Fire

MAIN INSTRUMENT PANEL

Warning Light
56.) Engine Accessory Section Fire Warning Lights
57.) RH Auxiliary Power Plant Fire Warning Light
58.) Manifold Pressure Purge Valve Switches
59.) Carburetor Alcohol De-Icer Switches
60.) Propeller Circuit Breakers
61.) Propeller "Synchronizer Off" Warning Light
62.) LH Aux. Power Plant CO_2 Dis. Switch
63.) Eng. Section CO_2 Discharge Switch
64.) RH Aux. Power Plant CO_2 Dis. Switch
65.) Firewall Shutoff Valve Switches

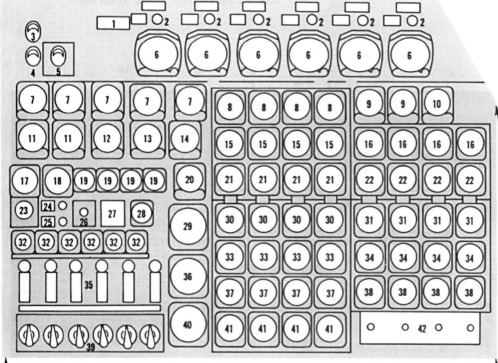

14.) Cabin Air Temperature Indicator
15.) Fuel Pressue Indicators
16.) Oil Quantity Indicators
17.) D-C Voltmeter
18.) A-C Voltmeter
19.) Propeller De-Icer Load Indicators
20.) Master Tachometer Indicator
21.) Oil Pressure Indicators
22.) Oil Temperature Indicators
23.) D-C Voltmeter Selector switch
24.) "Both Inverters Out" Light

33.) Manifold Press. Gages
34.) Cowl Flap Position Ind.
35.) Gen Switches and Warn. Lights (four engine); Two Auxiliary Power Plants
36.) Altimeter
37.) Torquemeters
38.) Carb. Air Temp. Gages
39.) Generator Output Control Rheostats (four engine); Two Auxiliary Power Plants

40.) Rate-Of-Climb Indicator
41.) Fuel Flowmeters
42.) Oil Cooler Air Exit Door Control Switches
43.) Hydraulic Control Panel
44.) Oil Dilution Switches
45.) Left Auxiliary Power Plant Control Switches
46.) Right Auxiliary Power Plant Control Switches
47.) Carburetor Air Filter Control Switch
48.) Prop. Selector Cont. Lever
49.) Fuel Booster Pump Switches
50.) Water Injection System

LOWER ELECTRICAL PANEL

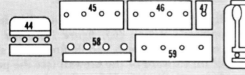

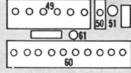
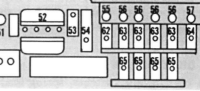

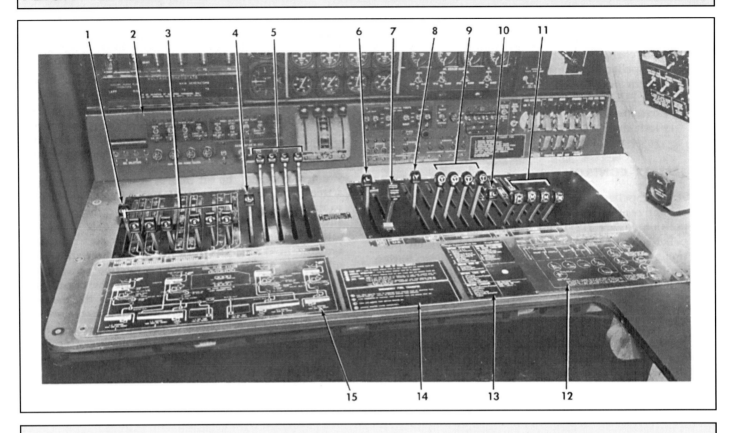

1. FUEL TANK SELECTOR VALVE CONTROLS LOCK LEVER
2. LOWER ELECTRICAL PANEL
3. FUEL TANK SELECTOR VALVE CONTROL LEVERS
4. CARBURETOR AIR PREHEAT CONTROLS LOCK LEVER
5. CARBURETOR AIR PREHEAT CONTROL LEVERS
6. PROPELLER MASTER RPM CONTROL LOCK LEVER
7. PROPELLER MASTER RPM CONTROL LEVER

8. THROTTLE CONTROLS LOCK LEVER
9. THROTTLE CONTROL LEVERS
10. MIXTURE CONTROLS LOCK LEVER
11. MIXTURE CONTROL LEVERS
12. DIAGRAM OF ENGINE ANALYZER PANEL PATTERNS
13. FLIGHT ENGINEER'S CHECK LIST
14. FUEL MANAGEMENT INSTRUCTIONS
15. FUEL FLOW SYSTEM SCHEMATIC

FLIGHT ENGINEER'S MAIN INSTRUMENT PANEL AND LOWER ELECTRICAL PANEL

AIRCRAFT AF51-133 AND SUBSEQUENT

MAIN INSTRUMENT PANEL

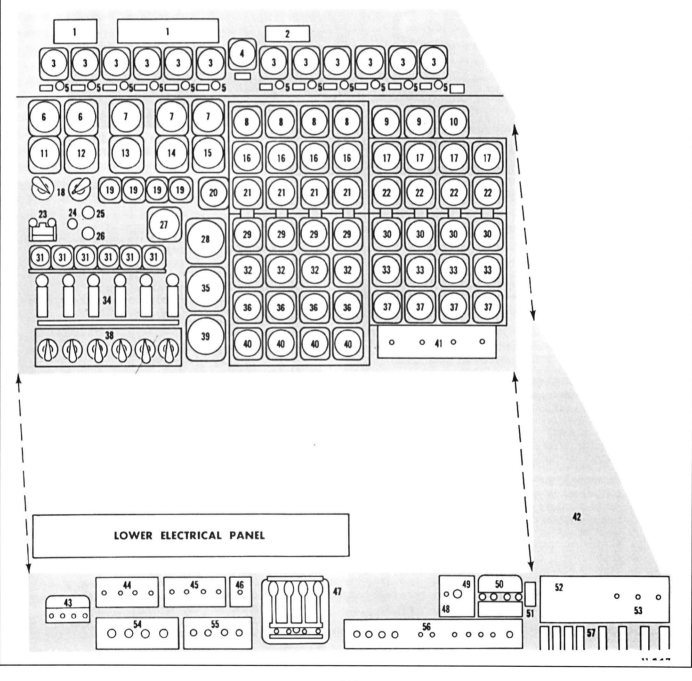

LOWER ELECTRICAL PANEL

1. TAKE-OFF WARNING LIGHTS
2. FUEL GRADE PLATE
3. FUEL QUANTITY INDICATORS
4. FUEL QUANTITY TOTALIZING INDICATOR
5. FUEL QUANTITY INDICATOR TEST SWITCHES
6. AUXILIARY POWER PLANT OIL PRESSURE INDICATORS
7. ANTI-ICERS HEATERS TEMPERATURE INDICATORS
8. WATER INJECTION SYSTEM PRESSURE INDICATORS
9. WATER INJECTION SYSTEM QUANTITY INDICATORS
10. HYDRAULIC PRESSURE INDICATOR
11. D-C VOLTMETER
12. A-C VOLTMETER
13. ANTI-ICER HEATER FUEL PRESSURE INDICATOR
14. CABIN AIR TEMPERATURE INDICATOR
15. FREE AIR TEMPERATURE INDICATOR
16. FUEL PRESSURE INDICATORS
17. OIL QUANTITY INDICATORS
18. VOLTMETER SELECTORS
19. PROPELLER DE-ICING LOAD INDICATORS
20. MASTER TACHOMETER INDICATOR
21. OIL PRESSURE INDICATORS
22. OIL TEMPERATURE INDICATORS
23. BATTERY SWITCHES
24. INVERTER SWITCH
25. "MAIN INVERTER OUT" LIGHT
26. "BOTH INVERTERS OUT" LIGHT
27. CLOCK
28. AIRSPEED INDICATOR
29. TACHOMETER INDICATORS
30. CYLINDER HEAD TEMPERATURE GAGES

31. AMMETERS (FOUR ENGINES; TWO AUXILIARY POWER PLANT)
32. MANIFOLD PRESSURE GAGES
33. COWL FLAP POSITION INDICATORS
34. GENERATOR SWITCHES AND WARNING LIGHTS
35. ALTIMETER
36. TORQUE PRESSURE INDICATORS
37. CARBURETOR AIR TEMPERATURE GAGES
38. GENERATOR OUTPUT CONTROL RHEOSTATS (FOUR ENGINES; TWO AUXILIARY POWER PLANT)
39. RATE-OF-CLIMB INDICATOR
40. FUEL FLOWMETERS
41. OIL COOLER AIR EXIT DOOR CONTROL SWITCHES
42. HYDRAULIC CONTROL PANEL
43. OIL DILUTION SWITCHES
44. LEFT AUXILIARY POWER PLANT CONTROLS
45. RIGHT AUXILIARY POWER PLANT CONTROLS
46. CARBURETOR AIR FILTER CONTROL SWITCH
47. PROPELLER SELECTOR CONTROL LEVERS
48. WATER INJECTION SYSTEM CONTROL SWITCH
49. WATER INJECTION SYSTEM READY LIGHT
50. COWL FLAP CONTROL SWITCHES
51. CB DISCHARGE SWITCH
52. FIRE EMERGENCY INSTRUCTIONS
53. FIRE DETECTOR TEST SWITCHES
54. MANIFOLD PRESSURE PURGE VALVE SWITCHES
55. CARBURETOR ALCOHOL DE-ICER SWITCHES
56. PROPELLER CIRCUIT BREAKERS AND "SYNCHRONIZER OFF" WARNING LIGHT
57. FIREWALL SHUTOFF VALVE SWITCHES

FLIGHT ENGINEER'S STATION-TYPICAL

AIRCRAFT AF51-5188 THROUGH AF51-5197

1. MAIN INSTRUMENT PANEL
2. HYDRAULIC CONTROL PANEL
3. ENGINE ANALYZER PANEL
4. COLD AIR ORIFICE
5. OVERHEAD ELECTRICAL PANEL
6. ENGINEER'S STATION LIGHT RHEOSTATS
7. HEATER CONTROL PANEL
8. INTERPHONE CONTROL PANEL
9. FLEXIBLE TABLE LIGHT

10. RED FLOOD LIGHTS (4)
11. CIRCUIT BREAKER PANEL
12. A-C FUSE PANEL
13. ASH TRAY
14. ANEMOSTAT
15. OXYGEN REGULATOR
16. OXYGEN FLOW INDICATOR
17. CONTROL TABLE
18. FUEL SYSTEM CONTROL PANEL
19. LOWER ELECTRICAL PANEL

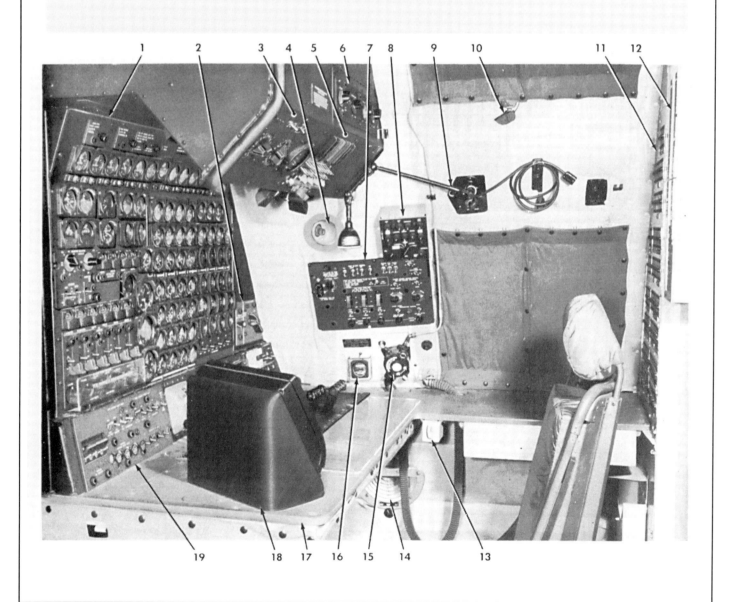

FLIGHT ENGINEER'S STATION -- TYPICAL

AIRCRAFT AF51-5198 AND SUBSEQUENT

1. MAIN INSTRUMENT PANEL
2. HEATER CONTROL PANEL
3. COLD AIR ORIFICE
4. ENGINE ANALYZER SCOPE
5. FLIGHT ENGINEER'S STATION LIGHT RHEOSTATS
6. INTERPHONE CONTROL BOX
7. CIRCUIT BREAKER PANEL

8. A-C FUSE PANEL
9. FUEL SYSTEM CONTROL PANEL
10. CONTROL TABLE
11. OXYGEN REGULATOR
12. ASH TRAY
13. LOWER ELECTRICAL PANEL
14. FLEXIBLE TABLE LIGHT

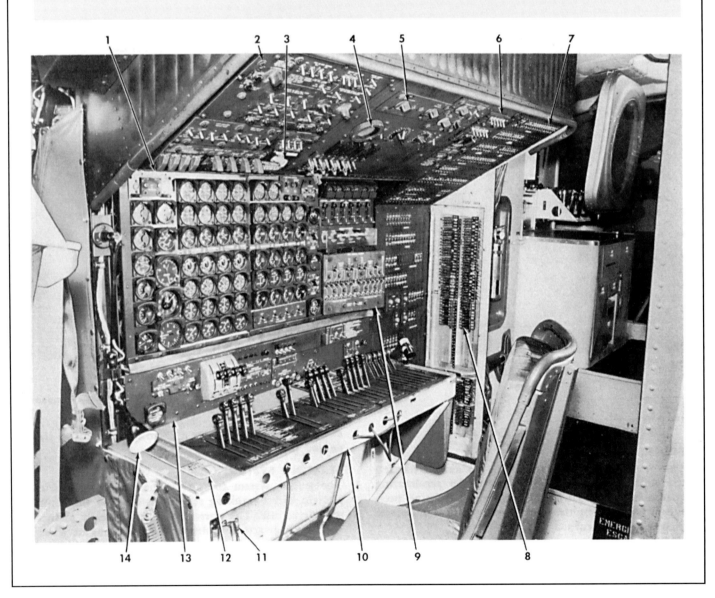

RADIO ANTENNAS

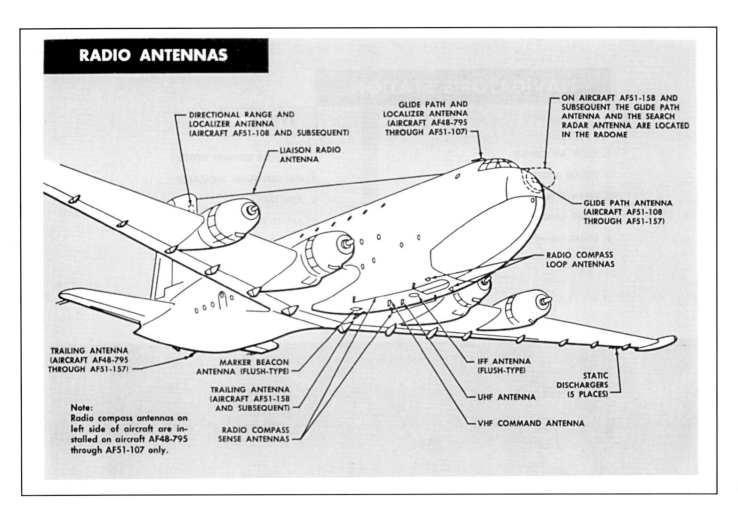

DIRECTIONAL RANGE AND LOCALIZER ANTENNA (AIRCRAFT AF51-108 AND SUBSEQUENT)

LIAISON RADIO ANTENNA

GLIDE PATH AND LOCALIZER ANTENNA (AIRCRAFT AF48-795 THROUGH AF51-107)

ON AIRCRAFT AF51-158 AND SUBSEQUENT THE GLIDE PATH ANTENNA AND THE SEARCH RADAR ANTENNA ARE LOCATED IN THE RADOME

GLIDE PATH ANTENNA (AIRCRAFT AF51-108 THROUGH AF51-157)

RADIO COMPASS LOOP ANTENNAS

TRAILING ANTENNA (AIRCRAFT AF48-795 THROUGH AF51-157)

MARKER BEACON ANTENNA (FLUSH-TYPE)

TRAILING ANTENNA (AIRCRAFT AF51-158 AND SUBSEQUENT)

RADIO COMPASS SENSE ANTENNAS

IFF ANTENNA (FLUSH-TYPE)

UHF ANTENNA

VHF COMMAND ANTENNA

STATIC DISCHARGERS (5 PLACES)

Note:
Radio compass antennas on left side of aircraft are installed on aircraft AF48-795 through AF51-107 only.

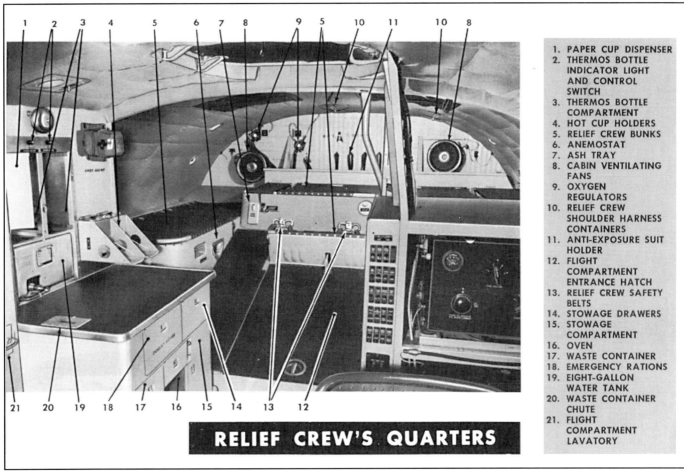

1. PAPER CUP DISPENSER
2. THERMOS BOTTLE INDICATOR LIGHT AND CONTROL SWITCH
3. THERMOS BOTTLE COMPARTMENT
4. HOT CUP HOLDERS
5. RELIEF CREW BUNKS
6. ANEMOSTAT
7. ASH TRAY
8. CABIN VENTILATING FANS
9. OXYGEN REGULATORS
10. RELIEF CREW SHOULDER HARNESS CONTAINERS
11. ANTI-EXPOSURE SUIT HOLDER
12. FLIGHT COMPARTMENT ENTRANCE HATCH
13. RELIEF CREW SAFETY BELTS
14. STOWAGE DRAWERS
15. STOWAGE COMPARTMENT
16. OVEN
17. WASTE CONTAINER
18. EMERGENCY RATIONS
19. EIGHT-GALLON WATER TANK
20. WASTE CONTAINER CHUTE
21. FLIGHT COMPARTMENT LAVATORY

RELIEF CREW'S QUARTERS

NAVIGATOR'S STATION

TYPICAL

1. COLD AIR ORIFICE

2. LORAN SCOPE

3. FLEXIBLE TABLE LIGHT

4. SPARE LAMP BOX

5. DOME LIGHTS MASTER SWITCH

6. PORTABLE OXYGEN BOTTLES

7. OXYGEN FLOW INDICATOR

8. ASH TRAY

9. APS-42 RADAR SCOPE

10. OXYGEN REGULATOR

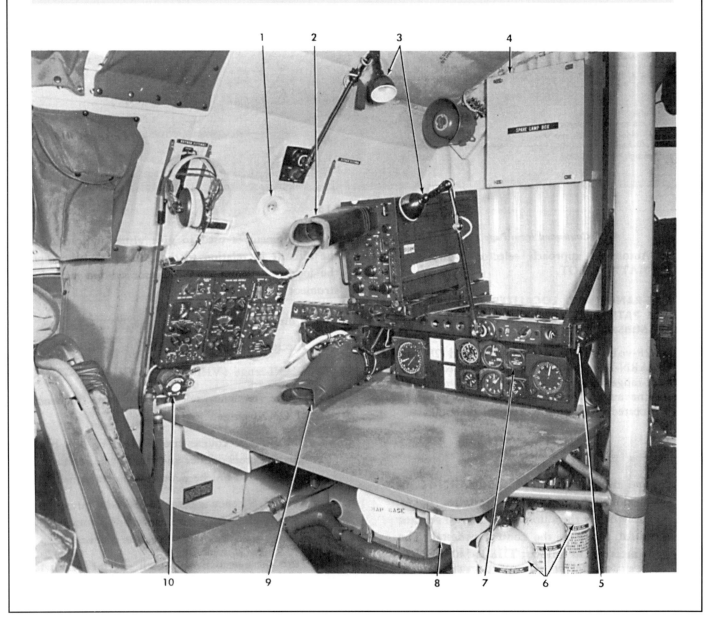

RADIO OPERATOR'S STATION

TYPICAL

1. FLIGHT COMPARTMENT LADDER CONTROL SWITCH
2. RADIO EQUIPMENT CIRCUIT BREAKER PANEL
3. RADIO RACK
4. FLEXIBLE TABLE LIGHT

5. FLARE CHUTE
6. OXYGEN FLOW INDICATOR
7. OXYGEN REGULATOR
8. TRANSMITTING KEY
9. ASH TRAY

117

C-124 NOSE GEAR

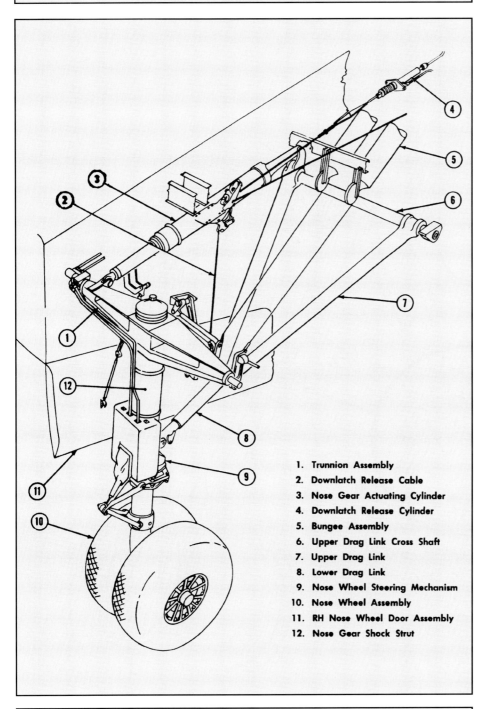

1. Trunnion Assembly
2. Downlatch Release Cable
3. Nose Gear Actuating Cylinder
4. Downlatch Release Cylinder
5. Bungee Assembly
6. Upper Drag Link Cross Shaft
7. Upper Drag Link
8. Lower Drag Link
9. Nose Wheel Steering Mechanism
10. Nose Wheel Assembly
11. RH Nose Wheel Door Assembly
12. Nose Gear Shock Strut

C-124 TAIL SKID

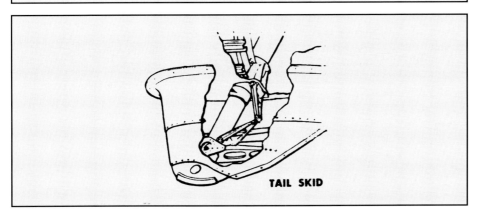

TAIL SKID

Alighting [Landing] Gear Description

The alighting [landing] gear is composed of three major units: two freely retractable main gears with dual wheels and a fully retractable nose gear with dual steerable wheels. Each of the main gear wheels is equipped with a hydraulically actuated expander-tube-type brake. The main and nose gears are extended and retracted by hydraulically actuated struts which are controlled by the alighting gear control lever, located on the pilot's main instrument panel on aircraft and subsequent; and located on the control pedestal on aircraft A. The nose gear extends hydraulically, as it is pushed down and against the air stream; the main gear extends by its own weight, down and with the air stream. Both the nose and main gear uplatches normally are released hydraulically; the down latches are actuated hydra-ulically. Both the nose and main gear doors are actuated in conjunction with the alighting gear. A faired, non-retracting tail skid, supported by a shock strut, protects the fuselage tail section from possible damage in the event of a tail-down landing.

Brake System General

The brake system can be operated by either the hydraulic system, which is the system normally used, or by the emergency air brake system which can be used in the event of a hydraulic system failure.

Note From The Author: A shuttle valve separates the main and emergency systems.

Hydraulic System General

A pressure-type hydraulic system is installed to retract the main gear, operate the main gear doors, the nose gear, the main alighting wheel brakes, the nose wheel steering, the nose loading cargo doors (opening, closing and latching), the bottom cargo doors, the nose loading ramp (retraction, latching, and lateral tread adjustment), the wing flaps, the windshield wipers, the surface snubbers, and the flight deck retractable ladder. A separate hydraulic system operates

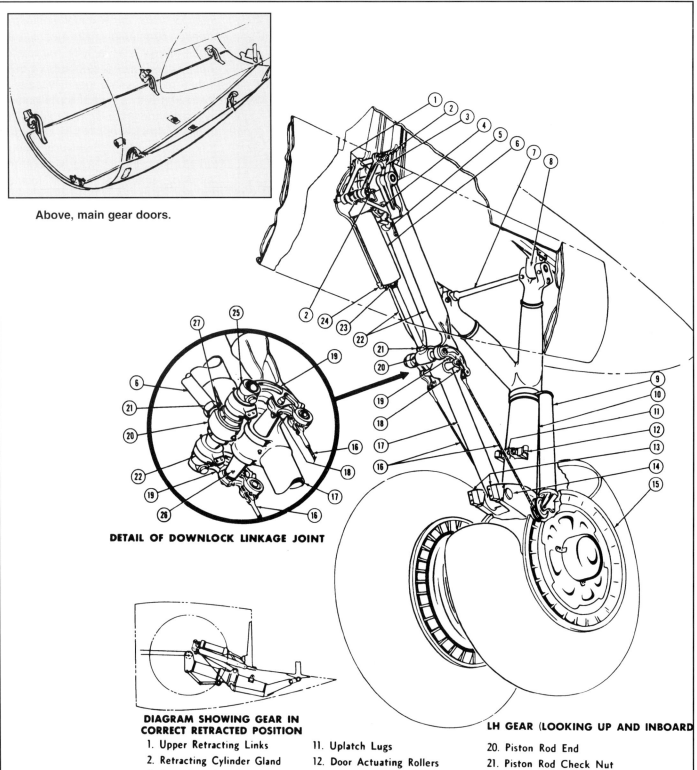

Above, main gear doors.

DETAIL OF DOWNLOCK LINKAGE JOINT

DIAGRAM SHOWING GEAR IN CORRECT RETRACTED POSITION

LH GEAR (LOOKING UP AND INBOARD

1. Upper Retracting Links
2. Retracting Cylinder Gland
3. Front Spar Fittings
4. Lower Retracting Links
5. Uplatch Mechanism
6. Main Gear Retracting Cylinder
7. Shock Strut Cross Shaft
8. Shock Strut Attach Fitting
9. LH Bungee
10. Main Gear Shock Strut
11. Uplatch Lugs
12. Door Actuating Rollers
    (Airplanes 42 and Subsequent)
13. Landing Gear Bumpers
14. Lower Drag Link Attach Pin
15. Main Wheel Assembly
16. Bungee Cables
17. Lower Drag Link
18. Short Latch Link
19. Long Latch Link
20. Piston Rod End
21. Piston Rod Check Nut
22. Upper Drag Links
23. Piston Rod Packing Nut
24. Cylinder Head Elbow
25. Downlock Eccentric Shaft
26. Downlock Shaft
27. Retainer

the aileron hyd-raulic booster system. On aircraft 30 and subsequent, the windshield wipers are electrically operated. The surface snubbers are operated by a separate hydraulic system on aircraft 165 and subsequent.

Hydraulic system pressure is normally supplied by four engine-driven, piston-type hydraulic pumps, two on each inboard engine. An auxiliary hydraulic electric pump (driven by an electric motor) is provided to operate the hydraulic system in the event of four engine-driven pump failures or when the aircraft is on the ground and the engines are not running. Normal system operating pressure is 2700 to 3000 (plus or minus 50) psi; the pressure is shown on hydraulic system pressure gages on the pilot's side instrument panel and on the flight engineer's hydraulic control panel. Hydraulic fluid, Specification MIL-O-5606, is used in the hydraulic system. Shear seal and slide-type operating valves are used in the hydraulic system. A brake emergency air system providing differential braking is installed to operate the brakes in the event of complete failure of the main and emergency hydraulic systems.

Heating and Ventilating (Aircraft A through 79) Description

Heating and ventilating of the flight deck and main cabin areas is accomplished by circulating heated air supplied by combustion-type heaters and by supplying cold ventilating air at ambient temperatures. Electrically driven ground blowers make possible the operation of the heating and ventilating system on the ground when ram air is not available. The

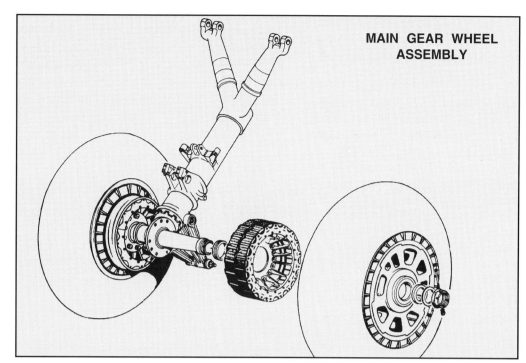

MAIN GEAR WHEEL ASSEMBLY

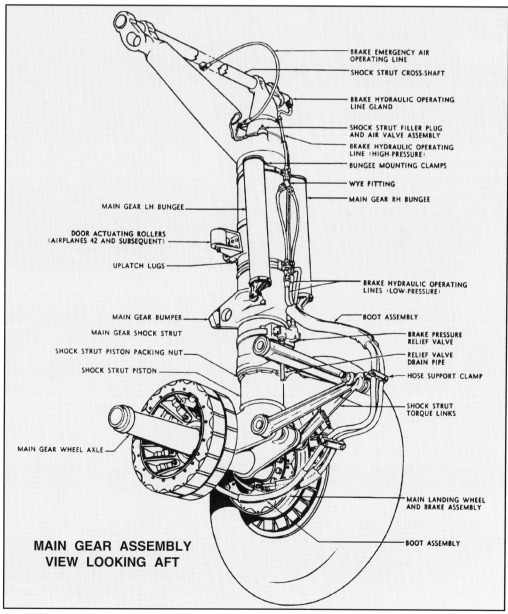

BRAKE EMERGENCY AIR OPERATING LINE
SHOCK STRUT CROSS-SHAFT
BRAKE HYDRAULIC OPERATING LINE GLAND
SHOCK STRUT FILLER PLUG AND AIR VALVE ASSEMBLY
BRAKE HYDRAULIC OPERATING LINE (HIGH-PRESSURE)
BUNGEE MOUNTING CLAMPS
WYE FITTING
MAIN GEAR RH BUNGEE
MAIN GEAR LH BUNGEE
DOOR ACTUATING ROLLERS (AIRPLANES 42 AND SUBSEQUENT)
UPLATCH LUGS
BRAKE HYDRAULIC OPERATING LINES (LOW-PRESSURE)
MAIN GEAR BUMPER
BOOT ASSEMBLY
MAIN GEAR SHOCK STRUT
BRAKE PRESSURE RELIEF VALVE
SHOCK STRUT PISTON PACKING NUT
RELIEF VALVE DRAIN PIPE
SHOCK STRUT PISTON
HOSE SUPPORT CLAMP
SHOCK STRUT TORQUE LINKS
MAIN GEAR WHEEL AXLE
MAIN LANDING WHEEL AND BRAKE ASSEMBLY
BOOT ASSEMBLY

MAIN GEAR ASSEMBLY VIEW LOOKING AFT

heaters for the flight deck and main cabin can be set to regulate automatically the interior temperatures at a comfortable range of 15.6° C to 27.7°C (60° to 82° F), either through their respective electrical bridge circuits or by the heater control switches. Auxiliary ventilation for the main cabin during loading operations and prior to take-off is provided by two axial-flow ventilating fan blowers located in the bulkhead between the flight compartment and the main cabin. By opening the astrodome and placing the fans in operation, a stream of outside air can be circulated along the top of the fuselage for the entire length of the cabin.

The leading edge of the empennage and the wing are maintained in an ice-free condition by heated air supplied by combustion-type heaters and distributed through ducts in the leading edge structures. Neither the tail nor wing anti-icer heaters are equipped with ground blowers, as overheating of the structures would occur during ground operation because of the lack of cooling airstream over the surfaces. Inadvertent operation of the leading edge anti-icer is prevented by a switch on each main gear which, when the weight of the aircraft is on the gear, opens a relay in the main junction box and cuts all electrical power to the anti-icer heaters.

The double-panel windshield also is kept in an ice-free condition by heated air, which is ducted up through the supporting structure and into the space between the windshield panes.

Fuel is supplied to all heaters from the No. 3 main fuel tank by means of either the normal or auxiliary electrically driven fuel pumps in the No. 3 nacelle. The controls for each heater fuel system are installed in the individual heater control containers."

Heater Controls and Warning Lights (Description)

"With the exception of the on-off controls of the 100,000 Btu-per-hour windshield and anti-icer heater and the cockpit heating and ventilating-air

FLIGHT ENGINEER'S HEATER CONTROL PANEL — AIRCRAFT AF48-795 THROUGH AF50-1268

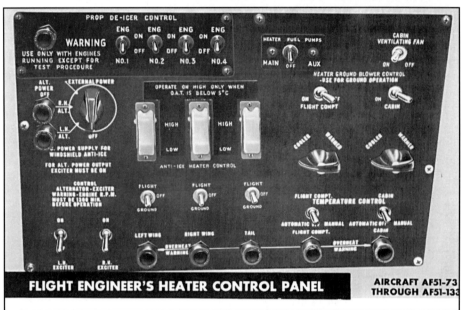

FLIGHT ENGINEER'S HEATER CONTROL PANEL — AIRCRAFT AF51-73 THROUGH AF51-133

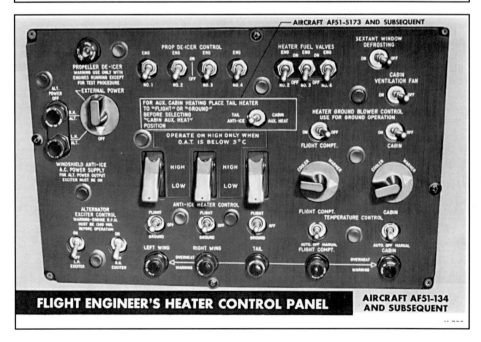

FLIGHT ENGINEER'S HEATER CONTROL PANEL — AIRCRAFT AF51-134 AND SUBSEQUENT

controls, all the heater controls, warning lights, and heater CO^2 fire protection discharge switches are located on the flight engineer's heater control panel and are clearly placarded as to system and function. The windshield anti-icer heater is turned on and off by a cable control to the right of the co-pilot's section of the main instrument panel.

Power Plant and Related Systems Description

The aircraft is equipped with four Wasp Major engines conforming to AF designation Model R-4360. R-4360-35A engines are installed on aircraft A, R-4360-20WA engines on aircraft 1 through 204, and R-4360-63 engines on aircraft 205 and subsequent. The major differences in the three engines are in the accessory or rear section and the propeller reduction gear, with the R-4360-20WA engine incorporating a spacer case, an automatic engine control, and a variable speed blower system. All engines are equipped with a water/alcohol injection system for added take-off power. The engines are four-row, radial, air-cooled, tractor-type power plants, with 28 cylinders helically arranged around the crankshaft in four rows of seven banks. From front to rear, the major sections of the engine case are: the propeller shaft case section, the magneto drive case section, the crankcase section, the cylinder section, the blower case section, the spacer case section (R-4360-20WA only), and the accessory drive case section. The propeller case section may also be referred to as the front section; the combination of the magneto drive case, crankcase, and cylinder sections may be referred to as the power section; and the blower case, spacer case (if any), and accessory drive case sections may be referred to as the rear section. The ignition for the R-4360-20WA and R-4360-35A engines is supplied by seven separate magneto units; one complete unit for the four cylinders in each of the seven banks. The ignition for the R-4360-63 engine is supplied by four separate magneto units; one complete unit for the seven cylinders in each of the four rows of cylinders. The cylinders are arranged in four rows and seven banks; the rows are identified alphabetically, A through D, from front to rear; the banks are identified numerically, one (the number of the bank in which the top cylinder is located) through seven clockwise as viewed from the rear. Each cylinder is identified by a letter and a number, the letter identifying the row and the number identifying the bank in which the cylinder is located. On the quick engine change, the demountable unit is removed. The unit includes the engine, the engine mount, engine accessories, piping, electrical installation, oil cooler, air induction system, cowling, cowling flaps and drive units, and propeller slip-ring control. The demountable unit does not include the propeller, the oil tank, or the hydraulic pump installation.

Fuel System (Aircraft A through 139) Description

The fuel system provides fuel for the engines, for engine oil dilution, for the auxiliary power plants, and for the combustion heaters, and in aircraft A, for the propeller feathering system. The fuel equipment includes six integral wing tanks with a total capacity of 11,100 U.S. (9243 Imp.) gallons, a booster pump and a selector valve for each tank, four engine-driven fuel pumps, four fuel strainers, and the necessary controls, piping and fittings. A number of tank-to-engine fuel flow combinations are possible.

Fuel System (Aircraft 140 and Subsequent) Description

The fuel system provides fuel for the engines, for engine oil dilution, for the auxiliary power plants, and for the combustion heaters. The fuel equipment includes 12 integral fuel tanks with a total capacity of 11,128 U.S. (9265 Imp.) gallons, a booster pump and a shutoff valve for each tank, four engine-driven fuel pumps, four fuel strainers, and the necessary controls, piping and fittings. A number of tank-to-engine fuel flow combinations are possible.

Water/Alcohol Injection System

Description

An engine water/alcohol injection system is installed in the aircraft to provide power from the engine in excess of normal take-off ratings and is used during take-off, or under emergency conditions when greater horsepower than is normally available is required. The system consists essentially of two water/alcohol tanks with a capacity of 30 U.S. (24.97 Imp.) gallons each, one located in each wing; four water/alcohol electrically driven supply pumps, one for each engine; two strainers; four water/alcohol regulators; four derichment valves; and the necessary pipes, fittings, and electrical control system. On aircraft 1 and subsequent, the engine is equipped with a variable-flow water injection regulator. On aircraft A, the R-4360-35A engine is equipped with a constant-flow water injection regulator.

Oil System

On aircraft A through 164, lubricating oil is furnished to the four engines by four independent but similar oil systems, one in each nacelle section. The principal units of each system are a hopper-type supply tank; and engine-driven oil pump; an oil cooler; a thermostat assembly and an electric actuator for the oil cooler air exit door control; quantity, pressure, and temperature indicators; an oil dilution solenoid valve; a firewall shutoff valve, and the necessary tubing, switches, wiring, etc. Oil is supplied to the engine under pressure by the integral engine-driven pump and is returned to the tank through the cooling system. The system is filled with oil, Specification MIL-O-6082, grade 1100 (winter and summer). On aircraft 165 and subsequent, each nacelle is equipped with a dual oil cooler unit and an oil flow divider in place of the single oil cooler unit.

Propellers

The Model C634S-C402 Curtiss Electric propeller installation is the full-feathering, reversible-pitch, constant-speed type, having a 3-bladed propeller, 16 feet 6 inches in diameter. Electric energy is used to operate

ORANGEPEEL COWLING

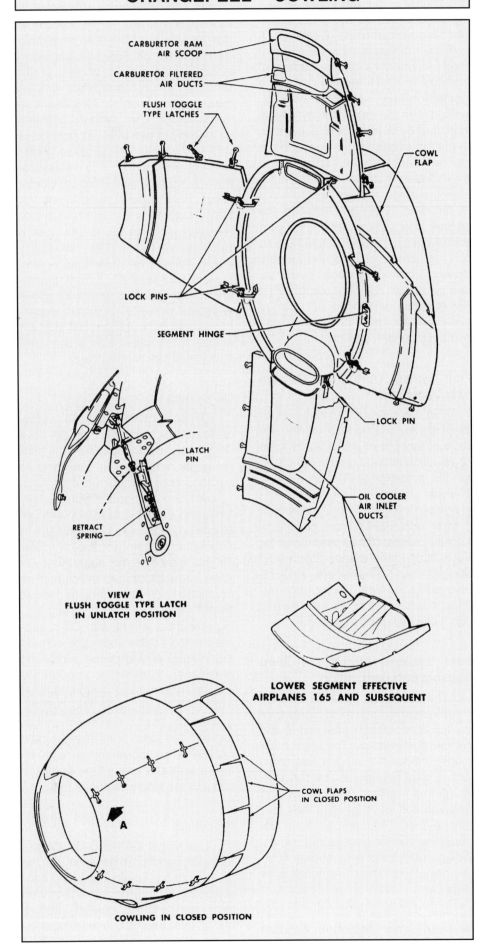

CARBURETOR RAM
AIR SCOOP

CARBURETOR FILTERED
AIR DUCTS

FLUSH TOGGLE
TYPE LATCHES

COWL
FLAP

LOCK PINS

SEGMENT HINGE

LOCK PIN

LATCH
PIN

RETRACT
SPRING

OIL COOLER
AIR INLET
DUCTS

VIEW A
FLUSH TOGGLE TYPE LATCH
IN UNLATCH POSITION

LOWER SEGMENT EFFECTIVE
AIRPLANES 165 AND SUBSEQUENT

COWL FLAPS
IN CLOSED POSITION

A

COWLING IN CLOSED POSITION

the electro-mechanical systems, which maintain constant engine rpm by means of automatic changes in the angle of the propeller blades. The propeller is of unit-type construction and has a blade-angle control system of the synchronizer type. The propeller proper is comprised of five major assemblies: the hub assembly, the blade-and-cuff assemblies, the power gear assembly, the power unit (blade-angle changing) assembly, and the attachment assembly. The synchronizer control system, normally a constant-speed control system, consists of a synchronizer unit installed in the lower forward baggage compartment, an alternator mounted on each engine nose section, a synchronizer tachometer, a master rpm control, switches, and the necessary wiring and conduits. In addition, an electric anti-icer system, which consists basically of electric heating elements, is installed on the leading edge of each propeller blade, and an anti-icer timer assembly and one contactor assembly for each nacelle are provided.

Electrical System

The electrical system is a 24-to-28-volt, single-wire system, with the negative return for all circuits grounded to the aircraft structure. Direct-current power is obtained from four engine-driven generators, two auxiliary power plants and two storage batteries. The inverters are installed to supply 115-volt, 400-cycle a-c power for the operation of the a-c electrical equipment. The inverters are operated by the 24- to 28-volt direct current system. Power distribution is provided by bus bars and feeder cables, with circuit protection being provided by fuses and circuit breakers. Major control switches are located in the flight deck control panels and main deck switch panels.

Note: According to the AN 01-40NVA-2, aircraft A (the prototype) through 79 were delivered from the production line without the wing-tip combustion heaters or the nose mounted radar. Aircraft 80 through 164 came off the production line without the nose mounted radar but had the wing-tip mounted heaters.

Aircraft 165 and subsequent came off the line with radar and heaters. Almost all aircraft were later upgraded to the late production standard, so far as combustion heaters and radar were concerned.

Above, wing tip heater. (Nick Williams) Below, wing-tip heater with access door open. (USAF via Craig Kaston)

The Test Birds

Probably the best known of the C-124 test vehicles was the YC-124B, originally built as a C-124A, Serial No. 51-072. The airplane was extensively modified to test the application of turboprop engines to use on long-range military aircraft. The plane was used by the Air Research and Development Command (ARDC) to give the service experience with aircraft employing this type of powerplant.

It's interesting to note that at least two other cargo types were being tested at about this time, both with trial installations of turboprop engines. One was the Lockheed YC-121F Super Constellation and the other was the Boeing YC-97J.

The YC-124B, was equipped with the YT34-P-1 engines and began flight tests in early 1954, ceasing these operations in early 1956. As might have been expected, the airplane demonstrated significantly im-proved performance and greatly enhanced lifting capability. In spite of this, the C-124 fleet was never modified to take advantage of the benefits of the more powerful (and much simpler!) engines. Instead, the Air Force chose to develop newer long and medium-range transports that could be designed around the new engines and thus take full advantage of their capabilities.

The C-133, built by Douglas, met the requirements for a long range transport, though not without an initial period of teething problems. Lockheed's C-130 Hercules met the requirement for a medium-range transport so well that it's become a classic among cargo aircraft in both the military and civilian sector.

It's interesting to note that, in addition to the basic pure cargo version of the turboprop C-124, there was a proposed air refueling

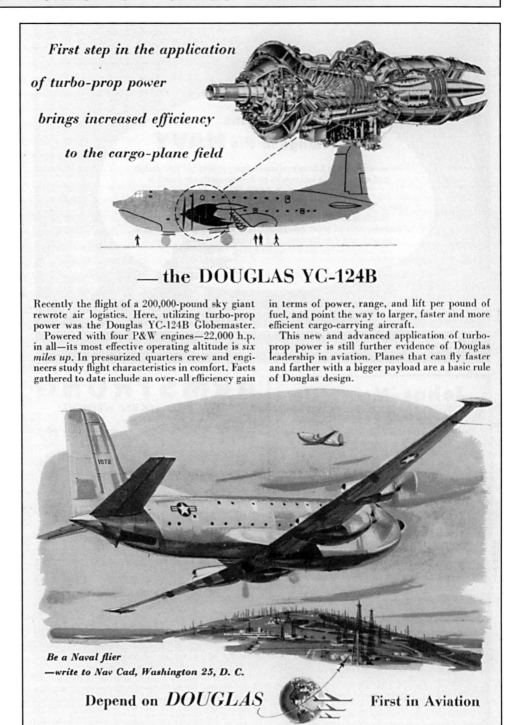

tanker model. Though it was never built, even in prototype form, the project did progress to the design study stage. Readers will remember that Boeing produced and flew the prototype KC-135A in the early '50's and that airplane met, and continues to meet, the Air Force's basic tanker needs.

One of the beauties of the turboprop engine, simplicity aside, is that it can be operated efficiently at high altitudes.

Thus, it provides the almost instantaneous response to throttle movements, characteristic of the reciprocating engine, with the relative light weight and simplicity of the jet. Because the turboprop can be flown at higher altitude, it lends itself to application to aircraft whose design features include cockpit and cabin pressurization. With that in mind, the engineers at Douglas studied the feasibility of modifying the C-124 to

YC-124B
TURBOPROP

Above, YC-124B at the Douglas plant while being prepped for its first flight on 2 February 1954. (Douglas via Earl Berlin) At right, YC-124B 51-072 at Edwards AFB during an open house on 19 May 1955. The prop tips had been painted red. (William Swisher) Below, YC-124B cruises over Southern California. Note the horizontal stabilizers were canted up on the YC-124B. (via Craig Kaston)

Above and below, YC-124B being chased by a Douglas AD-5 during its first flight from Santa Monica to Edwards AFB on 2 February 1954. (Douglas via Harry Gann)

make it a fully pressurized airplane. Though the idea proved feasible, the weight penalty wasn't acceptable and the YC-124B ended up being the only version of the Globemaster II to have this feature. This pressurization problem (the weight penalty) may have been one of the contributing factors in the Air Force's reluctance to employ a turboprop Globemaster II in the tanker role.

It appears the Air Force was more interested in a turboprop tanker version of the C-124 than it was in a pure cargo carrying model, at least at first. A 1951 Standard Characteristic Sheet bears this out by stating that the KC-124B was intended to be a cargo plane with provision for equipment with in-flight refueling gear.

Another C-124, this one a "C" model and not quite so radically modified, was used for powerplant tests. In this case, the new engine was the

Above and below, close-up of the YC-124B engines at Edwards AFB on 19 May 1955. (Lloyd S. Jones)

T57 turboprop, intended to be the powerplant driving the proposed C-132, a very large cargo plane featuring the fuselage of the C-124 (early on, at least) combined with swept wings similar to those later used on the DC-8 airliner. Though the C-132

was never developed beyond the design stage, the engine was built, run on ground test rigs and finally cleared for flight test.

Burnie Dallas was the pilot who delivered the airplane to the modification center. These are his comments, taken from a letter he wrote to me in September, 1988:

"In the early spring of 1954, flying from Larson, I flew and delivered 52-1069 to Logan International, Boston, MA; they transferred the aircraft to Wrenchler plant to be used as a test bed for this company's engine, ... With that engine hung in the radome [it] sure looks like hell and the exhaust pipe is just as bad, but she flew anyway by getting the true airspeed up to approximately 210 knots, At this speed the turboprop was rotating, then you would feather the inboard engines, fire up the turboprop, When it got up speed then you feathered the outboard engines, then Shaky was pulled through the air by this one engine. This aircraft #375, you will note that this bird was not listed as an active C-124."

Mounted in the nose of the C-124C, serial number 52-1069, the engine had sufficient power to pull the airplane along on its own, with the airplane's four reciprocating engines shut down and feathered.

Flight tests were conducted as follows: The airplane took off and climbed to test altitude on the power of the four R-4360s. Once at the proper altitude, the two inboard engines were shut down and the test engine was started. Once the test engine was running at full power, the outboard engines were shut down and the test engine did all the work.

It appears the test engine never went into production. After the test program was completed, the C-124C test vehicle was retired to Davis-Monthan AFB and subsequently scrapped.

Yet another variant of the C-124 bears mentioning here. It was called the C-124X. As finally built, it bore no resemblance to the C-124. In fact, what was initially called the C-124X was produced as the C-133 Cargomaster.

Globemaster III

There was, at one time, a plan to produce a new cargo plane; a radical departure from the C-124 as we know

it. Eventually designated C-132 and, sadly, never built, it would have been everything Old Shaky wasn't.

Illustrations of the airplane show a double-decked cargo plane appearing very much like a turboprop powered C-5A. Old Shaky's characteristic radar thimble was mounted on the nose and the fuselage was a double-lobe structure, somewhat similar to that seen on the Boeing C-97 and Lockheed Constitution. The program was dropped due to projected costs. The Air Force decided the smaller, less expensive C-133 would meet future airlift needs.

One more reason is offered, this one by the author, for the rejection of the C-132 design. The Air Force had, in the 1949-1950 time frame, been flying the very large XC-99 cargo derivative of the B-36 "Peacemaker" bomber. Though dependable and able to carry its full cargo load for less cost per ton-mile than any other airlifter then in service, the airplane was, for its time, just too big to put into production. The problem wasn't in engineering or cost. Experience with the

Above, the T57 test bed aircraft in flight. These were the intended powerplants for the C-132 then on the drawing boards. (via Harry Gann)

plane showed that there was seldom a need to fill the airplane to its volume or weight capacity. There just wasn't that much cargo being moved by air, there apparently being no urgent need.

In the years that followed, with greater emphasis on getting large quantities of troops, equipment and munitions to world-wide hot spots in the shortest possible time, airplanes like the C-5A became "must haves" and military planners no longer thought in terms of dependence on medium-sized cargo planes. The more modern C-17 continues to reflect the emphasis on very large cargo planes and quick reaction to trouble, wherever it occurs.

Below, C-132 mock-up at the Douglas plant. (via Craig Kaston)

YC-124B TURBOPROP TRANSPORT

C O N D I T I O N S			BASIC MISSION I	MAX FUEL MISSION II	DESIGN ALT MISSION III	DESIGN MISSION IV	FERRY RANGE V
TAKE-OFF WEIGHT		(LB)	234,150	235,000	217,000	200,000	170,963
FUEL AT 6.0 LB/GAL (GRADE 100/130)		(LB)	52,479	66,492	50,229	48,129	66,492
PAYLOAD (CARGO)		(LB)	77,200	64,037	62,300	47,400	---
WING LOADING		(PSF)	93.3	93.6	86.5	79.7	68.1
STALLING SPEED (POWER OFF)		(KNOTS)	110	110	106	102	94
TAKE-OFF GROUND RUN AT SL	(1)(3)	(FT)	4,570	4,590	3,825	3,160	2,200
TAKE-OFF TO CLEAR 50 FT	(1)(3)	(FT)	6,480	6,540	5,250	4,250	2,920
RATE OF CLIMB AT SL	(2)	(FPM)	1,550	1,545	1,750	1,985	2,460
RATE OF CLIMB AT SL (ONE ENGINE OUT)	(2)	(FPM)	935	925	1,080	1,250	1,600
TIME: SL TO 20,000 FT	(2)	(MIN)	22.7	23.0	19.0	16.0	11.8
TIME: SL TO SERVICE CEILING	(7)(2)	(MIN)	44.4	44.4	44.2	43.3	29.4
SERVICE CEILING (100 FPM)	(2)	(FT)	24,100	24,000	25,900	27,800	31,200
SERVICE CEILING (ONE ENGINE OUT)	(2)	(FT)	17,400	17,300	19,600	21,900	25,900
COMBAT RANGE	(4)	(N MI)	1,755	2,350	1,790	1,880	3,495
AVERAGE SPEED		(KNOTS)	276	275	275	272	265
INITIAL CRUISING ALTITUDE		(FT)	19,900	19,800	22,550	25,100	29,300
FINAL CRUISING ALTITUDE		(FT)	26,150	27,900	28,250	30,400	34,500
TOTAL MISSION TIME		(HR)	6.44	8.61	6.64	7.03	13.32
COMBAT RADIUS	(4)	(N MI)	1,000	1,320	1,000	1,000	---
AVERAGE SPEED		(KNOTS)	269	270	268	266	---
INITIAL CRUISING ALTITUDE		(FT)	19,900	19,800	22,550	25,100	---
FINAL CRUISING ALTITUDE		(FT)	34,500	34,500	34,500	34,500	---
TOTAL MISSION TIME		(HR)	7.65	9.99	7.69	7.76	---
FIRST LANDING WEIGHT	(5)	(LB)	205,000	198,000	190,000	174,900	---
GROUND ROLL AT SL	(3)(6)	(FT)	3,230	3,115	3,000	2,760	---
TOTAL FROM 50 FT	(3)(6)	(FT)	4,430	4,300	4,140	3,830	---
COMBAT WEIGHT	(5)	(LB)	127,800	133,963	127,700	127,500	110,856
COMBAT ALTITUDE		(FT)	34,500	33,800	34,500	34,500	34,500
COMBAT SPEED	(2)	(KNOTS)	290	287	290	290	303
COMBAT CLIMB	(2)	(FPM)	325	300	330	335	560
COMBAT CEILING (500 FPM)	(2)	(FT)	32,130	31,300	32,150	32,200	34,600
SERVICE CEILING (100 FPM)	(2)	(FT)	36,760	35,900	36,780	36,810	39,500
SERVICE CEILING (ONE ENGINE OUT)	(2)	(FT)	31,900	31,050	31,920	31,950	34,300
TAKE-OFF GROUND RUN AT SL	(1)(3)	(FT)	1,150	1,270	1,150	1,150	850
TAKE-OFF TO CLEAR 50 FT	(1)(3)	(FT)	1,525	1,680	1,520	1,520	1,120
RATE OF CLIMB AT SL	(2)	(FPM)	3,520	3,340	3,520	3,530	4,130
MAX SPEED AT OPTIMUM ALTITUDE	(2)	(KNOTS)	332	331	332	332	334
OPTIMUM ALTITUDE		(FT)	13,800	13,300	13,800	13,800	15,150
BASIC SPEED AT 25,000 FT	(2)	(KNOTS)	324	322	324	324	328
LANDING WEIGHT	(5)	(LB)	110,245	110,856	110,050	109,950	110,856
GROUND ROLL AT SL	(3)(6)	(FT)	1,730	1,740	1,725	1,720	1,740
TOTAL FROM 50 FT	(3)(6)	(FT)	2,530	2,550	2,525	2,535	2,550

DIMENSIONS

WING
Span — 173.3 ft.
Incidence (Root) — 5° 15 ft.
(Tip) — 3° 15 ft.
Dihedral — 6°
Sweepback (LE) — 4° 44 ft.
LENGTH — 129.7 ft.
HEIGHT — 51.2 ft.
TREAD — 34.2 ft.
Prop Ground Clearance — 4.8 ft.

FUEL / OIL

LOCATION	NO. TANKS	GAL.
wing outbd.	4	2,724
wing inbd.	6	4,896
wing aux.	2	3,462
	Total	11,082
GRADE		100/130
SPECIFICATION		MIL-F-5572
OIL		
nacelle	4	80
GRADE		1100

CHART NOTES

(1) Take-Off Power
(2) Max Power
(3) Take-Off Sea Level
(5) For Radius Mission if Shown
(6) Without Reverse Thrust
(7) For Ferry Mission V

ELECTRONICS

VHF Command	AN/ARC-3
UHF Command	AN/ARC-27
Liaison	AN/ARC-8
Radio Compass	AN/ARN-6
Loran	AN/APN-9
Localizer	AN/ARN-14
Glide Path	AN/ARN-18
Interphone	AN/AIC-8
Marker Beacon	AN/ARN-12
Radio Beacon	AN/APN-76
Emerg. Sea Rescue	AN/CRT-3
I.F.F	AN/APX-6
Inter. Responder	AN/APN-12A
Search	AN/APS-42
Emergency Keyer	AN/ARA-26

POWER PLANTS

FOUR YT34-P-I
Pratt & Whitney
Turboprops

ENGINE RATINGS

SLS	ESHP	RPM	MIN
T.O:	5,500	11,000	5
MIL:	5,360	10,750	30
NOR:	4,675	10,500	Cont

WEIGHTS

Loading	LB	L.F.
Empty	101,930 (E)	
Operating	104,471	
Design	200,000	2.5
Combat (basic)	127,800	3.3
Max T.O. (ovrld)	235,000*	2.0
Max T.O. (norml)	235,000*	2.0
Max Landing	205,000	

(E) Estimated
* Limited by wing stucture

Air National Guard C-124 Squadrons and Groups

105th Tactical Airlift Squadron / 118th Tactical Airlift Group - Tennessee

125th Military Airlift Squadron / 138th Military Airlift Group - Oklahoma

128th Military Airlift Squadron / 116th Military Airlift Group - Georgia

133rd Military Airlift Squadron / 157th Military Airlift Group - New Hampshire

155th Military Airlift Squadron / 164th Military Airlift Group - Tennessee

156th Military Airlift Squadron / 145th Military Airlift Group - North Carolina

158th Military Airlift Squadron / 165th Military Airlift Group - Georgia

183rd Air Transport Squadron / 172nd Air Transport Group - Mississippi

185th Military Airlift Squadron / 137th Military Airlift Group - Oklahoma

191st Military Airlift Squadron / 151st Military Airlift Group - Utah

Note: The "weekend warrior" image is dying off, in large part due to the equipment of Air National Guard units with the same types of modern aircraft the active duty units are flying, and due to the proven professionalism of the Air Guard crews and technicians. Modern Air National Guard units have proved themselves equal too and, in many cases, better than their active duty counterparts. This superiority is a reflection on the teamwork, tenure of duty and application to their military jobs of the experience and knowledge gained in off-duty employment. This is especially true of aircrew members, many of whom are full-time airline pilots with thousands of hours of flying experience in all kinds of weather conditions.

OKLAHOMA AIR GUARD

The 125th TFS flew North American F-86D Sabre Dogs from 1957 until January 1960, when the squadron was redesignated the 125th ATS and issued Boeing C-97G Stratofreighters. After participating in the Berlin Airlift, the squadron transitioned to the C-124C in February 1968. The unit continued to fly the C-124C until 25 January 1973, when they reverted back to a fighter squadron and were equipped with North American F-100Ds.

The following aircraft were assigned to the 125th ATS: 52-0996,

Above, C-124C 52-1061 from the 125th MAS, 138th MAG, Oklahoma ANG was seen at Tours, France, on 17 October 1968. (via Stephen Nicolaou)

52-0998-1000, 52-1033, 52-1057, 52-1060-1061, 52-1065, 52-1083, and 53-0009.

Retired Major General Bobby E. Walls remembered the C-124 well, though his opinion of the airplane wasn't very high. General Walls was (and from the tone of his letters, still is, despite his "retired" status) a confirmed fighter pilot and the closest he got to saying anything nice about big cargo planes, to this author, was his statement that, "... the C-97 was a Cadillac beside 'Old Shaky'." During his association with the C-124, General Walls had one bad experience that stands out in his mind and this, no doubt, contributed to the dislike for the Globemaster II.

General Walls describes how his unit got its C-124s and the impact the transition had on the personnel.

"We were an Air Defense unit, flying F-86Ds, when the decision was made to change three Air Defense and three Tactical Fighter units to the role of strategic airlift. This happened in late 1959, and in February 1960 the first crews arrived at Travis AFB, California, to transition into C-97 aircraft. This was the first time in history that the reserve forces were involved in heavy, four-engine operations—worldwide.

We flew the C-97 until sometime in 1968, at which time we transitioned into the C-

124. The change was made either by going to training at Tinker AFB, Oklahoma, or by home station training. Most of the Air Technicians (full time employees) went to Tinker for their checkout. We had an ATC [Air Training Command] unit come to Tulsa for the ground school portions of the training, and used our own people for the actual flying checkout. Just as soon as we had qualified crews, we started the almost daily flights to Southeast Asia. If I remember correctly, our wing had a departure for SE Asia about every three days, and this was accomplished in a non-EAD status. The crews were put on active duty (title 10) for the duration of their trip only—usually ten - eleven days.

Most of the aircrews were, naturally, not too happy with the transition. We had several crewmembers that were old C-97 people, and you will admit that the C-97 was a Cadillac beside 'Old Shaky'. We received authorization, early in the C-97 program, to hire retired Air Force flight engineers. To my knowledge, this is the only time that a retired person could be an active member of the reserve units. Flight engineers were in such demand that this was absolutely necessary. Of course, each unit had air advisors (active duty types) assigned to each crew position and some in maintenance."

General Walls' most memorable experience with the C-124 was related in the story below. He was kind enough to relate it to me in a candid format. The story is very authentic and, from my perspective, doesn't appear to have been embellished with "imagined" details to make the story more exciting.

The Flight of 999

"On approximately 11 or 21 Nov 1970, we left Tulsa with a crew of eight (8) in a C-124C aircraft, tail no. 999. Our mission was to fly from Tulsa to Travis AFB, CA; Hickam AFB, HI; Wake Island; Yokota AB, Japan and return. The crew consisted of:

Lt. Col. Bobby E. Walls Aircraft Commander/Pilot

Major David L. Hall 1st Pilot/Pilot

Major Donald B. Durbin 2nd Pilot/Co-pilot

Lt. Lisenby Navigator

MSgt William D. Shephard 1st Engineer

TSgt Nelvin Hankins 2nd Engineer

SSgt Frank Blair Loadmaster

SSgt Philip Cowan Loadmaster

We had trouble along the way, and we were going to be running late on return to Tulsa. Several crew-members were not Air Tech (full-time) so we needed to get back so they could get to their civilian jobs by Monday. Upon arrival at Yokota AB, we asked about our out-bound cargo and they stated that they had very little for us. We then asked for them (ACP) to request routing for an over-fly of Midway Island into Hickam. If the winds were favorable we could make it non-stop to Hickam and catch up on our schedule. If needed, we could land at Midway for a fire-ball into Hickam.

After spending our allotted ground time (I think around 48 hours) we arrived at operations about 2300 hrs. As advertised, the aircraft had a short fuel load for Wake Island, not as requested. I asked the ACP controller to initiate the request again and ask for an expedited answer. After about two hours the request was granted—if no cargo space was needed for the flight. Yokota had about 500# [pounds] so we asked for an onload of the cargo plus a full load of fuel for the leg to Hickam. Winds were favorable. After all this jacking around we finally got ready to go to the aircraft. When we arrived there we had a C-141 parked in front of us on-loading cargo. This delayed us to the point that we were going to have a crew duty time problem. We finally got ACP to get them moved. I thought about this time that the flight Gods did not want us to fly that night and I did think about a cancel. However, things did work out and we leaped into the murky black.

About 4 hrs and 50 minutes into the flight I told Dave Hall that he had the watch as I was going back and eat my flight lunch. I had just sat down to eat when the engineer (Hankins) stated that we were losing engine #2. I put my lunch aside and started getting into my flotation gear (I can't swim a lick). Before I could get into it and into the left seat the engineer stated that we were losing engine #3 (this makes BOTH inboards). I then started putting on ANOTHER flotation gear.

By this time Bill Shephard had arrived on deck, so he took the engineer's seat and I took over the pilot's position with Dave Hall in the right seat. We contacted Fuchu airways for primary radio control and for emergency assistance. We, of course, immediately started losing altitude from 9000 ft. Fuchu cleared all altitudes below us. The rest of the crew not engaged in the actual emergency started gathering gear to throw over-board. They opened the elevator doors, removed the elevator from the hole and proceeded to dump cargo. We had an engine trailer on board, the largest item, and had Hell getting rid of it. It had stuck in the elevator hole and we had nothing except a wooden stick to pry with.

At about 1500 ft we passed over some type of fairly large ship. After passing by it I had just about decided to ditch. We tried to contact the ship but no luck. After I mentioned ditching, Hall, Shephard and some of the others confessed that they weren't too good in the swimming department. After a consultation, I decided to press on.

We finally got rid of the trailer at about 400 ft above the water. We were then able to maintain some semblance of flying speed. Bill Shephard and I had been fighting with the throttles for about 30 minutes—I would push them full forward and he would look at the temperature and pull them back some.

We finally got a C-141 for RESCAP and they escorted us to Marcus Island. While enroute to Marcus we talked to an Air America aircraft inbound to Marcus. The captain talked with us, advised of the reef around the island and how hard it was to see. He stated that after we landed that he would land, off-load, pick us up and take us back to Yokota.

We finally found the island. Now, with both engines out on the inboard, all we had was emergency hydraulics from an electric pump—not much. We could only get about 10% of the flaps available and had only two applications of the brakes—and reverse. All this on an island with the runway stopping at the water on both ends and only a little over 4000 ft. available.

The Air America captain was right. The dike was difficult to see—as a matter of fact, I never did see it until after I got out of the aircraft—but I hit it with the main gears. I wanted to put that sucker down on the very first brick available, and I did.

We got it stopped in minimum distance, backed off into a revetment (after installing the gear pins so that the gear wouldn't collapse after the impact with the dike). Air America landed, picked us up and delivered us back to Yokota.

Of course, we had a hell of a lot of paper work to fill out. Also, everyone had tossed all their gear, except minimum personal baggage, overboard so claims had to be made for that. A lot of Christmas shopping had to be re-accomplished and we were put aboard a C-141 for Hickam-Travis.

MAC had a lot of questions to ask and we answered them, but not all to their satisfaction. My recommendation to all was (1) that nobody try that long of a flight again. Fuel cannot be dumped in case of emergency. (2) that all cargo aircraft have several iron pry-bars aboard."

On the positive opinion side, the comments of retired Major General Stanley F. H. Newman are appropri-

ately presented. General Newman served with the Oklahoma Air National Guard, and was with the unit during the unexpected and untimely retirement of Old Shaky. His comments are recorded here, taken from a letter he sent to me in September '88.

"My Okla ANG organization, 185th Mil Alft Sqdn, 137th Mil Alft Gp, & 137th Mil Alft Wing, was equipped with the C-124C from 1 April 1968 to 9 December 1974. During that period, I was Group Commander, then Wing Commander. The 138th MAG (Tulsa) was part of our wing during the early part of that period, but converted to F-100Cs. After that, our wing consisted of the 137th MAG (Okla City), 164th MAG (Memphis) and the 165th MAG (Savannah) .....

As the last three units to fly the C-124, we found ourselves in a unique position of being the only people who could airlift outsized cargo to those places unsuitable for the C-5A. Consequently, we flew many SAAM missions throughout the free world ... and continued support of the Vietnam War to many bases in South Vietnam. The wing and its three groups were awarded the Air Force Outstanding Unit Award during this period.

Our ownership of that great bird came to a sudden and unexpected termination [the] summer of 1974. Our NDI people came to me one day with a report that they had found cracks in the wing spar of one of our aircraft. To play safe, I had all of our C-124s checked out and all of them at Okla City had the same problem. We advised our other two groups at Memphis and Savannah of our finding and they in turn checked all their aircraft. Only one C-124 (at Savannah) was free of the problem. After a short period of time, all 3 groups were authorized a one-time

flight and ordered to fly the aircraft to the Davis-Monthan boneyard. All three groups stared at empty ramps for some time until replacement C-130s were received.

While the flying was great as the last Shakey units, Logistics support was another story. When the last C-124 left the active MAC fleet, support vanished overnight. Experienced C-124 maintenance troops also seemed to disappear except at our home stations. Consequently, we were forced to carry a rather large spares kit and include home station maintenance experts on each crew. Engine overhaul reliability was the poorest I have ever seen and engines frequently failed during the first few flying hours after installation. Those of us doing maintenance functional check flights began to refer to our C-124s as the "Douglas Tri-Motor." Towards the end, we frequently found it necessary to fly out to Davis-Monthan and cannibalize parts from the C-124s store there. Needless to say, it was rarely a dull mission.

We, the 137th, had an interesting long range flight from Yokota AB, Japan, to Okla City, stopping only once at Hickam

Above, 185th TAS C-124C 52-1077 was seen in France in 1969. (S. Nicolaou) Below, 185th TAS C-124C 52-1084 on 7 June 1974. (Craig Kaston)

AFB, Hawaii. (Might have been a C-124 record).

Treat Old Shakey kindly—she was a unique and gallant lady."

As the 185th FIS, the squadron flew North American F-86D/Ls from May 1958 through 1 April 1961, when the squadron became the 185th ATS and was equipped with the Boeing C-97F/G. The unit was also equipped with C-97Es "Miss Oklahoma City" and "Talking Bird", which were retained even after the squadron transitioned to C-124Cs and became the 185th MAS in May 1968. C-130As replaced the C-124 in December 1974.

The following C-124Cs were flown by the 185th TAS: 52-0943, 52-1026, 52-1028-1029, 52-1037, 52-

1039, 52-1042, 52-1053, 52-1057, 52-1060, 52-1067, 52-1074, 52-1076-1077, 52-1079, 52-1084-1085, 52-1089, 53-0006, 53-0009, 53-0030, 53-0032, 53-0041, 53-0043 and 53-0046.

TENNESSEE AIR GUARD

The 105th became the 105th ATS on 1 April 1961 when it equipped with C-97Gs. The squadron was redesignated the 105th MAS on 1 January 1966, when the unit transitioned to the C-124C. The Globemaster IIs were replaced with Lockheed C-130As in March 1971.

The 155th TRS was equipped with the Republic RF-84F when they transitioned to the Boeing C-97 on 1 April 1961 and became the 155th MAS. The C-124Cs took over in May 1967 and were replaced with the Lockheed C-130A in late 1974.

Above, C-124C on 29 April 1972. (via Kaston) Below, 164th MAG C-124C 52-0997 "Memphis". (Steven Toby via Earl Berlin) Bottom, 164th MAG C-124C 52-1022 "Memphis" on 18 March 1973 at D-M AFB. (William Swisher)

GEORGIA AIR GUARD

The 128th TAS were flying the North American F-86L when the squadron became the the 128th ATS on 1 April 1961. The 128th flew the Boeing C-97F until being replaced with the C-124C on 1 January 1966 and being redesignated the 128th MAS. On 4 April 1973, the squadron became the 128th TFS and was equipped with North American F-100D.

The 128th MAS was the first Air Guard squadron to receive the C-124. C-124C 53-0001 was received from the 58th MAS, 436th MAW.

Aircraft flown by the 128th MAS were: 52-0945, 52-0947, 52-0956, 52-0975, 52-0979, 52-0992, 52-0994, 52-1059, 53-0001, 53-0003, 53-0012, 53-0022, 53-0037 and 53-0047.

The 158th FIS was flying F-84Fs until 1 April 1962, when the squadron was redesignated the 15th ATS and was assigned the Boeing C-97F. In 1967, the unit became the 158th MAS when it re-equipped with the C-124C. The squadron traded in its Globemaster IIs for Lockheed C-130s on 19 September 1974. This was the last ANG unit to fly the C-124C, with the last two retired being 52-1066 and 53-0044.

The 158th MAS flew the following C-124Cs: 52-0994, 52-1000, 52-1025, 52-1032, 52-1035-1036, 52-1043, 52-1046-1049, 52-1051, 52-1057, 52-1065-1067, 52-1071-1072, 52-1074, 52-1076, 52-1086, 53-0008, 53-0018, 53-0029, 53-0032, and 53-0044/0045.

GEORGIA ANG

Above left, 128th MAS C-124C 53-0003 over Hickam AFB, Hawaii, in 1969. (Nick Williams) Upper left, 116th MAG C-124C 53-0012 at Davis-Monthan AFB, Arizona, on 17 March 1969. (William Swisher). Lower left, 116th MAG C-124C 53-0037 at Dobbins AFB, Georgia. (Norm Taylor collection via Earl Berlin) At left bottom, 158th MAS C-124C 52-1049 seen at Travis Field, Savannah, Georgia, on 24 July 1969. (Norm Taylor collection) Above, C-124C 52-1000 with MAC on its tail taxis at Norton AFB, CA. (Craig Kaston) At right, 158th MAS C-124C 52-1036 at AMRAC on 18 July 1972 (via Earl Berlin) At right, 158th MAS C-124C 52-1066 at St. Louis, MO, on 21 October 1970. (Norm Taylor collection via Earl Berlin) Below, 158th MAS C-124C 52-1057 at its Georgia base. (via Craig Kaston)

133RD MAS/157TH MAG NEW HAMPSHIRE AIR NATIONAL GUARD

NEW HAMPSHIRE AIR GUARD

133 FIS was flying the North American F-86L when, on 1 September 1960, the squadron transitioned to the Boeing C-97A and was redesignated 133rd ATS. In February 1968, the squadron received the C-124C and became the 133rd MAS. C-130s replaced the C-124s in April 1971.

C-124Cs assigned were: 52-1057, 53-0004-0005, 53-0027, 53-0029-0030, 53-0032, 53-0034, 53-0039, 53-0043, and 53-0049.

156TH MAS/145TH MAG NORTH CAROLINA AIR NATIONAL GUARD

NORTH CAROLINA AIR GUARD

As the 156th FIS flying the North American F-86L, the unit was reorganised as the 156th AAS in January 1961. The 156th AAS first flew Fairchild C-119Cs, and then Lockheed C-121Cs starting in 1962. In January 1964, the squadron was designated the 156th ATS and then in January 1965 it was designated the 156th MAS. The unit flew the C-124C from April 1967 until May 1971. The C-124Cs were replaced by Lockheed C-130Bs.

The 156th MAS/145th MAG flew the following C-124C aircraft: 52-0946, 52-0970-0971, 52-0985, 53-0013-0014, 53-0017-0018, 53-0024-0026.

At top, C-124C 53-0034 at Pease AFB on May 1969. (via Craig Kaston) Above, 156th MAS C-124C 53-0018. (Nick Williams collection) Below, 156th MAS C-124C 52-0971 at Charlotte, North Carolina, on 29 March 1969. (Norm Taylor collection via Earl Berlin)

191ST MAS/151TH MAG UTAH AIR NATIONAL GUARD

UTAH AIR GUARD

The North American F-86L equipped 191st FIS became the 191st MAS on 1 April 1961 and was equipped with Boeing C-97C/Gs. The squadron converted to the C-124C in February 1969. On 20 October 1972, the unit became the 191st ARS flying Boeing KC-97Ls.

C-124s assigned were: 52-0952-0954, 52-0956, 52-0975-0976, 52-0987, 52-1010, 52-1084-1085, 53-0004-0006, 53-0046, and 53-0049-0050.

183RD MAS/172ND MAG MISSISSIPPI AIR NATIONAL GUARD

MISSISSIPPI AIR GUARD

The 183rd TRS was redesignated the 183rd Aeromedical Evacuation Squadron on 15 November 1957. They flew the Fairchild C-119F until becoming the 183rd ATS and flying the C-121C in mid-1961. The squadron moved to Jackson Municipal Airport in January 1963. In February 1967, the C-124C replaced the Lockheed Constellations. Lockheed C-130Es replaced the Globemaster IIs in May 1972.

C-124C aircraft flown by the 183rd MAS were: 52-1054, 53-0002, 53-0007, 53-0009, 53-0011, 53-0015-0016, 53-0019-0020, 53-0023, 53-0025, and 53-0034.

At top, 191st MAS C-124C 52-0953 at Davis-Monthan AFB on 11 May 1971. (William Swisher) Above, 183rd MAS C-124C 53-0015 at Davis-Monthan AFB on 11 May 1971. (William Swisher) Below, 172nd MAG C-124C being filmed prior to making the "ANG'S 1,000th MISSION TO VIET NAM". (USAF)

AIR FORCE RESERVE

The C-124 served with the Air Force Reserve every bit as faithfully as she did with the active duty units and those of the Air National Guard. From 1961 to 1974, Air Force Reserve units, totalled 19 squadrons in 19 groups assigned to 9 wings. In the early years, these units contributed their services and supplemented the active duty forces. In later years, with the active duty C-124 units converted to C-141s and C-130s (aircraft the reserves would fly in the years following the retirement of the C-124), the Air Force Reserve units, along with those of the Air National Guard, were the only ones able to carry outsize cargo until the introduction of the Lockheed C-5A. Even after the C-5A became established in front line squadrons, the C-124 continued to provide outsize cargo airlift and might have continued to do so into the late 1970's had not wing fatigue cracks forced the retirement of the fleet.

On May 8, 1961, the first five Air Force Reserve squadrons were reorganized to become C-124 units. These squadrons were previously equipped with the Fairchild C-119 Packet, often erroneously referred to as the "Flying Boxcar," the official name of its C-82 predecessor. The conversion process promised to be a very challenging experience but the reserves proved they were up to it and it wasn't long before they were flying Shakys with the best of them.

The first five squadrons to convert were the 77th, 78th, 303rd, 304th, and 305th TCSs. The 77th belonged to the 916th TCG, 512th TCW. The 78th also belonged to the 512th TCW but was assigned to the 917th TCG. The 303rd, 304th and 305th TCSs were all assigned to the 442nd TCW but were assigned to the 935th, 936th and 937th TCGs, respectively. It's also important to note the squadrons changed from Medium airlift status to Heavy airlift status with the conversion.

Changes and enhancements to the Reserve C-124 fleet came on November 30, 1965, when Special Order G-124 directed the following changes, which would go into effect on December 1st of the same year: Headquarters 442nd, 445th and 512th TCWs became Headquarters 442nd, 445th and 512th ATWs. Headquarters 918th, 935th, 936th, 916th, 917th, 937th, and 940th TCGs became Headquarters (numerical designation) ATG. The 941st and 942nd TGPs-M, became ATGs-H. The previously mentioned seven groups remained Heavy airlift units.

The following units were also affected by Special Order G-124 and gained Air Transport Squadron, Heavy, designations: 77th, 78th, 303rd, 304th, 305th, 314th, and 700th

Above, C-124A 49-0255 takes off from Hickam AFB, Hawaii, in 1968/69. Nose doors had 100,000 painted in large numbers on the underside of each cargo door. (Nick Williams)

TCSs (all Heavy); 97th and 728th TCSs, Medium. The 314th converted to C-124s in April, the 700th in July, the 728th in August, and the 97th in December.

Special Order G-130, dated 10 December, 1965, made the following changes: 337th TCS of the 905th TCG (both Medium) became Air Transport Squadron and Air Transport Group, respectively, using their assigned numerical designations. Records indicate the group and its squadron didn't convert to the C-124 until April, 1966.

Special Order G-142 brought further changes in designation. Air Transport squadrons, groups and wings became Military Airlift units.

The December conversion of C-119 units wasn't limited to those listed above. Air Force Letter (AFOMO 487n), dated 1 December 1965, ordered the transfer of the 915th TCG-M, from the 435th TCW-M (deactivated) to the 445th ATW-H. Transfer to the new wing was accompanied by conversion from the C-119 to the C-124 and the squadron became a heavy airlift unit. AFOMO

At right, AFRES 442nd MAW C-124C 51-5188. (via Earl Berlin) Bottom, 452nd MAW C-124C 51-0167 at Norton AFB, CA, open house in May 1970. (Douglas via Harry Gann)

501n-1 ordered the conversion to the C-124.

A message sent on 16 February 1966, origin unclear, announced plans to convert more C-119 units to the larger C-124. Units affected were the 459th TCW; 901st, 904th, 909th, 932nd, and 945th TCGs; and the 73rd, 336th, 731st, 733rd, and 756th TCSs. It's important to realize not all of these groups and squadrons were assigned to the 459th Wing. The 901st belonged to the 94th Wing, as did the 904th. The 909th belonged to the 459th Wing and would later be joined by the 911th. The 932nd Group belonged to the 442nd Wing and the 945th Group was claimed by the 452nd TCW.

Designation changes continued. A Department of the Air Force Letter, dated 14 March 1966, directed the 79th TCS and 915th TCG to be redesignated 79th MAS and 915th MAG, respectively. The change was to go into effect on or about 8 April 1966.

The conversion process continued with the transformation of the 921st and 938th TCGs from C-119s to C-124s. The 938th had, in fact, been chosen earlier to convert but plans changed and the process didn't go into effect until 1 July under provisions set down by Special Order G-55. For the 938th, the conversion process was easier than it was for the 921st because the former unit had already begun making the necessary changes.

These units, their parent wings (452nd and 459th) and their individual squadrons (67th, assigned to the 921st; 312th, assigned to the 938th) lost their Troop Carrier designations and gained Military Airlift designations instead.

Yet another unit was affected by Special Order G-55. The 349th TCW-M, became the 349th MAW. The 349th's initial groups were the 940th and 941st. Assigned flying squadrons were the 314th and 97th, respectively.

By the time the conversion was completed, 19 squadrons had exchanged airplanes and the Air Force Reserve found itself effectively involved in the heavy airlift business, outsize cargo being its specialty. A total of 21 groups were ultimately involved, supervised by ten wings.

The following chart shows the arrangement of the squadrons, groups and wings that flew the C-124 for the Air Force Reserve. Note that, once the units formed and were operational, there wasn't much moving around of organizations until 1969 and after.

Squadron	Group	Wing
67	921	433
73	932	442
77	916	512
78	917	512
(446 in Apr '71)		
79	915	445

97	941 (939 Jul '69)	349
303	935	442
304	936	442
305	937	442
312	938	349
314	940	349
(452 in Jan '68)		
334	904	459
(445 in Jun '68)		
(452 In Dec '69)		
337	905	94
(459 in Feb '72)		
700	918	445
714	942	452
731	901	94
(302 in Jul '72)		
733	945	452
756	909	459
758	911	459
(94 in Apr '71)		

The 19 Military Airlift Squadrons were assigned to the following bases:

67th   Kelly AFB, TX
July 1966 - June 1971

73rd   Scott AFB, IL
April 1967 - July 1969

77th   Donaldson AFB, SC
May 1961 - April 1963
Carswell AFB, TX
April 1963 - February 1972

78th   Barksdale AFB, LA
May 1961 - February 1972

79th   Homestead AFB, FL
April 1966 - July 1971

97th   McChord AFB, WA
December 1965 - June 1969

303rd   Richards-Gebaur AFB, MO
May 1961 - June 1971

304th   Richards-Gebaur AFB, MO
May 1961 - October 1974

305th   Tinker AFB, OK

312th   May 1961 - May 1972
Hamilton AFB, CA
July 1966 - June 1969

314th   McClellan AFB, CA
April 1965 - January 1968

336th   Stewart AFB, NY
Oct 1966- Dec 1969
Hamilton AFB, CA
Dec1969 - Mar1972

337th   Westover AFB, MA
April1966 - Feb1972

700th   Dobbins AFB, GA
July1965- June1969

728th   March AFB, CA
Aug1965 - Jan1972

731st   Hanscom Fld, MA
Jan 1967 - Oct 1972

733rd   Hill AFB, UT
Oct 1961 - Jan 1973

756th   Andrews AFB, MD
Oct 1966 - June 1971

758th   Pittsburg IAP
Jan 1967 - April 1971

AIR FORCE RESERVE
OPERATIONS

The Air Force Reserve used an impressive number of C-124s, peak inventory being 158 aircraft in operation in late June 1967. But the significance isn't in the numbers. It's in the missions flown, the recorded accomplishments and the time and effort given by those who are commonly called "Weekend Warriors", as are their Air National Guard counterparts.

The C-124 entered the Air Force Reserve inventory in 1961 and late that year, though not completely adapted to their new mounts, the first five squadrons, their parent groups and wings were called to active duty in response to the Berlin crisis. Using more than 40 C-124s, the Reserve units flew more than 12 million passenger miles and 18+ million ton miles under the control of the Tactical Air Command. On August 27, 1962, the units were released from active duty and returned to Reserve status.

The Reserve C-124 units responded to the Cuban Missile Crisis in 1962, flying troops and their equipment to their home stations after the crisis off the Florida coast came to an end. Interestingly, the Reserve C-124 units weren't called to active duty during this period. The same would not hold true when the Reserves faced their next major crisis some six years later.

January 1968 was a tense month in an already tense period of U.S. history. The Vietnam war was in full swing and our nation was in turmoil. In the midst of this, we faced what came to be known as the Pueblo Crisis. Five Air Force Reserve C-124 groups and two wings were activated and weren't returned to Reserve status until June the following year. The units flew almost 2.5 million passenger miles and more than 37 million ton miles to points all over the world. 422 of the 4,200+ missions were flown in support of U.S. operations in Southeast Asia. Almost 2,800 missions were flown, by a sixteen plane detachment assigned as a provision-

Below, 904th MAG C-12C 52-1044 on 9 April 1972 at Hamilton AFB. (Smalley via William Swisher)

al squadron, from Mildenhall, England to points in Europe and Africa. More than 10,000 tons and 15,000 passengers were flown and 10,500 flying hours were racked up.

The C-124 crews from 1964 on did their part to help MATS (later MAC) carry out its airlift mission to Southeast Asia. Granted, most of the Reserve missions were to the area were generated as part of their normal training, but many missions were flown on a purely volunteer basis when the active duty folks needed a helping hand to handle the increased volume of cargo and passengers.

Air Force Reserve C-124 crews began flying missions to Southeast Asia at a modest rate, at first, something like 15 per quarter, beginning

the second quarter of 1964. But the rate picked up and the Reserve crews proved beyond any doubt that they and their airplanes were equal to any task the active duty folks assigned.

Wings and Groups Mobilized In January 1968

349th MAW, 938th MAG— Hamilton AFB, California

445th MAW, 918th MAG— Dobbins AFB, Georgia

433rd MAW, 921st MAG—Kelly AFB, Texas

349th MAW, 941st MAG— McChord AFB, Washington

459th MAW, 904th MAG— Stewart AFB, New York

Above, 756th MAS/909th MAG C-124C 51-0136 in the rain at Andrews AFB, MD. (Norm Taylor collection via Earl Berlin) Below, 909th MAG C-124C 51-0140 undergoing maintenance. (AAHS via Craig Kaston)

By 1969, the Military Airlift Command was phasing the veteran C-124 out of active service, its role being taken over by the giant Lockheed C-5A Galaxy. MAC found itself running short of experienced C-124 pilots at a time when it needed them most. To fill in the gaps, the Air Force Reserve supplied 51 pilots who served tours of active duty of varying lengths, the contribution encompassing the period from May to October of that year. The operation was called "Cold Shaky".

Reserve C-124 Missions Flown To Southeast Asia

Year Missions	Hours	Tons	Pass
1 - 6 '65 43	—	—	—
1 - 6 '66 64	4,619	1,916	361
FY '67 264	20,922	7,031	1,238
FY '68 228	17,571	4,255	397
FY '69 181	14,415	3,309	188
FY '70 210	17,884	4,981	572
FY '71 183	14,178	4,057	488
FY '72 118	5,473	1,526	191
FY '73 4	332	40	—

The following year, the C-124 fleet would be retired from the Air Force Reserve and Air National Guard. Wing fatigue cracks were discovered in the majority of the fleet and correction of the problem wasn't considered cost effective.

To better appreciate how well the Air Force Reserve C-124 units per-formed as a whole, let's take a look at a typical unit, the 911th Military Airlift Group (a component' of the 459th Military Airlift Wing). Like most Reserve C-124 groups, the 911th transitioned into "Shaky" from the C-119 Packet. The unit received its first C-124 on October 15, 1966, and continued flying the giant cargo planes until November 1972. By that time, the unit was well into transition into the smaller and simpler C-123 Provider and was faced with two major challenges. The primary challenge, of course, was that of readying itself for operations with the "newer" equipment (the C-123 having been around for a number of years but "new" to the 911th). The second challenge was possibly the most difficult, that being the maintenance of the aging C-124s. Here, the problem was more logistical than mechanical. The supply inventory, with respect to the C-124, was drying up and the mechanics had to make do with what they had, often improvising to meet mission demands. A look at the statistics that follow shows that they did the job well, for the most part, and kept the old girl flying to the end.

1969 — Last Half

	Jul	Aug	Sep	Oct	Nov	Dec
Average Aircraft On Hand	8	7	7	7	8	8
Flying Hours Scheduled	498	489	417	484	430	327
Hours Flown	447	462	265	265	389	318
Operational Ready Rate (%)	72.7	71.4	72.3	74.6	72.1	83.7
Tons Airlifted	180	203	141	91	111	77.6

The first quarter of 1970 saw the unit maintaining a high 81.7% Operational Ready Rate, other statistics being about normal. The second quarter Operational Ready Rate was 75.5% while the rate for the third quarter was 71.3%. The last quarter of the year saw the rate drop to 69.1%. It's important to note that the Operational Ready Rate "norm" for the command is 71.0% and the 911th exceeded the standard most of the time. The group didn't do as well in 1971, quarterly Operational Ready Rates for the first, second, third and fourth quarters being 62.5%, 61.8%, 55.1% and 57.7% respectively. Late in the first quarter of 1972, the 911th began the transition to the C-123s.

The unit had begun transferring the C-124s out as it anticipated the arrival of replacement aircraft. Thus, by March there were only two C-124s on hand. Despite this low number of aircraft, the unit showed a marked improvement in Operational Readiness Rate during the last two months of the quarter. The rate for January was a low 53%. In March, the rate climbed to 79.5% and in February it was an incredible 93.7%. Even more impressive is the fact that AFRES Headquarters had allotted the unit 300 hours for the quarter but had also given permission to disregard that maximum if the unit felt it necessary. Thus, the 911th flew a total of 431 C-

Below, 917th MAG C-124C 52-0964 on 5 April 1972. This was the last C-124 from Barkesdale AFB to arrive at MASDC. (via Earl Berlin)

At right, 945th MAG C-124C 52-1032 at Kelly AFB, TX, on 1 September 1972. (Norm Taylor) Below right, 941st TCW AFRES C-124C 51-0111 at McChord AFB, WA, on 27 April 1966. (N. Taylor)

124 hours and provided a fitting grand finale for a remarkable and much respected lady.

The Air Force Reserve flew more than a half-million hours with the C-124. That total doesn't include those flown by the unit while on active duty. As remarkable as the number of hours flown is, the low number of accidents recorded is even more impressive. Aircraft 50-0086 was the only C-124 involved in a major accident while flying with the Reserve forces. The airplane was destroyed but there were no injuries or fatalities. Strangely, instructor pilot error was discovered to be the cause.

Readers who recall William Farrar's comments about flying C-124s for SAC will appreciate the piece that follows. It was included in the same letter that contained the piece about SAC.

"Air Force Reserve: The first reserve outfits started to convert to Shakeys in '61. The 442nd Troop Carrier wing, Richards-Gebaur AFB (TAC) was the first such unit. They converted from C-119s. My first-ever military flight was with this unit, in a C-46, when I was an ROTC cadet at the University of Kansas.

The 442nd was recalled to active duty for a year by JFK for the Berlin Wall Crisis, during their C-124 conversion, and I joined after they were deactivated. Shortly thereafter, in '63, the wing was assigned to MATS, as were all other Reserve and Air Guard units with C-124s. Our gaining control was 22nd AF at Travis, and thus we started to fly their routes into the Pacific. This became very popular with the crews, especially flights to Tachikawa AB, Japan (now closed, but west of Tokyo near Yokota).

With my background, I quickly upgraded to AC [Aircraft Commander] status, and remained so all the time in the unit. I did some IP [Instructor Pilot] upgrading flights, but did not have the time to pursue this seriously because of my civilian job, which required travel (U.S. Food & Drug Adm. Investigator, covering four states from Kansas City District Office; I retired from this on June 3rd). The 442nd

converted to C-130s in 1971, reverted to TAC, then back to MAC later, as did all the C-130 units, both active and reserve. I retired from flying, and the reserves, in '79.

Flying for the reserves was a lot of fun, on the whole. There was, of course, a lot of hard work involved, and you had to utilize your time carefully. I did as much flying, sometimes more, than on active duty, and certainly did more international flying there. After the MAC routes started, I regularly went to the Far East twice a year, with short over-water missions (Alaska, Panama, Hawaii, etc.) usually twice also. The long flights took me to Vietnam, Philippines, Japan and Korea. A few east-bound missions slipped in too, and I went to the UK and Frankfurt [Germany]. Domestic flights were almost always going somewhere, so the amount you flew was mostly up to the individual, and how much one wanted to get involved.

This was when reserve bumming became an honorable profession. With your monthly week-end drills (4 days pay), 36 additional flying training periods annually, 15 days annual active duty, up to 89 days additional active duty annually, any schools (survival, simulator, etc.) you could slip in, special days that did not count against the other 89, a person could make a tolerable living doing this, and many did. I don't recall exactly the crew manning authorization, but I think it was 2-1/2 per plane, but don't rely on this

figure. In any case, we had a lot of crewmembers, many of whom lived well outside the KC [Kansas City] area, including Chicago, Memphis, St. Louis, and Omaha. Regular airlifts were flown to these cities for the regular UTA (unit training assembly) weekends. They were picked up Friday night and returned Sunday evening (sometimes very late). I'll talk about the Chicago airlift later.

In those days, however, most of us had gainful employment. There were many teachers, farmers, gov't employees, and businessmen in flying slots. There were of course, many with WW II experience, though these guys started retiring out in the late '60s. Not too many airline pilots in the 124 program for some reason, though some of the finest pilots I have ever flown with were involved. These were local TWA or Braniff crewmembers.

It took 'Big-Mac' a while to realize that the reserves could carry their load, but once we got started, especially over the Pacific, we were doing anything they wanted, and our unit had planes out in 'The System' nearly the year around.

A lot of crewmembers came and went during that period in the unit. Some should never have tried flying beyond their dollar ride. Because of the unusually high crew manning authorization, recruiting became desperate for bodies for a while, and some older pilots and navigators were signed on who had not flown for several years, and in fact still

wanted to use WW II or Korean procedures. I remember returning back from Japan on one trip with a brown shoe nav who had to be retrained totally after he was recruited from his insurance sales profession in a small Kansas town. He was finally pronounced fit to go, and I got him on a trip to Tachi [Tachikawa] for his initial line check. A few hours west of California he totally lost his bearings, and kept telling me (I was the AC), that the Farallon Island beacon was 100 miles away. This happened several times, and I never could pick it up on the ADF [Automatic Direction Finder]. Finally, I assured everyone that if we kept going east we were bound to hit North America. Ultimately we did and landed at Travis; he failed the check ride, but eventually was brought up to speed, and finished his career in the unit.

Young loadmasters were easy to recruit; they heard all the stories about the Japanese bath houses, cheap beer, and eager Jo-sans. In those good old days, $1 brought 360 yen. However, the long hours, hard work with the loads, and long, boring legs wiped out many. My point in all this is that recruiting and training new crewmembers was an ongoing process and a serious job. MAC check rides were common through the system, and one of their people could get on the airplane for a no-notice ride. The reserves always held their own on these, if the man had been trained by the unit and qualified there.

You want some stories, I could probably use up all this cheap typing paper [it was, but the letters were wonderful!] I have if I didn't do anything else for a week, with the stories of one kind or another. I'll give you a couple of short situations which were continuing, and one incident that sticks in my mind rather strongly.

Tachikawa AB, Japan, had been the Japanese research base during and before WW II. It had one runway, which ran north and south. It was only a little over 5000 ft. long. For take-off you could add about another 1000' usable length, by swinging your tail over the fence, and taxiing onto an over-run which included a base perimeter road. There were traffic lights to keep car traffic out of your way. Over the fence, north of the field, was a large vegetable farm, maybe 10 to 20 acres. The owner of this apparently had communist sympathies, because left-wing demonstrators were allowed to place tall poles in the field, which had red banners, and script on them vilifying the imperialist Americans. When you would struggle off the runway there, at 185,000 lbs. max gross weight to Wake Island, some of these people would leap out of some small caves they had dug to live in, grab some poles and poke them toward

you. I can't imagine what four R-4360s at max power did to their hearing, but as far as I know, no one bellied in the vegetables, which would have harmed them more. It was always sort of fun to see them down there, and after a while you felt as though they were friends.

Earlier, I mentioned flying to Chicago for an airlift. A reserve training squadron for navigators had been stationed at O'Hare Field (there remains there both reserve and Air Guard C-130 units even now), but it was deactivated about '65 or so, leaving all those guys without slots. Someone in the 442nd went up there, and recruited many of them, as the manning then was short on this position. To get them, however, the wing had to provide an airlift for UTA's, and this did in fact continue as long as we had the C-124s. This went into O'Hare and picked them up on the Guard ramp, and dropped them off on Sunday nights. I flew that Sunday flight many times, as I lived locally, and more important was a fairly junior pilot then. This was not a choice mission. O'Hare, as you probably know, is a busy airport and all the commercial traffic was jets, who fly a lot faster than Shakeys. If they were working two or more runways it wasn't too much problem. Often though the winds would make only one runway usable, and that really made traffic tight. We would go down final at about 130k [130 knots] (gear down and speed under 145k). The jets flew final at 150 - 160k. The implications were obvious. To keep a 727 off your tail, you had to keep up a good speed, and after touchdown, get off the runway fast. I'll never forget the tower in rapid-fire speech directing me to take the outer over the bridge to the guard ramp. Take-offs were even worse. I can remember being up to 15th in line to depart, with arrivals coming in between every departure, at about two minute intervals. They would get into number [one] position, after idling for quite a while. You had to baby those 4360's to max power, or face a probable abort on the runway, really messing up the traffic flow. Many an airline driver would ask, in a stressful manner, when that big monster was going to move, while he was descending towards the runway rapidly. Ultimately, some of us who flew the trip often complained so much that the pick-up point was changed to Glenview NAS [Naval Air Station], which was somewhat more inconvenient for the passengers, but a relief to our nerves. One cold winter night, because of snow and ice on the runway at O'Hare, we had to dump them at Milwaukee. Participation was worth the trouble for those guys though, and most of them were outstanding crewmembers and participated well.

My big story now. In late '66 I got on a trip with a destination of Kimpo AB, Korea; this is actually Seoul IAP [International Airport], and was also a ROKAF base, with fighters. We took the normal route to Tachikawa, and left from there to Kimpo very early one morning. With the time change, this made our arrival about 0800. Though I was not the designated AC, I was flying the plane in the left seat of that leg. The CP [co-pilot] was a big, loud, excitable guy, all three of which are the opposite of me. As you may know, Seoul is only a few miles from the DMZ, and this airport is on the west edge of the city. It has one runway, running roughly SE-NW. At that time, MAC had a reg requiring a GCA approach for any of their planes into here, regardless of the weather or landing runway. The GCA was set up to land on the SE runway. That morning, however, landing was actually to the NW, or just opposite as the GCA, which we started. It was operated by USAF controllers, who broke us off about half-way down, and turned us over to the tower, Korean manned. On the approach, however, before this breakoff, two ROK F-86s, on their dawn patrol take-off, flew off the airport, and passed us rather closely in the opposite direction. This really excited the CP, who had already come close to a stroke as we were approaching final, and thus getting close to the DMZ area. He was convinced that we would be the first-ever C-124 shot down by the North Koreans. Obviously, that didn't happen and the Sabres didn't run into us either.

I broke off for a visual pattern to the active, and then we saw another flight of F-86s on the runway. The CP started babbling to the tower about our landing clearance, and the Sabres departure; no answer. I turned final; no departure and no clearance. At about 4-5000 feet I initiated a go-around on my own, and re-entered traffic. By this time, the fighters had departed and the tower controller spoke to us, with landing clearance. On the roll-out they gave us wrong turning instructions, and I taxied right onto a dead-end narrow taxi-way. Finally, an American voice came on, got us turned around and to our parking space. We stayed around there a few hours, bought some brassware and other Korean items in the BX, and got back to Tachi without incident. The guy who had been CP flew that leg."

Flying for the reserves, obviously, had its moments; it was clearly rewarding as well. The reserves did an outstanding job with the C-124 and their exploits will go down in the history of military airlift operations.

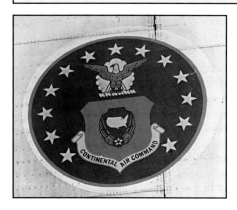

It is uncertain what criteria was used to assign reserve C-124s to the Continental Air Command (CAC). It appears that each unit provided four aircraft from 1961 through 1964, and eight thereafter until the CAC was inactivated on 8 January 1968.

At top right, CAC C-124C 50-1259 over Hickam AFB. The Continental Air Command stripe on the tail was usually white bordered by dark blue. (Nick Williams) Above right, CAC 733rd MAS 945th MAG C-124C 51-0073 at Elmendorf AFB, AK, on 29 June 1967. (Norm Taylor via Earl Berlin) At right, CAC 942nd MAG C-124C 51-0166 at an air show in the late 1960s. (via Earl Berlin) Below, CAC 442nd MAG C-124A 50-0093 at Richards-Gebour AFB open house on 23 September 1967. (AAHS via Craig Kaston)

Above, GC-124A 48-0795 at Sheppard AFB on 29 May 1963. (Lionel Paul Collection) Below, the C-124 fleet awaits the scapper's torch at Davis-Monthan AFB, AZ, on 10 May 1971. (USAF photo Samuel Parker collection via Earl Berlin)

C-124A 48-0795 became an instructional airframe in 1955 when it was assigned to the Air Training Command (ATC) at Sheppard AFB. It was re-designated GC-124A along with GC-124A 49-0237. 48-0795 was struck from inventory in April 1964 and 49-0237 was used from May 1953 through early 1970.

SURVIVORS

52-0943 — Seoul Air Museum, South Korea

52-1000 — Travis AFB Museum

52-1066 — Air Force Museum (currently carrying serial number 51-0135 and AF Reserve markings).

51-0089 — Warner Robins AFB Museum (Was on loan to Confederate AF in Texas)

52-0994 — McChord AFB Museum

52-1004 — Pima Air Museum

52-1072 — Charleston AFB Museum

51-0119 — Last known to be at Bradley Air Museum (8/75)

53-0044 — Civilian Aircraft Las Vegas, Nevada)

53-0050 — Aberdeen Proving Ground

52-1000: There've been some interesting stories behind these "museum pieces". The story behind 52-1000 is perhaps the most interesting. This airplane was located at the Aberdeen Proving Ground, Maryland, when it was inspected for possible restoration. 52-1000 was one of three C-

124s that were inspected and was found to be in the best over-all condition. The restoration cost was estimated and a figure of $150,000 was arrived at. The Travis AFB Historical Society voted to raise the money and the project went into high gear.

Just getting the airplane ready to leave the Aberdeen Proving Ground was a major undertaking. Though the airplane was deemed suitable for restoration, the job wasn't going to be easy. Practically all the cockpit instruments were gone. The rudder had fallen off the plane and was badly damaged. All four engines had to be replaced. The condition of the aircraft brought its share of surprises but mother nature added another for good measure when a bear was

found hibernating in one of the wings and had to be removed before work could continue.

Keep in mind the initial "restoration worthiness" inspection took place in late August 1982. On November 15, 1983, 52-1000 took wing after sitting on the ground nearly 12 years. Her first stop was Dover AFB, Delaware. She sat on the ground there for three days before the weather cleared enough to allow her to continue her journey.

Next stop was Dobbins AFB, Georgia. There, volunteers, many former C-124 crew members and mechanics possessing the kind of expertise to finish the restoration, went to work to really bring the mighty Globemaster II back to life.

Plans, at that time, called for the restored airplane to fly to Scott AFB, Illinois, then to Norton AFB, California, before making its final flight to Travis. The airplane is now on display at the Travis AFB Museum.

50-0994: The story behind McChord AFB's C-124 is a little simpler. The airplane was delivered to the museum on October 9, 1986. Volunteers from the Air Force Reserve, active Air Force and some retirees put the airplane back in shape at Selfridge Air National Guard Station in Michigan. The airplane had been used as a training aid for 13 years prior to restoration, being owned and employed by the Detroit Institute for Aeronautics.

As with the Travis AFB Museum's "Shaky", the McChord AFB plane needed lots of tender loving care and a healthy supply of parts and money to get her to her final destination. Engines had to be borrowed from Travis AFB in order to get the old girl back in the air. But back in the air she went and today she's a proud part of the growing McChord AFB aircraft display.

52-1066: Perhaps the best known C-124 "museum piece" is that on display at the United States Air Force Museum at Wright-Patterson AFB, Ohio. This airplane, serial number 52-1066, was flown by the Georgia Air National Guard before being retired to the Davis-Monthan storage facility in 1974. Made flyable at Davis Monthan, the airplane was flown to the Air Force Museum in August, 1975, by Colonel Arther E. Eddy, the same pilot who flew her to retirement in Arizona only a year before.

Today, the Air Force Museum's C-124 carries a different set of markings. Now carrying the serial number 51-0135, she is painted in Air Force Reserve markings to better represent the Reserve Globemaster IIs that flew much needed supplies to Southeast Asia. But under the new markings still lies the old 52-1066, a hard-working lady who served the active duty Air Force and the Air National Guard for a good many years.

Above, C-124C 52-1000 at Travis AFB in April 2000. (William Swisher) Below, C-124C 52-0994 as received by the Detroit Institute of Aeronautics, with Georgia Air Guard painted on its side. (Fred Dickey) Below middle, at a later date Detroit Institute of Aeronautics replaced Georgia Air Guard on the fuselage side. (Max Bell 1985) Bottom, 52-0994 taxis out at Willow Run, MI, in 1986 on its way to Selfridge ANG Base for maintenance prior to flying to the McChord AFB museum. (Max Bell)

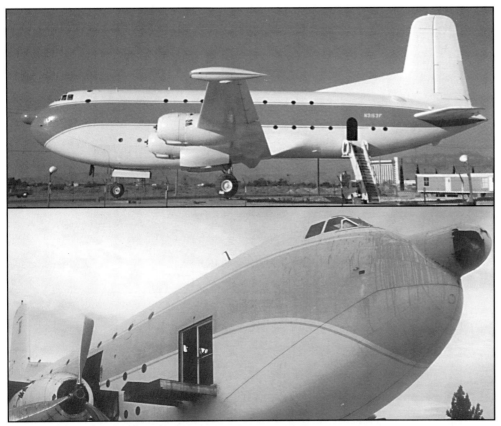

Above, the Air Force Museum's C-124C 52-1066 was painted as 51-0135 to represent the Air Force Reserves' (AFRES) contribution during the Viet Nam war. (USAF)

At left, C-124C 53-0044 at McCarran Field, Las Vegas, NV. The aircraft had been brought to the airport to be converted into a theme restaurant and was mounted on blocks and painted white with medium blue trim. It carries civilian registration number N3153F. (Harry Gann) At left, the aircraft today in year 2000 with paint peeling and and corrosion evident. Note the patio door and platform for entry, which was never completed. (Scott Bloom)

Below, C-124C 52-1004 in fresh Military Airlift Command (MAC) paint scheme in 1999 at the Pima Air and Space Museum. The aircraft had been there since the museum's inception on 8 May

AIRMODEL / COMBAT MODELS C-124 1/72nd SCALE GLOBEMASTER II

The kit was first issued by Airmodel in the 1970s before being acuired by Combat Models. It is a vacuform kit, which because of its size is very difficult to build. The kit comes with a very good set of drawings and currently sells for $34.95 plus shipping. It can be ordered from Combat Models, 400 3rd Street, West Easton, PA 18042. A detail update kit can be purchased from Jerry Rutman, HC88 Box 38, Pocono Lake, PA 18347. It consists of resin and white metal parts and has everything needed to complete the kit. Send $1.00 for a price list of his products.

Above, Airmodel kit by Max Bell. Below, Combat Model by Mike Riehl. Bottom, Combat Model by Ben Howells.

WELSH MODELS VACUFORM 1/144 SCALE C-124A/C KIT MT4

I would recommend this kit along with the companies other excellent products such as the Martin Mars. These kits are well thought out and a pleasure to build.

This vacuform kit is complete with resin and white metal detail parts. The kit provides resin engine cowls, thus solving one of the major shortcomings of most vacuform kits. The aircrafts fuselage is formed as a C-124A prior to the addition of the thimble nose radome. A white metal thimble nose radome is provided for radar fitted C-124As and C-124Cs. The other white metal detail parts included in the kit are: flapjack fairings, tail bumper, de-icing air intakes and wingtip combustion heater pods, landing gear and wheels, and propellers.

The kit includes decals for three different versions: a early Military Air Transport Service (MATS) C-124A (50-083) assigned to the Continental Division, a C-124C (52-1049) from the 1705th Air Transport Group (ATG) Continental Division of the Military Air Transport Service (MATS), and a C-124C (52-1074) assigned to the Oklahoma Air National Guard.

To purchase the Welsh Model C-124 write to:

D.R. wade Welsh Models
93, Fonmon Park road
Rhoose, Barry
South Glamorgan, U.K.
Phone/Fax 01446-710113

Above and below, this Welsh models vacuform kit was built by Max Bell.